Elonei Mamre

Elonei Mamre

The Encounter of Judaism and Orthodox Christianity

Edited by

Nicholas de Lange
Elena Narinskaya
Sybil Sheridan

LEXINGTON BOOKS/FORTRESS ACADEMIC
Lanham • Boulder • New York • London

Published by Lexington Books/Fortress Academic
Lexington Books is an imprint of The Rowman & Littlefield Publishing Group, Inc.
4501 Forbes Boulevard, Suite 200, Lanham, Maryland 20706
www.rowman.com

86-90 Paul Street, London EC2A 4NE, United Kingdom

British Library Cataloguing in Publication Information Available

Library of Congress Cataloging-in-Publication Data Available

ISBN 978-1-9787-1398-7 (cloth) | ISBN 978-1-9787-1399-4 (ebook)

To the memory of

Father Sergei Hackel
Rabbi Louis Jacobs

Their commitment to dialogue,
rooted in knowledge of their own religious tradition
and sensitive openness to the other's,
contributed greatly to the initiative that resulted in this book,
and serves as a model and an inspiration to the rest of us.

Contents

Introduction

Nicholas de Lange

Elonei Mamre ('oaks of Mamre') is the name given in the Hebrew Bible (Gen 13:18) to the place near Hebron where Abraham pitched his tent and built an altar to the Lord. (In the Greek translation, the oak is singular and Mamre seems to be its name.) It was here that 'the Lord appeared to him' and that he received a visit from 'three men' who foretold the birth of Isaac (Gen. 18:1–2). An old tradition explains the name Mamre as meaning 'vision' (perhaps the same tradition which explains the name Israel as 'man who sees God'). Both Jewish and Christian interpreters have speculated on the meaning of this vision, and the identity of the 'three men.' One of the earliest Christian writers, Justin Martyr, reports a debate with a Jew, Trypho, on this very subject (*Dialogue*, 56). The Jew maintains that Abraham saw God and also saw three 'angels' or messengers, while the Christian insists that he saw the Word of God accompanied by two angels. The difference may seem small but it has large consequences. A later, and very influential, Christian explanation interprets the 'three men' as the Holy Trinity. This is how the scene is depicted in what is surely the most famous of Russian icons, by Andrei Rublev (Grypeou & Spurling 2009). In choosing this title for our book we partly had in mind this exegetical encounter, but more importantly we wanted to point to the person of Abraham as a kind of patron figure for Jewish–Christian relations.

Is religion a glue or a barrier? Internally, it operates to hold believers together and foster a sense of unity and of mutual responsibility and support. That is not to say that religious issues have not frequently led to disputes and even violence between factions sharing the same religion. But the same sense of inner unity often seems to sharpen the external barriers between one religious group and another. The history of Christian–Jewish relations offers many examples of both tendencies. There is a great deal of common ground between these two religions which have grown from the same seed. One may speculate that it is this very closeness that has exacerbated antagonisms between them.

In this book we want to explore, through a plurality of voices, both the glue and the barriers. The book arose out of, and is intended as a contribution to, dialogue between Jews and Christians, specifically Orthodox Christians. Dialogue between Jews and Christians began in earnest after World War II, out of a shocked realization that Christianity had to bear some responsibility for the antisemitism that had led to the Nazi genocide, and an earnest endeavor to prevent something similar occurring again in the future. Before that time there were polemics and controversies, but genuine dialogue—in which both sides listen—was rare or nonexistent. (A first step had been taken in the foundation of the National Council of Christians and Jews in the United States of America in 1927.) A pioneering meeting was held at Oxford in August 1946, which ultimately led to the creation of the International Council of Christians and Jews (Simpson & Weyl, 1995). In the summer of 1947 an 'International Emergency Conference on Anti-Semitism' took place in the Swiss village of Seelisberg. The documents agreed by this conference, and most notably the 'Ten Points of Seelisberg,' can be seen in retrospect as 'The Foundation of the Jewish-Christian Dialogue' (Rutishauser, 2007). Another key event was the declaration 'Nostra Aetate' issued after the Second Vatican Council, in 1965. These and other initiatives were taken by Roman Catholic and Protestant Christians with the participation of Western European and North American Jews, with no significant representation of Orthodox Christians, or indeed of Eastern European Jews. We therefore feel that there is an urgent need for greater understanding and dialogue between Jews and Orthodox Christians.

This book grew out of the work of a group of Jewish and Orthodox Christian theologians which has been meeting regularly over many years for the purpose of encounter and dialogue. The group arose at the initiative of David Kessler, the South-African born proprietor of the London *Jewish Chronicle*, and the first meeting was held at University College London on 25 November 1997. It was organized by Professor John Klier and Father Yves Dubois, and chaired by Rabbi Dr Louis Jacobs. The other participants were Bishop Basil of Sergievo, Archpriest Sergei Hackel, Dr Andrew Louth, the Revd Jonathan Gorsky, Rabbi Dr John Rayner and the undersigned. Bishop Kallistos of Diokleia was invited but was unable to be present. In preparation for the meeting a small library of relevant books was sent to each participant (the cost being borne by the Kessler Foundation) and written responses to this reading matter were solicited and circulated. The discussions were deep and wide-ranging, and were notable for a mood of trust and openness. Other similar meetings followed, and eventually a regular rhythm was established;

the venue was moved to the Faculty of Divinity in Cambridge and the group was cautiously enlarged.

The participants no doubt had their own reasons for choosing to participate in this exercise in dialogue. My own motives are complex. I fell in love with Greece during my first visit to the country as a classical student in the 1960s, and became fascinated by its religion, with its wonderful combination of Jewish and classical elements. (In those days we still read John Lawson's remarkable book *Modern Greek Folklore and Ancient Greek Religion*.) This fascination led to a doctorate on Jewish–Christian relations in the early Patristic period, and then to a research position in the Parkes Library in the University of Southampton, a center devoted to the study of Jewish–Christian relations. Gradually the history and religious culture of the Jewish minority in the Byzantine empire became my main academic research interest, and relations between Jews and Christians naturally occupied a large place in this work.

The contributors to this volume, with a couple of exceptions, have all been members of this group, and most of the chapters originated as papers read to meetings of the group, and consequently benefited from discussion with other members. In selecting the topics for the book, out of a large number that have featured in our meetings, we have focused on two main areas: theology and worship, because these are the subjects to which we have returned again and again. Indeed, they were the main subjects of the first meeting of the group described above.

We begin with the endlessly fascinating subject of mysticism, and indeed it is appropriate that we start our quest with a reminder of the essential unknowability of the Godhead. It has been said that mysticism is the point at which Judaism and Christianity, and indeed Islam, come closest together. Mystical theology is commonly considered an essential characteristic of Orthodoxy, while there is a current view that it is alien to Judaism. In fact, a strong mystical vein runs through Judaism, as a glance at a Jewish prayer book will quickly reveal. Marcus Plested refers, appropriately, not only to Philo and Paul, but to the *Merkabah* literature and the *Zohar*. Two important questions for further discussion are raised by this chapter. The first is whether the key difference between the two religious traditions in question is not the presence or absence of mystical theology, but rather its precise importance and centrality in each. It is surely telling that Orthodox Christians tend to read the Song of Songs as celebrating the mystical union between the soul and Christ (or the Church), whereas in rabbinic Judaism it is read as an allegory of the covenant between God and Israel, centering on the exodus from Egypt. This allegorical interpretation looks forward not to union with God but to the redemption of the world in the Messianic age. The second question concerns precisely the mystical union with the divine as the mystic's goal. Marcus Plested concludes by expressing his doubt about the existence in Judaism of what he calls 'a developed metaphysical basis for mystical union,' and this concurs with the verdict often attributed to Gershom Scholem, the great specialist on Jewish mysticism (Scholem 1941). Occasionally, however, Scholem seems to allow that some Jewish mystics envisaged the possibility of mystical union, and this corrective has been endorsed by other specialists.

Apophatic theology, which approaches the divine through the negative way, is sometimes traced back to the Jewish thinker Philo of Alexandria, and it certainly has roots in Greek philosophy. The Jewish rationalist tradition, in engaging philosophically with the unknowability of God, brings us close in some ways to the apophatic dimension of Orthodox theology. The classic Jewish exponent of the negative way is Moses Maimonides, and Daniel Davies is an able guide through the complexities of his thinking about this difficult but important subject (see also Jacobs 1973: 38–55).

The unity of God is another subject which is often presented as a stumbling block to understanding between Jews and Christians; it frequently featured in medieval controversies (Jacobs 1973: 21–37). Yet both Judaism and Christianity, like Islam, insist adamantly on the unity of God as a theological principle, even while both feel compelled to explore different aspects of the Godhead in its relationship with the created order. Andrew Louth rightly insists that the God of the Hebrew Bible is not necessarily the unique God of the philosophers, but rather the greatest of all the gods, the only one truly deserving of our worship. This formulation is still familiar to Jews today in the prayer book, where the service for reading the Torah each Sabbath begins 'There is no one like you among the gods, O Lord.' Just as familiar, though, if not more so, is the statement, impossible to express in English: 'The Lord our God, the Lord is One' (Deut 6:4). This belief is so deeply ingrained in Judaism that it is sometimes referred to as 'the Jewish creed.' No doubt the repeated polemics of the Middle Ages contributed to making it a non-negotiable and central element in Jewish theology. Yet the Bible also uses many different (and sometimes contradictory) images of God, and it sometimes requires an effort to reconcile these. There is surely room for a good deal of further discussion by Jews and Christians together about what exactly they mean by the unity of God.

Another misleading belief is represented in the cliché: 'Judaism is a religion of law, Christianity is a religion of love.' Those who live and worship within both faiths know very well that both law and love are ingredients within our beliefs and practices. Many years ago, when I taught Anglican ordinands about Judaism, I used to enjoy giving them for discussion (without revealing the source) an extract from a well-known book about Orthodox Christianity, summarizing the rules for Lenten fasting. Invariably their response was that the text indicated an obsessive concern with legal minutiae that was typical of Judaism; they were astonished to learn that it described Christian rules. On the other hand the biblical command 'You shall love the Lord your God' (Deut 6:5) is recited by observant Jews every morning and evening. Prominent in the daily prayers is one thanking God 'who loves his people Israel.' Law and love surely go hand in hand. We invited two of the members of the group, Andrew Louth, an Orthodox Christian priest, and Norman Solomon, an Orthodox Jewish rabbi, to reflect on this dyad for us.

One of the most contentious issues in Jewish–Christian dialogue is what has been termed *supersessionism*, the claim that, as Andrew Louth puts it in his chapter on the 'New Israel,' that 'the old religion is to be replaced by the new religion that confesses Christ.' This claim is so deeply rooted in Christian thought, from the New Testament on, that it is remarkable to observe how firmly it has been rejected, particularly since the Shoah, by influential western Christian theologians, and been articulated in influential official statements. The attempt to engage with this long and complicated tradition is surely an essential prerequisite to true dialogue. Situating supersessionist teachings within their historical context, as Andrew Louth does, is a very helpful first step. There is surely a long way to go before this obstacle to Jewish–Christian relations is removed.

Perhaps the most difficult topic of all to confront in this dialogue is that of the (real or supposed) anti-Jewish prejudice that sometimes appeared to be ingrained in the Christian sources. That is not to say that there are no signs of anti-Christian sentiment in the Jewish sources, but they are easier to deal with in that they tend to be a response to actual discrimination or maltreatment, whereas on the Christian side anti-Judaism generally seems to reflect not a personal grudge but ideological beliefs. In the post-War dialogues between Jews and Protestants the Christian side has often evinced a straightforward willingness to jettison or condemn this part of its heritage. Roman Catholics moved more cautiously, but they too, at least at an institutional level, have embraced change. The situation in the Orthodox churches, with their veneration of tradition, is quite different. It is possible, even today, to read or to hear from the pulpit anti-Jewish teachings of the most primitive, ignorant and virulent kind. These sometimes emanate from the highest representatives of the religion. The late Metropolitan Ioann Snychev of St Petersburg, a member of the ruling Synod of the Moscow patriarchate, espoused views which have not unfairly been labelled antisemitic, and he is only one, admittedly extreme, example (de Lange 2006; Tabak, Problems). In 1991 the Patriarch of Moscow and All Russia Aleksi II delivered a speech to an audience of rabbis in New York in which he addressed the Jews as 'brothers' and strongly rejected antisemitism; this potentially important gesture was outspokenly criticized both in the Russian Church abroad and within the Moscow patriarchate, and thirty years later it seems to have had very little effect (Tabak, Relations).

The record of the Constantinople patriarchate in this respect has been more positive. There is material in this topic for a whole book; we have touched on it in a number of chapters, while recognizing that it is an issue that pervades the whole of Jewish–Orthodox dialogue.

In this context, Elena Narinskaya, taking the example of St Ephrem the Syrian, a prolific and influential early Christian author, explores the paradox of a figure who voices strident anti-Jewish sentiments while owing a great deal to the Jews of his day. (A similar paradox can be observed in other fathers, notably Origen: de Lange 1976.) She situates his hostility to Judaism against the background of the struggle of a new and insecure church to seek an identity for itself, recognizing its debt to Judaism while marking out its own path. Such an approach is not intended to defend, let alone exonerate, Ephrem, but to understand him better. Elena Narinskaya is clear on this point: 'what I am struggling to find an excuse for is the church accepting its anti-Jewish legacy.' She concludes by arguing that an urgent task is for the church to eliminate the anti-Jewish language still present in its liturgy (particularly the services for Holy Week), where it serves to perpetuate prejudice and hatred. (We shall return to this topic below.)

Taking up this challenge, we decided to devote a substantial part of this volume to the subject of worship, beginning with yet another prominent feature of Orthodox Christianity which provokes discomfort for Jews: the veneration of images. The Bible and post-Biblical Jewish writings polemize against the manufacture and worship of idols: this was one of the main Jewish complaints against the pagan Greeks and Romans. Yet early Byzantine Judaism was apparently not hostile to images. The archaeology of ancient synagogues, both in the Land of Israel and elsewhere, has revealed numerous examples of mosaic floors showing biblical scenes, and even one spectacular synagogue, now reconstructed in the National Museum in Damascus, whose walls are covered with such images (Simon 1986: 17–28; Prigent 1990). It has been cogently argued that there was a close connection between Jewish and Christian iconography (Simon 1986: 382, 388; Prigent 1990). But whereas Orthodox Christianity survived the onslaught of iconoclasm, Judaism did not, and the use of images was definitively abolished in synagogues (Prigent 1990: 32–5). In any case, although human figures had been tolerated, and even some pagan symbols, the closest the Jewish iconographers approached to representing the Godhead was to show the hand of God descending from the sky. It is different in the church. As Elena Narinskaya puts it, 'icons penetrate and represent the very essence of Orthodox Christian identity,' and there is no hesitation about representing God visually, in his incarnate form. Challenging though this may be for Jews, they must surely learn to understand and accept the strong attachment of Orthodox Christians to icons, and the strong theological basis for this attachment. Daniel Weiss responds in a positive spirit, basing himself on rabbinic texts and on arguments drawn from Jewish theology. He comes to the possibly surprising conclusion that even in this ostensibly intractable area dialogue is possible, and he suggest that 'better awareness of the *shared conceptual dynamic* of iconic thinking can help Jews perceive Orthodox Christians as different from themselves in various ways, but not as operating with a categorically foreign theology.'

The subject of worship indeed clamors for our attention, being such a central feature of the corporate and individual life of Jews and Orthodox Christians. Once again, it is the veneration for tradition which is the major obstacle to change. Metropolitan Kallistos of Diokleia, a regular participant in our discussions, read us a very useful paper on this subject in 2003, outlining the main issues. Unfortunately his health did not allow him to develop it into a fuller treatment, so we decided to include it as it was given, as it distinguishes the various issues and offers some signposts towards change.

One of the positive aspects of Jewish–Orthodox Christian dialogue is that it offers room to Orthodox Jewish participants, because of the commitment to tradition that they both share. Orthodox Judaism is not totally resistant to liturgical change. For example, in the *Aleinu* prayer the British Orthodox prayerbook has omitted the words, referring to the 'nations of the world,' ' . . . who worship vain and worthless beings, and make supplication to a god who cannot save,' on the grounds that they might cause offense to Christians. However, as Howard Cooper explains, the more liberal branches of Judaism have undertaken thoroughgoing revision of the traditional prayers, and some have explored novel approaches to worship. The Jewish minorities in countries where Orthodox Christianity prevails have hardly been touched by these new trends, which indicate some of the ways in which worship can potentially be made more relevant to new generations with different needs. Notable forerunners in this approach were the Hasidim of eighteenth-century Poland. In a similar vein, Jeremy Schonfield offers a personal interpretation of the annual cycle of fasts and feasts in the Jewish calendar, in the hope that it may serve as a model for exploring parallel narratives in other faith traditions.

The biblical Psalms offer common ground for Jews and Christians. Yves Dubois explains their use in Orthodox Christian worship. His account takes us back to the early days of the Church, when it was still very close to Judaism. Indeed, it is possible that the practice of reading the entire psalter in the course of a week is a relic of an ancient Jewish practice, now lost (see further on this topic de Lange 2014). Jewish readers, familiar with the Psalms from the synagogue worship, will find familiar elements here.

Michael Hilton looks back at the matrix out of which Judaism and Christianity both evolved. From that common ground the two religions branched out in different directions, and yet, surviving in small islands in a Christian sea, Judaism was not impervious to influences from the majority culture. The perspective here is mainly a western one, but an analogous investigation of Judaism in Orthodox lands would reveal similar instances of influence from the environment. It would also show how much both religions owe to the background in ancient Greek religion and Roman law (de Lange 2015, 151–3; de Lange 2002). There is also room for a study showing how much Orthodox Christianity owes to Judaism: is it a coincidence, for instance, that both make the year begin in September, when the biblical injunction is for it to start in April (Ex 12:2) (de Lange 2014)?

Reverting to the question of the hostility to Judaism detected in the Orthodox liturgy, Michael Azar confronts the issues head-on, identifying the texts in question and asking what can be done about them. Eschewing simple solutions to a complicated problem, he stresses that, on the positive side, it is not true that Orthodoxy consistently resists all change to the liturgy. The decentralized structure of the Church presents obstacles to change, but at the same time offers some practical leeway.

The last two chapters are concerned with the 'blood libel' the false accusation by Christians that Jews murder Christian children to use their blood for ritual purposes. They originated in a session of our group held in June 2004. John Klier, a leading historian of Russian Jewry who was one of the moving forces behind our group, sadly passed away in 2007; his paper is reproduced here as he delivered it. George Wilkes has kindly elaborated the paper he delivered for this publication. The libel has a long history, often resulting in shocking violence against Jews, but this history belongs mainly in Western Europe and specifically in German-speaking lands, so it may seem surprising to find it discussed in a book about Orthodox Christianity. Sadly, in the course of the nineteenth and early twentieth centuries there were a number of incidents in countries where Orthodoxy was the dominant religion. John Klier, examining the Russian examples carefully, concludes that the involvement of the Orthodox church was minimal, and identifies political motivation. George Wilkes, broadening the enquiry to take in the Greek Orthodox church, adopts a similar tack. Once again, historical research can serve as an antidote to theological generalization.

Behind the blood libel there lurks a bigger problem: the pogroms. Before Auschwitz occupied the foreground of our minds, the name of Kishinev played a similar role as shorthand for the discrimination and violence practiced against Jews. The Orthodox church, the Russian government, and even the Tsar were commonly blamed for this atrocity, in which the blood libel and the *Protocols of the Elders of Zion* were implicated. Once more, the myths do not stand up to careful historical scrutiny (see Zipperstein 2018), but the Russian pogroms, especially for Jews of eastern European origin, still cast a very long shadow. More painstaking historical research is needed if these stumbling blocks on the path to better relations between Jews and Orthodox Christians are to be removed.

In this volume we have tried to lay foundations for continuing dialogue. In a companion volume, *Tois Pasin ho Kairos: Judaism and Orthodox Christianity Facing the Future*, we consider some of the challenges posed to both faiths by the changing world in which we are living.

BIBLIOGRAPHY

de Lange N. 1976. *Origen and the Jews*. Cambridge.

de Lange N. 2006. 'The Orthodox Churches in dialogue with Judaism,' in *Challenges in Jewish–Christian Relations*, ed. J. K. Aitken & E. Kessler, 51–62. New York/Mahwah NJ.

de Lange N. 2014. 'Byzantium and the Judaic Tradition,' in *Byzantine Culture. Papers from the Conference 'Byzantine Days of Istanbul,' May 21–23 2010*, ed. D. Sakel, 29–35. Istanbul.

de Lange N. 2015. *Japheth in the Tents of Shem: Greek Bible Translations in Byzantine Judaism*. Tübingen.

de Lange N. 2022. *Jews in the Byzantine Empire*. Athens.

Grypeou E. & H. Spurling. 2009. 'Abraham's Angels: Jewish and Christian Exegesis of Genesis 18–19,' in *The Exegetical Encounter between Jews and Christians in Late Antiquity*, ed. E. Grypeou & H. Spurling, 181–203. Leiden & Boston.

Lawson J. C. 1910. *Modern Greek Folklore and Ancient Greek Religion: A Study in Survivals*. Cambridge.

Prigent P. 1990. *Le Judaïsme et l'image*. Tübingen.

Rutishauser C. M. 'The 1947 Seelisberg Conference: The Foundation of the Jewish–Christian Dialogue,' *Studies in Jewish–Christian Relations* 2/2 (2007), 34–53.

Scholem G.G. 1941. *Major Trends in Jewish Mysticism*. Jerusalem.

Simon M. 1986. *Verus Israel: A Study of the Relations between Christians and Jews in the Roman Empire (AD 135–425)*, tr. from French by H. McKeating. Oxford.

Simpson W.W. & R. Weyl, 1995. *The Story of the International Council of Christians and Jews. A Brief History of the ICCJ, 1946–1995. Heppenheim.*

Tabak Y. 'Problems and Prospects of Christian–Jewish Dialogue: A Russian Perspective.' Available on www.jcrelations.net (accessed 25 October 2021).

Tabak Y. 'Relations between the Russian Orthodox Church and Judaism: Past and Present.' Available on www.jcrelations.net (accessed 25 October 2021).

Zipperstein S. J. 2018. *Pogrom: Kishinev and the Tilt of History*. New York.

SUGGESTIONS FOR FURTHER READING

Averintsev S. 2006. 'Some Constant Characteristics of Byzantine Orthodoxy,' in *Byzantine Orthodoxies*, ed. A. Louth & A. Casiday, 167–78. Aldershot.

Gurevich A., ed. 1995. *Pravoslavnaya tserkov' i yevrei* [The Orthodox Church and the Jews]. Moscow.

Jacobs L. 1973. *A Jewish Theology*. London.

Jacobs L. 1995. *The Jewish Religion: A Companion*. Oxford.

Kratzert T. 1994. *Wir sind wie die Juden: der griechisch-orthodoxe Beitrag zu einem ökumenischen jüdisch-christlichen Dialog*. Berlin.

Külzer A. 1999. *Disputationes graecae contra Iudaeos. Untersuchungen zur byzantinischen Dialogliteratur und ihrem Judenbild*. Stuttgart.

Lowe M., ed. 1994. Orthodox Christians and Jews on Continuity and Renewal (Immanuel 26/27). Jerusalem.

Papademetriou G. C. 1991. Essays in Orthodox Christian–Jewish Relations. Lima OH.

Parkes James. 1934. *The Conflict of the Church and the Synagogue: A Study in the Origins of Antisemitism*. London.

Rudney A. 1995. 'Conditions for Dialogue between Jews and Christians in Russia' (translated by Emma Watkins), *Religion, State and Society: The Keston Journal*, 23:1, 11–17.

Schreckenberg Heinz. 1990. *Die christlichen Adversus-Judaeos-Texte und ihr literarisches und historischen Umfeld (1.–11. Jh.)* (2nd edition). Frankfurt am Main.

Shanks H., ed. 1992. *Christianity and Rabbinic Judaism: A Parallel History of Their Origins and Early Development*. Washington DC.

Chapter 1

Mysticism in the Orthodox Christian Tradition

Marcus Plested

The Orthodox Christian tradition has long been distinguished by its rich mystical theology and pronounced accent on mystical experience as a goal set before all baptized Christians. This quest for a direct and deifying encounter with the ultimately unknowable divine other has taken many forms and had many eloquent exponents over the millennia. I can scarcely cover all of these within the confines of this chapter but will offer instead a selection of examples that will give some impression, at least, of the chief characteristics of the Orthodox mystical tradition. I shall also offer some comments on its principal theological underpinnings. My principal examples will be from the fourth century: St Gregory of Nyssa and Macarius (Macarius-Symeon, pseudo-Macarius). In both cases I will emphasize their use of material from the Old Testament or Hebrew Bible and make occasional and very inexpert connections to forms of Jewish mysticism.

Before going much further I should say something about the term 'mysticism.' The word derives ultimately from the Greek *mueo*—'to close the eye, to initiate into the mysteries.' While the abstract term 'mysticism' is not one we find in the Church Fathers, or indeed in classical philosophy, terms such as 'mystery,' 'mystic' and 'mystical' have a have a long history within Christian usage. For the purposes of this chapter I shall use all of these terms, including the neologism 'mysticism,' to denote some aspect of the pursuit and experience of union with the divine—with the unknown and yet somehow well-known God.

In contemplating the topic of mystical experience, I am drawn in the first instance to the Egyptian desert, to what is often called the 'golden age' of monasticism. While a celibate lifestyle has only ever been a very marginal

1

and atypical feature of Jewish religious practice, the fourth century witnessed a veritable explosion of Christian monasticism both in Egypt and elsewhere. Monasticism was to become a dominant feature of the life and spiritual character of the Christian Roman Empire down to its fall in 1453 and remains omnipresent and deeply embedded in Orthodox life and thought to the present day. And while not every Orthodox monk or nun has experienced God directly, there are certainly many who have and who have articulated that experience in some manner or other. Going back to the miraculous cruelty and clarity of the Egyptian desert, where there is precious little to separate man and God, we find Abba Longinus expressing this arresting thought:

> A woman knows she has conceived when she stops losing blood. So it is with the soul, she knows she has conceived the Holy Spirit when the passions stop coming out of her. But as long as one is held back in the passions, how can one dare to believe that one is sinless? Give blood and receive the Spirit. (*Apophthegmata Patrum* 1975, 123)

This vivid and uncompromising piece of advice from fifth-century Egypt neatly conveys the idea that strenuous ascetic effort is almost invariably a prerequisite for mystical experience. It also emphasizes the fact that mystical experience is inescapably an embodied experience. We do not approach God as disembodied intellects but as a psychophysical whole.

Union with God is a recurrent feature of the New Testament: from Christ's high-priestly prayer that 'all may be one' (Jn 17:21) to St Paul's own mystical experience of ineffable reality (2 Cor 12:2–4) and the injunction to become 'partakers of the divine nature' in 2 Peter 1:4. But it is in the writers of the Alexandrine tradition, in figures such as Clement and Origen of Alexandria, that mystical experience gravitates to the very center of Christian theology. Here we pause to acknowledge the irony—if that is the word—that these writers are heavily indebted to a Jewish theologian: Philo.

For Philo, God remains radically unknowable in himself but draws the creature closer to himself through his mediating powers and operations (especially his word (*logos*) and wisdom (*sophia*)) which stand in-between the created and uncreated realms. For Philo, the Hebrew prophets instance the ecstasy this process entails—one is to be drawn out not only of the world of sense but also of oneself in 'ecstasy and divine possession and madness'—a form of consciousness that is best conveyed through the motif of darkness, through the eclipse and eviction of the mind:

> For when the light of God shines, the human light sets; when the divine light sets, the human dawns and rises. This is what regularly befalls the fellowship of the prophets. The mind is evicted at the arrival of the divine Spirit, but when

that departs the mind returns to its tenancy. Mortal and immortal may not share the same home. And therefore the setting of reason and the darkness which surrounds it produce ecstasy and inspired frenzy. (*Who is the Heir of Divine things?* 264–5, Philo 1932: 419)

We should be careful to note that this is not a *unio mystica*, properly speaking. Philo's Jewish and classical inheritances combine to preclude anything like the Christian doctrine of *theosis* or deification, predicated as this is on the incarnation. As expressed by St Irenaeus of Lyons: 'God became what we are so that we might become what he is' (*Against the Heresies* 5, preface, Irenaeus of Lyons 1969: 14). Even where Philo uses deification-type language, he is careful to add that this is not to be construed as participation in the divine nature as such (cf. *Every Good Man is Free* 43, Philo 1941: 35–7). For Philo, the soul of the mystic—even that of Moses, the greatest of them all—is not deified but is rather raised above the usual human condition to an intermediary position between created and uncreated natures, between God and man.

St Clement of Alexandria adopts much of Philo's language of mystical encounter including the motif of divine darkness as a fitting expression of the utter incomprehensibility of God. He had no qualms, however, in speaking quite unambiguously about human deification using the same exchange formula we find in Irenaeus. Mystical experience also looms large in Origen's teaching. Origen takes the three books of Proverbs, Ecclesiastes, and the Song of Songs to refer to the three stages of ascent to God, that is, to the acquisition of the virtues, to the proper understanding of the natural world and, finally, to union (or reunion) of the soul with God. It is in large measure through Origen that deification became the normative construal of salvation within the Greek patristic tradition, being taken up by figures such as St Athanasius and the Cappadocian Fathers. All subsequent doctrinal debates, both Trinitarian and Christological, tended to revolve around precisely this question: only if God (in the fullest possible sense of the term) has truly become human (also in the fullest possible sense of the term) can humans hope to become divine.

The great Cappadocian theologian St Gregory of Nyssa (c.332–c.395) stands squarely within this tradition. While it is St Gregory the Theologian who first coins the noun 'theosis,' it is his friend Gregory of Nyssa who gives us perhaps the most extensive and penetrating exposition of the mystical life. Among his best-known works are his homilies on the Song of Songs and his *Life of Moses*—a work that clearly owes something to Philo. In Gregory's *Life of Moses* the biblical narrative of Moses is treated on a number of levels, most significantly as a paradigm of the soul's ascent to a unitive and deifying experience of God. Gregory's treatment takes it as axiomatic that ascetic endeavor is a *sine qua non* of mystical experience. Every aspect of Moses' life is seen as a preparation for his ascent of the mountain and as a pattern for us to follow. Thus the crossing of the Red Sea, to take one of the most obvious examples, shows us that:

> Those who pass through the mystical water in baptism must put to death in the water the whole phalanx of evil [. . .]. Since the passions naturally pursue our nature, we must put to death in the water both the base movements of the mind and the acts which issue from them. (*Life of Moses* 2 125, Gregory of Nyssa 1978: 84)

The Egyptian army signifies the passions which must be slain if the intellect is to achieve the kind of focus it needs to apply itself to the mystical ascent. The soul must then go on to taste of the waters of Marah, 'the life far removed from pleasures'—a way of life that appears bitter and disagreeable at first:

> But if the wood be thrown into the water, that is, if one receives the mystery of the resurrection which had its beginning with the wood (you of course understand the cross when you hear the wood), then the virtuous life, being sweetened by the hope of things to come, becomes sweeter and more pleasant than all the sweetness that tickles the sense with pleasure. (*Life of Moses* 2 132, Gregory of Nyssa 1978: 86)

The bittersweet life of asceticism is very clearly a presupposition of any sort of authentic knowledge of God:

> The person who would approach the contemplation of Being [i.e. God—the source of all being] must be pure in all things so as to be pure in soul and body, washed stainless of every spot in both parts, in order that he might appear pure to the One who sees what is hidden. (*Life of Moses* 2 154, Gregory of Nyssa 1978: 92)

Such purity is required to cleanse what William Blake called the 'doors of perception,' to open the spiritual senses of the soul—senses corresponding in some measure to the physical senses but capable of direct apprehension of divine realities. As Gregory continues:

> He who would approach the knowledge of things sublime must first purify his manner of life from all sensual and irrational emotion. He must wash from his understanding every opinion derived from some preconception and withdraw himself from his customary intercourse with his own companion, that is, with his sense perceptions [. . .] When he is so purified, then he assaults the mountain. (*Life of Moses* 2 157, Gregory of Nyssa 1978: 93)

Moses—and the soul that imitates him—goes on to climb to the summit of the mountain and to penetrate the luminous darkness that stands for the true knowledge of God that transcends knowledge, the seeing that consists in not seeing.

> But as the mind progresses and, through an ever greater and more perfect diligence, comes to apprehend reality, as it approaches more nearly to contemplation, it sees more clearly what of the divine nature is uncontemplated. For leaving behind everything that is observed, not only what sense comprehends but also what the intelligence thinks it sees, it keeps on penetrating deeper until by the intelligence's yearning for understanding it gains access to the invisible and the incomprehensible, and there it sees God. This is the true knowledge of what is sought; this is the seeing that consists in not seeing, because that which is sought transcends all knowledge, being separated on all sides by incomprehensibility as by a kind of darkness. (*Life of Moses* 2 163, Gregory of Nyssa 1978: 95)

This kind of radical apophaticism was to be taken to a new pitch in Dionysius the Areopagite, most notably in his seminal *Mystical Theology*, a work that went on to shape much of the subsequent theology of both Greek East and Latin West. But while Gregory and Dionysius follow Philo in finding divine darkness a more suitable motif than that of light, it is clear that this darkness is no absence of light but rather a superabundance of light—a dazzling or luminous darkness. Attempting to convey something of the dizzying and vertiginous nature of such an encounter, Gregory offers a further arresting image:

> Imagine a sheer, steep crag, of reddish appearance below, extending into eternity; on top there is a ridge which looks down over a projecting rim into a bottomless chasm. Now imagine what a person would probably experience if he put his foot on the edge of this ridge which overlooks the chasm and found no solid footing nor anything to hold onto. This is what I think the soul experiences when it goes beyond its footing in material things in its quest for that which has no dimension and which exists from all eternity. For here there is nothing it can take hold of, neither place nor time, neither measure nor anything else; it does not allow our minds to approach. And thus the soul, slipping at every point from what cannot be grasped, becomes dizzy and perplexed and returns once again to what is connatural to it, content now to know merely this about the Transcendent, that it is completely different from the nature of things that the soul knows. (*Commentary on Ecclesiastes* 7, Gregory of Nyssa 1962, 127)

Here we see another distinctive feature of Gregory's account of mystical experience: his sense (often termed *epektasis*) that there is no end to the finite creature's progress into the depths of the infinite divine life:

> This truly is the vision of God: never to be satisfied in the desire to see him. But one must always, by looking at what he can see, rekindle his desire to see more. Thus no limit can interrupt growth in the ascent to God, since no limit to the Good can be found nor is the increasing of desire for the Good brought to an end because it is satisfied. (St Gregory of Nyssa, *Life of Moses* 2 239, Gregory of Nyssa 1978: 116)

Deification is, in other words, never a 'done deal' or finished state but rather an eternal process of ever-closer assimilation to the infinite deity.

I now turn to Macarius, with Gregory one of the great fountainheads of the Christian mystical tradition. Since at least the sixth century a large corpus of ascetic material (homilies, treatises, letters, questions and answers) has been ascribed to St Macarius the Great of Egypt, founder of the semieremitic monastic community at Scetis in the Wadi Natrun. Less commonly, some of the writings have been ascribed to St Macarius the Alexandrian or a certain Symeon (hence 'Macarius-Symeon'). The corpus has, however, been shown to be the work of an anonymous ascetic writing in Syria or Mesopotamia roughly between the 370s and the 390s. The author, whom for convenience I refer to as Macarius ('the blessed one') was a clearly a mystic of the highest order—so much so that Gregory of Nyssa copied one of his works (the *Epistola magna*) and passed it off as his own (the *De instituto christiano*). Macarius' writings attest in the most vivid and precise of terms to the reality of mystical experience and the burning need for each and every baptized Christian to strive towards such experience. While writing for a primarily monastic audience, Macarius (like Basil of Caesarea) never refers to 'monks' or 'nuns' but only to 'Christians,' thereby reinforcing the splendidly democratic character of his mystical vision.

Mystical experience, for Macarius, is not always a comfortable experience and involves both good and bad. Like Gregory, he makes this point through a transposition of the trials and travails of the Exodus narrative to the soul. The soul must undergo its own Passover, tasting both the sweetness of the lamb (divine grace) and the bitterness of the herbs (the 'invisible warfare' against the passions) (II 47.7–14). Macarius similarly transposes the sacrificial prescriptions of the Old Testament to the soul, arguing that she must in some sense be 'slain' in the putting to death of her passions (II 1.6). In order to share in the glory of the Lord, she must also participate in his sufferings:

> The Lord shows himself to the soul in two aspects, with his wounds and in the glory of his light. The soul contemplates the sufferings which he suffered for her; but she also contemplates the dazzling glory of his divine light and is transfigured from glory to glory in this same image, according to [the action of] the Spirit of the Lord, and grows in both aspects—in that of the sufferings and in that of the glorious light [. . .]. (III 3.3.2)

Macarius is one of very few to thus unite the themes of Transfiguration and Crucifixion. But for all his emphasis on the severity of the struggle with the passions, Macarius never lapses into any sort of body–soul dualism but rather maintains a sense of the human being as a psychophysical unity held together in the heart. The heart is, for Macarius, not only the physical and affective but also *intellectual* center of the human person—for it bears the intellect as charioteer and governor:

> For the heart governs and reigns over the whole bodily organism; and when grace possesses the pastures of the heart, it reigns over all the members and the thoughts [. . .] For there, in the heart, is the intellect, and all the faculties of the soul, and its expectation; therefore grace penetrates also to all the members of the body. (II 15.20)

The heart is thus axis on which the body is enabled to participate in the mystical life of the soul. It is the deepest and realest self and thus necessarily the locus of mystical experience:

> Although the heart is a small vessel, it contains dragons and lions, venomous beasts and all the stockpiles of evil, rough and uneven paths and chasms. Likewise God and the angels are there, as are life and the Kingdom, light and the apostles, the heavenly cities and the treasuries of grace. All things are there. (II 43.7)

The involvement of the body in mystical experience is further illustrated through a compelling account of the interiorization of the Lord's Transfiguration on Thabor:

> As the body of the Lord was glorified when he ascended the mountain and was transfigured into the divine glory and the infinite light, so too are the bodies of the saints glorified and resplendent. For as the glory that was within Christ covered his body and shone forth, in the same way the power of Christ that is [now] within the saints will overflow outwards upon their bodies. (II 15.38)

Mention of Thabor brings us on to another distinctive feature of the Orthodox Christian mystical tradition: the emphasis on the vision and experience of God as light. Along with his emphasis on the heart, Macarius is also known as one of the greatest exponents of a mysticism of light. Again, this is an aspect of mystical experience that has its Old Testament counterpart: the light that shone from Moses' face on his descent from Sinai being the product of his own vision of supernal light and a prefiguration of the resurrection glory of the body (II 5.10). For Macarius, the direct experience of the divine light is absolutely definitive Christian hope and incumbent on all Christians. As he explains:

> The blessed Apostle Paul, the architect of the Church, forever anxious for the truth and not wishing that those who hear the word should be impeded by ignorance, indicated with great exactitude and clarity the goal of the truth and made known the perfect mystery of Christianity in every believing soul, this being to receive through a divine operation the experience of the effulgence of the heavenly light in holy souls in the revelation and power of the Spirit. (I 58.1.1)

Let me now turn to a remarkable passage with obvious connections to the Jewish *merkabah* tradition. This is the passage which opens the most widespread collection of the Macarian writings (Collection II) and which conveys one of the guiding principles of the Macarian writings: *theosis* conceived in terms of God's indwelling in man. For Macarius, the vision of the prophet Ezekiel (Ez 1:10) is of the soul become the 'throne of glory,' or 'dwelling place' of God (II 1.2).

> The blessed prophet Ezekiel recounted a glorious and inspired vision or apparition which he saw, describing a vision full of ineffable mysteries. He saw in the plain a chariot of Cherubim, four spiritual living creatures [. . .]. That which the prophet actually saw was true and certain, but it signified and foreshadowed something else, a 'mystery hidden from ages and from generations' (cf. Col 1:26) [. . .] The mystery which he saw was of the soul which receives the Lord and becomes his 'throne of glory' (cf. Mt 19:28). For the soul which is found worthy to be a partaker in the Spirit of his light is illumined by the beauty of his ineffable glory and established as his seat and dwelling place. Such a soul becomes all light, all face, all eye, and there no part of her which is not full of the spiritual eyes of light. (II 1.1–2)

Macarius goes on to provide a rich variety of accounts of mystical experience. Here we may draw attention to a pronounced pneumatological dimension, a pronounced emphasis on the power and operation of the Holy Spirit. The following is just one of many possible passages:

> Those who have been found worthy to become children of God, to be born from above in the Spirit and to have Christ shining forth and reposing in them, are guided in varied and differing qualities of the Spirit. They are steered by grace in spiritual repose within the heart [. . .]. Sometimes it seems that they are a royal banquet rejoicing and exulting in an inexpressible joy and happiness. [. . .] Sometimes they are as if drunk with wine, drunk with the divine and spiritual drunkenness of the Spirit in heavenly mysteries. And then at other times they are full of weeping and lamentation as they intercede for man's salvation. For, burning with the love of the Spirit for all mankind, they take to themselves the

sorrow and grief of the whole Adam. [. . .] Grace guides the soul in very many different ways [. . .] so as to present it perfect, spotless and pure to the heavenly Father [. . .] When the soul attains spiritual perfection, totally purged of all the passions and perfectly united to and mingled with the Spirit [. . .] in ineffable communion, then the soul is itself vouchsafed to become spirit, being commingled with the Spirit. It then becomes all light, all spirit, all joy, all repose, all gladness, all love, all compassion, all goodness and kindness. It is as though it had been swallowed up in the virtues of the Holy Spirit as a stone in the depths of the sea is surrounded by water. Such people are totally mingled with and embraced by the Spirit, united to the grace of Christ, and assimilated to Christ. (I 13.2.1–4)

Such union with God, Macarius is careful to note, does not imply confusion of natures. The ontological gap between infinite and finite nature endures. As he explains:

He is God, the soul is not God. He is Lord, it a servant. He is Creator, it a creature. He is maker, it a thing made. There is nothing in common between his nature and that of the soul. But through his infinite, ineffable and inconceivable love and compassion, he has been pleased to dwell in this thing of his making, this intellectual creation, this precious and especial work. (II 49.4)

Neither God's dwelling in man nor man's dwelling in God eradicates the ontological gap between their respective natures. Man may be deified, but he is not thereby lost in the Godhead. Macarius explains that in the resurrection:

all the members become translucent, all are plunged into light and fire, and transformed; they are not, as some say, destroyed, they do not become fire, their own nature ceasing to subsist. For Peter remains Peter, and Paul remains Paul, and Philip remains Philip. Each retains his own nature and hypostasis, filled by the Spirit. (II 15.10)

Here we have the Christian doctrine of deification in a nutshell: humans remain created and finite by nature and hypostasis even as they are totally transformed in their plunge into the uncreated light and fire of the divinity.

The themes laid down in Gregory and (especially) Macarius remain normative and formative for the later Orthodox mystical tradition: the Trinitarian and Christocentric dimension of mystical experience, the involvement of the body, the language and theology of deification, the emphasis on the heart, the focus on ascetic endeavor, and the vision of God described in terms of light and/or darkness.

In the later tradition we see mystical experience gravitate to the very center of the whole Byzantine theological enterprise. For example, St Maximus the Confessor in the seventh century grounds his confession of the two wills—divine and human—of Christ not so much on abstract theological principles but on the lived experience of the saints of the synergistic and personalistic character of union with God. And in the eleventh-century figure of St Symeon the New Theologian we see this mystical tradition at its most vibrant and audacious, including several detailed accounts of his own experience of the divine light. For Symeon, to deny mystical experience as a universal calling was not only heresy but the summation of all heresies since it amounts to a total evacuation of the Gospel and the annulment of Christ's promises (*Catecheses* 29, Symeon the New Theologian 1965: 177–9).

In the fourteenth century the whole notion of the deifying vision of God as light came into question in the course of Hesychast controversy. It fell to St Gregory Palamas to defend the reality of this experience (an experience for which one must ready oneself through ascetic renunciation and the practice of the Jesus Prayer). With the mystical experience of figures such as Macarius and Symeon, together with that of monastics of his own time, Gregory argues for dogmatic distinction between the unapproachable and utterly unknowable nature or essence of God and God's self-revelation in his attributes, energies, or operations. His divine presence (corresponding perhaps in some sense to the *Shekhinah*) underpinning and sustaining the creation, for example, is to be understood in terms of energy or operation, not of essence. It would of course be instructive to compare this schema to the *sefirot* of the *Zohar* although the *sefirot* are clearly emanations, and not energies, of God. Palamas further explains that there are three forms of divine union. The first, according to nature, pertains only to the three persons of the Trinity. The second, according to person or hypostasis, pertains only to the two natures of Christ. The third, open to all rational creatures, pertains to energy or grace. The doctrine of the divine energies thus serves as the basis of the doctrine of deification.

Space being limited, I should like to conclude by underlining the point that the mystical tradition laid down in the figures I have mentioned has remained central to the Orthodox Christian tradition down to the present day—so much so that a twentieth-century Franco-Russian theologian, Vladimir Lossky, could claim very plausibly that there is no mysticism without theology and no theology without mysticism (Lossky 1957, 9). This, he claimed, was the essential difference between the Orthodox and the various western Christian traditions. While one might question his ingrained sense of East–West dichotomy, there is no doubting his basic premises. The very fact that he was able to make such a claim without being laughed out of court tells us something about the extent to which the Orthodox Christian tradition remains defined and characterized by the experience of its mystics. This, I think, could certainly not be said of the Jewish tradition: I do not believe mystical experience has ever occupied such a privileged place within mainstream Judaism nor that a similar statement to that of Lossky could possibly be applied within

Judaism. I would also note the difficulty of sustaining a theology of deification within a Jewish world-view. This brings us, I think, to another point of contrast: we do not have in the Jewish tradition a developed metaphysical basis for mystical union. As I hope to have shown, Orthodox Christians rapidly connected the possibility of mystical union with Trinitarian theology and Christology (and, later, to the essence–energies distinction). This metaphysical basis of mystical union is—so far as I am aware—absent (or at least marginal) within Judaism. But while I have concluded with some points of contrast, I do not deny that we are dealing with the same ultimate reality and the same hope of drawing ever closer to the one true God.

BIBLIOGRAPHY

Apophthegmata Patrum. 1975. *The Sayings of the Desert Fathers* tr. B. Ward. Oxford.

Gregory of Nyssa. 1962. *From Glory to Glory: Texts from Gregory of Nyssa's Mystical Writings*, tr. H. Musurillo. London.

Gregory of Nyssa. 1978. *Gregory of Nyssa: The Life of Moses*, tr. E. Ferguson and A. Malherbe. New York/Mahwah NJ.

Irenaeus of Lyons. 1969. *Contre les hérésies* 5, ed. and tr. A. Rousseau. (Sources Chrétiennes 153.) Paris.

Lossky, Vladimir. 1957. *The Mystical Theology of the Eastern Church*. Cambridge.

Macarius [References to Greek original; translations my own]:

    I = *Makarios/Symeon: Reden und Briefe* ed. H. Berthold. (Die griechischen christlichen Schriftseller der ersten drei Jahrhunderte 55–56.) Berlin 1973.

    II = *Die 50 Geistliche Homilien des Makarios* ed. H. Dörries, E. Klostermann, M. Kroeger. (Patristische Texte und Studien 4.) Berlin 1964.

    III = *Pseudo-Macaire: Oeuvres spirtuelles I: Homélies propres à la Collection III* ed. and tr. V. Desprez. (Sources Chrétiennes 275.) Paris 1980.

Philo of Alexandria. 1932. *Who is the Heir of Divine things?*, ed. and tr. F. Colson and G. Whitaker. (Loeb Classical Library 261.) Cambridge MA.

Philo of Alexandria. 1941. *Every Good Man is Free*, ed. and tr. F. Colson. (Loeb Classical Library 363.) Cambridge MA.

Symeon the New Theologian. 1965. *Catéchèses 23–34*, ed. B. Krivocheine and tr. J. Paramelle. (Sources Chrétiennes 113.) Paris.

Chapter 2

The God Who Can and Cannot be Said

Daniel Davies

Among representatives of negative theology in the Jewish tradition, Moses Maimonides is often thought to be the most extreme. In his *Guide for the Perplexed*, he states that only negations should be used to refer to God. 'Know that the description of God, may He be cherished and exalted, by means of negations is the correct description—a description that is not affected by an indulgence in facile language and does not imply any deficiency with respect to God in general or in any particular mode' (Maimonides 1963: 134). Moreover, even negations are only used if they are of a certain kind. 'Even those negations are not used with reference to or applied to Him, may He be exalted, except from the following point of view, which you know: one sometimes denies with reference to a thing something that cannot fittingly exist in it' (Maimonides 1963: 136). Maimonides then explains that denying divine attributes aims at showing that language cannot be applied to God because no attributes can exist in the divine. He explains that they do not simply indicate a privation, an example of which would be negating sight of a person and thereby attributing blindness. Instead, it is similar to negating sight of a wall, which is to deny that a wall is the kind of thing that sees. The same is true of negating attributes of God: God is simply not the kind of thing that can be said to have any sort of property, whether that is color, size, wisdom, life, or goodness. Maimonides even seems to use this method when writing of God's existence: 'of this thing we say that it exists, the meaning being that its nonexistence is impossible' (Maimonides 1963: 135). Neither existence nor nonexistence is appropriate to God. God's existence has nothing in common with the any existence that we encounter, so that the word 'exists' could only be used of both if we bear in mind that the meanings are entirely different. 'Existence is, in our opinion, affirmed of Him, may He be exalted, and of what is other than He merely by way of absolute equivocation' (Maimonides 1963: 118).

It is tempting to think that Maimonides must be saying either that we can come to some knowledge of God simply by saying what God is not without saying anything at all about what God is (Davies 1993: 27) or that we can have no knowledge at all of God (Pines 1979). There are passages in the *Guide* that appear to indicate that negations cannot provide any knowledge whatsoever of God. He writes, for example, that 'negation does not give knowledge in any respect of the true reality of the thing with regard to which the particular matter in question has been negated' (Maimonides 1963: 139). The 'true reality' and the essence of God is, in Maimonides' view, unknowable. The consequences of a negative theology lead to an account of God that is too thin for many believers. For example, Franz Rosenzweig wrote that once a theologian has completed the task of negation, 'negative theology and atheism can shake hands' (Rosenzweig 1971: 23). Some interpreters of Maimonides even argue that he was aiming at something similar, although that is a contentious interpretation (Davidson 2005: 412).

I do not think that the account of Maimonides as purely a negative theologian who merely wishes to turn our attention away from God and towards the world is a fair representation. It ignores some of his own clarifications and neglects the dialectical and rhetorical context of the chapters explicitly dedicated to the matter. In practice, Maimonides does not deny that God is the necessary existent and that such a being contains all perfections. Instead, he denies that divine, uncreated perfections can be of the same kind as created ones. He is not as negative as he is often made out to be. Saying that God's essence cannot be known is not the same as saying that nothing at all can be known about God. Maimonides explains that while God's essence is unknowable, it is possible to know that God is a necessary existent and the creator of all other existent beings. However, I will not explicitly engage with the debate in the literature on Maimonides in this chapter. Instead, I will suggest that the claim that atheism follows from negative theology fails to take into account ontological assumptions held by many in the Middle Ages. Furthermore, even if it is granted that God is unknowable, it need not automatically follow that God must also be unspeakable. It will turn out that Maimonides' account of God results in a negative theology but, for other thinkers, that very same account also allows certain terms to be used of God: the God who cannot be said is also the God who can be said.

Denial is a crucial aspect of negative theology. The reasons that Maimonides argues for divine ineffability are the same reasons that he argues in favor of negative attributes. Even if we are to stop at denials, an important part of the work has been done. Kenneth Seeskin writes that atheism 'is a risk that has to be run, because only through the process of denying inadequate conceptions of God can we reach the idea of true transcendence' (Seeskin 2000: 36). And affirming God's transcendence is an important task that, Seeskin argues, is at the very heart of Judaism.

If the aim is to arrive at a notion of divine transcendence that prevents idolatrous thoughts that associate the creator with something not divine, perhaps this strategy would prove sufficient. Asserting that God is transcendent could demand nothing more than simply denying that anything created, or anything either intelligible or imaginable, is to be associated with the divine. Seeskin explains that a genuine commitment to even such an apparently minimal notion of the divine is an extremely difficult task.

The negative move itself therefore has profound ramifications for our lives. If only God is worthy of worship, and God must constantly be distanced from anything that can be grasped, the symbols that humans need and that are part of religious life must constantly be kept distinct from the divine. A correct attitude toward life-goals, ideologies, material goods, and even spiritualities would involve appreciating the value of created things and treating them accordingly by committing to the appropriate degree. Bearing in mind that God is the only being worthy of absolute worship challenges us to keep in mind constantly that the values we hold and the way in which we commit to them must be subjected to constant re-evaluation in light of what is most important, God's transcendence.

While Seeskin is correct to point out the importance of this aspect of negative theology, he recognizes that it is not identical to atheism: the idea of God is not empty but is 'an idea whose full meaning is too much for our minds to grasp' (Seeskin 2017: 52). Since negation alone does not tell the whole story, is there anything more that can be said?

I would like to suggest that the assessment that atheism follows from a negative theology is based on an assumption about existence that Maimonides and many others throughout history did not share, even though it is prevalent in modern thought. Today, it is common to suppose that the existence affirmed or denied of any object is the same as that which is affirmed or denied of any other object. Existence is thought to be everywhere the same. Furthermore, existence is not an empirical feature of an existing object, so the slogan 'exists is not a predicate' is often used to indicate that existence does not add anything and, therefore, existence cannot be a real property. It is considered the emptiest of features, adding nothing to any existing thing. Instead, existence has been called an 'on/off' feature. "Existence is an on/off property: 'either you're there or you're not'" (Hughes 1990: 26). There is no difference between the existence of one kind of object and that of another.

On the basis of such a view, negative theology does indeed seem to lead close to atheism. If existence has a single meaning, denying that God possesses existence in the same way as creatures do is to deny that God exists at all. Many medieval thinkers, possessed of a different set of ontological assumptions, were able to deny that God possesses creaturely attributes without denying God altogether. God was said to be distinct from creation not by virtue of lacking being but by possessing the fullness of being, a corollary of God being indistinct from God's existence. However, this is a concept that benefits from the idea there are modulations in existence, a point that is denied by the belief that existence is an empty property.

Below, I will explain that Maimonides distinguishes God's manner of existence from that of all creatures by classing it as necessary. However, before considering whether it makes sense to speak of a Necessary Existent, it is worth considering how to characterize existence when it belongs to familiar objects, i.e., contingent, created beings. The claim is that in all created beings there can be essential and accidental attributes but, at an even more fundamental level, there must be a distinction between what the being is and its very existence. The distinction is reflected in the fact that an answer to the question what something is differs from the answer to the question whether something is (Burrell 1993: 40). It is possible to explain what a dinosaur or a dodo is, for example, without asserting that it still exists. A definition of these objects accounts only for what they are, and the definition is said to denote the essence of a thing. Existence is not taken as part of the definition and is therefore distinguished from essence.

Distinguishing existence from essential attributes leads Maimonides to assert that existence is accidental to created beings: 'It is known that existence is an accident attaching to what exists. For this reason it is something that is superadded to the quiddity of what exists. This is clear and necessary with regard to everything the existence of which has a cause. Hence its existence is something that is superadded to its quiddity' (Maimonides 1963: 133).

Such a position raises an obvious difficulty because it sounds as though Maimonides is saying that existing, concrete individuals are the subjects of their existence. He was criticized by, among others, Hasdai Crescas, who argued that it is absurd to treat existence as an accident, since accidents inhere in a subject. Were existence an accident, existence would require a pre-existing subject, which is impossible. If the subject is to receive existence as an accident, it must be assumed already to have existence—but it is that very existence that is supposed to be added on afterwards.

A not inconsiderable doubt occurs according to the opinion of one who says that the existence in the rest of the existing things [besides God] is other than the quiddity, and that it is an accident occurring to it. This is because if the existence is an accident, it follows necessarily that it exists in a subject. The existence would therefore have existence . . . It would follow necessarily that if this accident bestows the existence and the continuity on the essence it would be prior to the subject in terms of the essence . . . But it has already been posited as an attribute! This inconsistency cannot hold. (Crescas 1990, 96)

While it might be undemanding to say that existence is not an accidental attribute at all and simply leave it at that, it is worth considering what Maimonides meant by characterizing it as such.

As Crescas explains, an accidental attribute is posterior to the object in which it inheres. It depends on that object in order to exist. With regard to some accidental features, the relationship is simple to depict. Consider color, for example. It is easy to see that an object's color depends on the object in a way in which the object does not depend on its color. A wooden fence might be painted red, for instance, and the fence's redness would depend on the fence's existence for its own existence. The reverse is not true. The fence does not need to be red in order to exist. This aspect of an accidental feature falls victim to Crescas' criticism, if existence is also said to be accidental. Were it an accident of this kind, existence would require an object that already exists.

However, there is a way in which existence can be likened to color. A color depends on its subject in order to be distinct from other instances of the same color. Several fences could be painted with red from the same can, but each fence would have its own instance of redness distinct from that of any other instance. In this sense, existence can indeed be likened to an accidental feature. The existence of an individual is distinct from that of any other individual by belonging to the instantiated particular. A distinction between the existence of one individual and that of another relies on the individuals in question, similar to the way in which the distinction between the different instances of redness relies on the individual fences.

Maimonides' characterizing existence as an accident is therefore useful but potentially misleading. In order to defend it, there is a need to find a way to portray this connection between essence and existence that preserves the relationship outlined here. Existence must be logically prior to a subject in terms of actuality but posterior in terms of individuality.

Although Maimonides himself does not enter into an extended discussion of existence, assuming instead that his readers will be familiar with the relevant issues, his view is supported by a number of current philosophers who have attempted to rehabilitate the notion that existence is a real property of individuals. This opinion is germane to a proper understanding of Maimonides' ontology. Barry Miller is one of this view's major proponents (Miller 2002). He argues that the relationship between an existing thing and its essence can be likened to that between a substance and its bound, which, together, result in an instance of existence. The bound restricts the kinds of properties that the object has, so that those properties admitted by the essence can be predicated of it. For example, a cat can have a certain set of properties, like consciousness, furriness, or laziness, but it cannot have the ability to fly or photosynthesize. The properties that can fittingly be ascribed to the cat are delineated by its definition. Other objects have other properties, which are similarly limited by their respective bounds.

If the relationship between existence and essence is depicted in such a way, Crescas' criticism can be met. The existence of an individual would depend on the individual, on the bound, in order to be distinct from other instances of existent things. However, since a bound is posterior to that which it binds, there is no need to say that existence is occurring to something that already exists.

Using an analogy of a bound for a definition will not help to understand God's existence, however, since Maimonides insists that God cannot be defined. And in distinguishing necessary from contingent beings, he states that existence bears an accidental relationship to essence only in the case of created beings. The Necessary Existent is uncreated and simple so, in God, no distinction can be made between essence and existence. 'As for that which has no cause for its existence, there is only God, may He be magnified and glorified, who is like that. For this is the meaning of our saying about Him, may He be exalted, that His existence is necessary. Accordingly, His existence is identical with His essence and His true reality, and His essence is His existence' (Maimonides 1963: 133).

In light of the above account of the relationship between existence and individuals, these statements seem to lead to absurdity. Any instance of existence must be determined by an essence, but if the existence itself is that which determines, there would be no instance of existence. Furthermore, if God's existence is nothing other than God's essence, and the essence is that which enables attributes to be assigned, God can have no attributes aside from God's existence. Maimonides' negative theology then kicks in, because the term 'existence' cannot mean the same when applied to an instance of existence as it does when applied to God, who does not instantiate any essence. It is therefore totally equivocal. No positive attributes can be assigned to God, and the consequent negative theology appears to deny even that God exists. Again, we can only speak in denials.

Let us return to Maimonides' critique of those who posit attributes in God. He argues that they ascribe attributes to God that are of the same kind as those that exist in creatures. They are mistaken because they assume that the kind of existence attributed to God is the same as that attributed to creatures, only more intense.

> According to what they think, the difference between these attributes and ours lies in the former being greater, more perfect, more permanent, or more durable

than ours, so that His existence is more durable than our existence, His life more permanent than our life, His power greater than our power, His knowledge more perfect than our knowledge, and His will more universal than our will. In this way both notions would be, as they think, included in the same definition. (Maimonides 1963: 130)

Since God's existence is necessary, Maimonides insists that it is a mistake to assign such attributes to God, and "the term 'existent' is predicated of Him, may He be exalted, and of everything that is other than He, in a purely equivocal sense" (Maimonides 1963: 131). However, applying terms purely equivocally seems to empty them of meaning and therefore leads to a common critique of Maimonides' view, which is that there seems to be no reason to use one word rather than another. Instead of saying 'God is powerful,' why not say 'God is lazy'? For both statements, the qualification that the term does not mean the same as what we understand must be added in any case. To the extent that Maimonides anticipates this criticism, he responds that the Bible employs terms that are considered perfections by the masses, so these are the terms that are generally permissible. The purpose of using only words indicating perfection is to avoid those that people might understand to teach that there are imperfections in the divine.

For they predicate of God what they deem to be a perfection in respect to Him and do not predicate of Him that which is manifestly a deficiency. When, however, the true reality is investigated it will be found—as shall be demonstrated that He has no essential attribute existing in true reality, such as would be super-added to His essence. (Maimonides 1963: 106)

Other theologians are not satisfied with this response, however. The difference between saying that 'God is wise' and that 'God is forgetful' cannot be simply that one is useful for educating the ignorant while the other is not. One such critic is Gersonides, who argued that certain terms are said primarily of God and only in posterior fashion of creatures (Gersonides 1987: 108). Maimonides' opposition to including divine attributes in the same definition as created perfections cannot be overlooked, however. If Gersonides is not to fall victim to the objection that Maimonides raises, it will be necessary to consider whether a perfection term applied to God can be excluded from the definition of created perfections that use the same word.

If Miller's new paradigm for how essence and existence are related to one another is accepted, it is plausible that existence is different in different individuals. It is therefore possible to say that it is not merely an on/off property. Its meaning depends on the kind of thing it is predicated of. In order to clarify this idea, a comparison can be made with the way in which the word 'good' is used. Like 'existence,' 'good' can be predicated of many different kinds of things. However, the word's meaning depends on the kind of thing it is said of. I mean something quite different by 'good' when I say that 'I am drinking a good cup of coffee' from what I mean when I say that 'I am sitting on a good chair' or that 'Superman is good.' We understand the meaning of the attribute because we also understand what the attribute is predicated of; we understand words through our experience, and we have direct experience only of contingent things.

Whereas 'good' has different meanings, depending on the object it is attached to, the contention that 'existence' can have shades of meaning is denied by those who argue that it is everywhere the same. On their account, there is no difference between the existence of an amoeba and that of a person. This is a point on which many medieval thinkers disagree with the majority of today's philosophers. They held that, since the instance of existence is delineated by the essence that it instantiates, existence too can be different in different things. If existence is related to existing things in the way suggested above, so that the kind of existence that one sort of substance has differs from the kind that another sort of substance has, there is a case to say that, like 'good,' 'existence' can range across different senses. Its meaning depends on the kind of thing it is predicated of. And if there are indeed such modulations in being, it would also be possible, potentially, to establish a hierarchy of being among existing things. It would be possible to order beings according to their ontological richness: a definition that is less restricting would allow for a greater number of properties. Many philosophers in other eras thought that there are degrees of reality. It is something that would need to be argued for today, but it nevertheless has support (Zangwill 2011: 530).

The possibility that such a scale could be drawn up leads to the question of how to portray the scale's maximum degree. We can ask whether it is possible for its perfection to differ essentially from the scale's members. If so, the limit would not fall under the same definition as those members. One way to depict how a scale of related things can have different kinds of maximal limits is by analogy with the two limits of speed. At one end of the scale is the speed of light, which is a limit beyond which there can be no greater speed. At the other end, however, the limit is not a speed at all, but is instead motionlessness. It is not included in the same definition as speed and is not a member of that scale. Nevertheless, even though motionlessness does not belong to the scale that it limits, it is related to that scale and, like light speed, can be considered the point at which the scale terminates.

Applying this distinction between different sorts of limits to the critique that Maimonides makes of attributes shows that the kind of attribute that he objects to is the kind that is a maximum of a scale. When people talk of God's power, they mean that it is simply greater and more perfect than that of creatures. It is therefore the same in kind as a created attribute and comprised in the same definition. However, if the perfection is not limited by the being attached to a limited, created being, it could be said not to be restricted by a definition. Returning to 'goodness,' for example, whereas the meaning of the word good is restricted to the kind of good that properly belongs to the subject it is predicated of, goodness itself is not. Furthermore, although we meet with instances of particular good things, we never come across an instance of pure goodness, unlimited by any bound.

If unrestricted, unlimited perfections are the kinds that Gersonides wishes to say are primarily said of God, he would be able to defend the view that they are said primarily of God and only derivatively of creatures. In order to explain such a move, it is helpful to distinguish between what such a term, which can be considered a perfection term, can mean in itself and what can be understood by such a term, a distinction that Maimonides never makes. When we say that something is good, and we understand what it is that is good, the term is used in a restricted sense. However, if it is also legitimate to talk of 'goodness,' we are using the term to refer to something that we do not understand.

While Maimonides never explicitly admits that certain terms are used more properly of the necessary existent than of created beings, he shares the view of other thinkers that God is to be identified with the divine existence and, therefore, shares the grounds used to make such a leap. Moreover, there is good reason to think that he also indicated that a Necessary Being is absolute and unlimited perfection, even though he denies that we can use words to capture that. His concern is to avoid defining or describing God in any way, and therefore to insist that words cannot be said to reveal any knowledge of the divine essence. Although he does not explicitly make this distinction, there is nothing in his philosophical assumptions or statements indicating that he would find it objectionable.

Maimonides denies that any divine perfection 'can be subsumed under the same definition' as created perfections. The question then becomes whether or not it is possible to use words that cannot be defined. Maimonides does not explicitly say that we can use words to represent something that we cannot understand by them except through 'a certain looseness of expression' (Maimonides 1963: 133), by taking liberties with language. However, if words like 'goodness' and 'existence' can be used to speak of what is unlimited, they are properly used of what cannot be understood. Maimonides' disagreement with those like Gersonides therefore concerns how we can use language, not what we can know of God's essence.

With a common conception of existence as an empty property, negative theology leads to a God that is an important corrective to temptations to worship anything intelligible and, therefore, created. Some consider belief in such a God to be close to atheism. However, adopting a conception of existence that accords more closely with many philosophers of former times, and may well become more popular in future, the God that challenges idolatrous ideas can be seen as the same as the God who is absolute and unlimited perfection. The traditional God of negative theology is transcendent and therefore the proper object of worship both because of our inability to understand the divine and the possibility that we might be able to talk of it.

BIBLIOGRAPHY

Burrell D. 1993. *Freedom and Creation in Three Traditions*. Notre Dame IN.

Crescas H. 1990. *Or Hashem*. Jerusalem.

Davidson H. 2005. *Maimonides: The Man and his Work*. Oxford, New York.

Davies B. 1993. *An Introduction to the Philosophy of Religion*. Oxford, New York.

Gersonides. 1987. *The Wars of the Lord* vol. 2, translated by S. Feldman. Philadelphia, New York, Jerusalem.

Hughes C. 1990. *On a Complex Theory of a Simple God: An Investigation into Aquinas' Philosophical Theology*. Ithaca NY.

Maimonides M. 1963. *The Guide of the Perplexed*, translated by S. Pines. Chicago.

Miller B. 2002. *The Fullness of Being: A New Paradigm for Existence*. Notre Dame IN.

Pines S. 1979. 'The Limitations of Human Knowledge According to Al-Farabi, Ibn Bajja, and Maimonides,' in *Studies in Medieval Jewish History and Literature*, ed. I. Twersky, 82–109. Cambridge MA.

Rosenzweig F. 1971. *The Star of Redemption*, translated by W. W. Hallo. London.

Seeskin K. 2017. 'No One Can See My Face and Live,' in *Negative Theology as Jewish Modernity*, ed. M. Fagenblat, 48–61. Bloomington IN.

Seeskin K. 2000. *Searching for a Distant God*. Oxford, New York.

Zangwill N. 2011. 'Negative Properties,' *Noûs*. 528–56.

Chapter 3

The Unity of God

Christians and the Trinity

Andrew Louth

Judaism, Christianity, and Islam, the three Abrahamic Religions, are often referred to as the three monotheistic faiths, or the three monotheisms. Christianity seems sometimes called on to defend its place in such company, for, although Christianity affirms the unity of God (the Nicene Creed begins: 'I believe in One God, the Father Almighty . . . '), it also associates with God, and as God, the Son of God and the Holy Spirit, and it was not long before Christians in the Greek East confessed God as *monas kai trias*, 'monad and triad,' in the Latin West *unitas et trinitas*, sometimes, as it were, condensed into *trinitas*, understood not as the Latin equivalent of the Greek *trias*, a set of three, but as a contraction of *tri-unitas*, 'three-oneness,' so that *trinitas* intimated both God's oneness and his threeness. As early as the second century, Justin Martyr defended the Christian ascription of divinity to God's *logos*, thus associating the *logos* with God as God, against the charges of the Jew 'Trypho' that such language qualified their monotheism. Such Jewish polemic against Christian claims to monotheism continued, though for the early centuries the evidence for this is, as with Justin, found in Christian responses to Jewish accusations, not in any extant Jewish anti-Christian literature (an example from the seventh century is a work by Leontios of Cypriot Neapolis, *Against the Jews, on the Trinity, Images, and Relics*, extracts from which in defense of images or icons survive in florilegia produced by the defenders of icon-veneration; what the Jewish arguments against the Trinity were, and how Leontios dealt with them, is not known: Thümmel 1992: 340–53). Muslim attacks on Christian betrayal of monotheism because of their confession of the Trinity seem to date back to the very beginnings of Islam, to judge from the way in which John Damascene is careful to present affirmation of God's oneness as fundamental to Christian belief, both in his *On the Orthodox Faith* and in his attacks on the iconoclasts (Louth 2002, 76–83).

I suppose this could be the starting point for a discussion of Christian monotheism and the Trinity (not least the way in which in some twentieth-century theology monotheism is regarded as a *temptation* for Christian theology, to be met by Trinitarianism as fundamentally challenging monotheism: a tendency that begins, I suppose, with Erik Peterson's *Monotheismus als politisches Problem* (Peterson 1951, 47–147) and resurfaces in 1972 in Jürgen Moltmann's *Der gekreuztige Gott*), but I am principally a historical theologian, most familiar with the first Christian millennium, and I want to focus my discussion there.

There are two bits of background that I want to fill in, before proceeding to my main topic: two bits of background that dovetail into each other. The first is a tendency in some recent scholarship to challenge the notion of 'Hebrew monotheism' as summarizing the faith of the Hebrew Bible, what Christians call the Old Testament. It is argued that this is to read back into the history of Hebrew religion what the Hebrew Bible came to be valued for in the period after the fall of the Second Temple. For, taken as a whole, the religion of the Hebrew Bible cannot really be regarded as 'monotheistic.' The insistence in parts of the Hebrew Bible on the 'one God' can sometimes be construed not as monotheism in the strict sense (as in the *shahada*: 'There is no God but God'), but as the affirmation that the God of the Hebrews, referred to as *YHWH*, is the most powerful among the gods (or sometimes, maybe, simply the God to whom the Israelites are to be loyal); not that there are no other gods. This morphs into a confession that there is no God but *YHWH*, that is, into monotheism, but this is true only of the later strata of the Hebrew Bible (and is indeed clearer in those parts of the Christian Bible not found in the Hebrew Bible—Wisdom and Maccabees, for example). (This is a very crude summary of what I gather is still a matter of discussion among scholars of the Hebrew Bible.)

After the fall of the Second Temple, religious traditions that valued the religious experience of the Hebrew people saw this experience as summed up in 'monotheism' and evolved a way of religious living that drew on the Hebrew Bible in the new context in which sacrifice and Temple had become impossible. These two traditions were, of course, what came to be called Rabbinic Judaism, in which the traditions of the Hebrew Bible were interpreted through the writings of the Mishnah and the Talmud, and what came to be known as Christianity, in which the traditions of the Hebrew Bible (or, for the vast majority of Christians, to be precise, the Greek translation of the Hebrew Bible known as the Septuagint) were interpreted in terms of what came to be called the 'New Testament' (in contrast with the 'Old'), and (I would argue) a body of writings, not ever clearly defined, known as the writings of the Fathers, consisting primarily of further commentary on the 'Old' and 'New' Testaments, all interpreted as witness to Christ—prophetic in the Old, apostolic in the New Testament—who, in his person and in his life, teaching, death on the Cross, and resurrection from the dead, fulfilled the religion of the biblical Temple.

The 'monotheism' of Rabbinic Judaism and Christianity did not, however, emerge in an intellectual and cultural vacuum. Although the Fathers regularly classify Greco-Roman paganism as polytheistic, the truth is more complicated: from around the first century of the Christian era (or the 'common' era, though to whom it is supposed to be common is not in the least clear to me) the philosophical traditions of the Greco-Roman world became deeply attracted by the conviction that it was unity, or the One, that had to be the ultimate explanation of anything and everything; any form of multiplicity or duality needed to find its explanation in a more fundamental unity (Athanassiadi & Frede 1999). Allied to this tendency was a heightened religious awareness, so that the 'principles' of the philosophy of Plato or Aristotle came to be conceived of in religious terms. As R. E. Witt memorably put it many years ago, late antiquity 'was attracted not so much by Plato the ethical teacher or political reformer, as by Plato the hierophant, Plato who (according to an old legend) had been conceived of Apollo and born of the virgin Perictione' (Witt 1971: 123). So principles like the Form of the Good, in Plato's *Republic*, 'beyond being,' or the mythical figure of the *dēmiourgos* ('fashioner') in Plato's *Timaeus*, 'whom no one can understand or, having understood, express,' or Aristotle's notion of the first cause, 'thought thinking itself,' the source of change and movement in the cosmos, who 'moves by being loved' are combined to form a conception of the one God, beyond human conception, impassibly governing the cosmos. The 'gods' are understood as divine powers, or influences, who exercise, or represent at the level of multiplicity, the rule of the one supreme God. This is a thoroughly monotheistic conception of the universe, which qualifies, but does not necessarily contradict, the traditional practices of Greco-Roman paganism. Some recent works suggest that it is this that should be regarded, in intellectual terms, as monotheism, which was assumed by the religions we nowadays regard as 'monotheistic,' namely, Judaism, Christianity, and eventually Islam. This, too, is a large and contentious field of scholarship, but the purposes of this chapter—what I want to take from this discussion—is that part of the intellectual background of the period in which both Rabbinic Judaism and Christianity emerged was a sense that the origin of everything was to be sought in a principle characterized by oneness or unity, regarded not just as a philosophical principle, but as the end and purpose of the intellectual life, to be attained by a life that cultivated a sense of unity or singleness (singleness of vision, one-centeredness).

In this, opposition and division were to be overcome so that intellectual vision itself could attain the singleness and simplicity, without which apprehension of the ultimate unity would remain forever beyond one's grasp—a union which transcended any residual duality in human thought, not least the duality between the knower and the known, in a union inexpressible in terms of knowledge, but perhaps glimpsed in analogies that drew on loving union or simple contact.

These two bits of background, put together, suggest that monotheism was not so much inherited by the thought of late antiquity from an earlier, clear conception of monotheism to be found, primarily, in the religion of the Hebrews, but rather a project that was worked out in different ways by the different religious traditions of late antiquity: emerging Rabbinic Judaism and Christianity, together with intellectual reflection, drawing on classical philosophy, in a different intellectual climate that was coming to value explicitly religious values.

These bits of background do not explain the forms that such monotheism took, nor the reasons that inspired the various forms of monotheism that emerged. As our concern is 'The Unity of God: Christians and the Trinity,' we need now to look at the pressures, primarily from within their own religion, that led Christians to formulate their doctrine of the Trinity. First, there is something one might call a monotheistic premise that is present in all Christian thought about the Godhead, which might be expressed as the conviction that the One God, worshipped and proclaimed by Moses and the prophets, and expounded in the Hebrew Scriptures, is identical with the Father of the Lord Jesus Christ. Much 'Christian' thought in the second century called this equation in question, either wanting to drive a wedge between the God revealed in the Old Testament and the God of the New Testament whom Jesus called 'Father,' or calling in question the very premise of monotheism, that there is one God, responsible for the cosmos and ruling it by his providence (*pronoia*)—or both, regarding whatever God is revealed in the Hebrew Bible as not measuring up to the exalted status of the one source of all that is. Again, this–often dubbed by scholars as 'gnosticism' or the 'gnostic problem' (using the word 'gnostic' in a much wider sense than any second-century thinker)–is not something I want to go into. I am content, for the moment, to speak about a 'monotheistic premise' to be found in the New Testament and later Christian thinkers. Secondly, there is a profound conviction that Jesus Christ, the one who died on the Cross under Pontius Pilate and rose from the dead, is to be so closely associated with God as to be properly called 'God.' An early example of this pressure to associate Christ with God the Father can be found in Paul's first letter to the Corinthians, where he exclaims, 'but for us God the Father is one, from whom is everything and we for him, and the Lord Jesus Christ is one, through whom is everything and we through him' (1 Cor. 8:6). In this passage, written perhaps no more than twenty years after the death of Christ, Paul associates Christ with the creative activity of God the Father, and makes this association precisely in the context of an affirmation of the oneness of God. Paul takes for granted the 'mono-theistic premise' and seeks to combine it with his conviction that Christ is to be regarded, not just as one who tells us about God, as his prophet, but one who manifests God and his nature as love. It is this that seems to me to lie at the heart of the growing clarity among Christians that the One God is Father, Son, and Spirit, or more precisely that there is one God the Father, but this demands being unfolded in the confession of the Son, or Word of God, who is God, and of the Holy Spirit, who proceeds from the Father as God. This leads to the confession that the one God is three, *ho trias,* the Trinity (though such explicit language does not emerge before the second century, with Theophilos of Antioch, whose notion of this triad—of God, his Word, and his Spirit—is, nevertheless, somewhat slant to the sense of God as Father, Son, and Holy Spirit that was already well attested).

One of the biblical passages that later became central to the perception of God as Trinity or *trias* is the passage referred to in the title of this volume: *Elonei Mamre*, the Oak(s) of Mamre. In Genesis 18, we read of the manifes-tation of God to Abraham at the Oak of Mamre in the form of three men (as they are first called). Abraham was sitting at the entrance to his tent at noon and, looking up, saw three men standing before him. However, Abraham addresses them not in the plural, but in the singular: *Kyrie* (I am following the LXX, which Philo used and after him the Greek Fathers). He welcomes them, washes their feet, and provides a meal. They promise Abraham that his wife Sarah will bear a son, at which Sarah, from the inside of the tent, laughs in disbelief. Abraham then accompanies them on their way to Sodom and Gomorrah, and the Lord reveals to him that he is going to punish these cities for their wickedness. Two of the men (now called angels, Gen. 19:1) travel onwards to the cities of the plain, while Abraham remains behind to plead with the 'Lord' for the inhabitants of the cities, gradually reducing the number of righteous inhabitants for the sake of whom the Lord will spare the cities.

The explicit mention of three, addressed as one, together with the asser-tion that only two of them go to wreak vengeance on the cities of the plain, while Abraham pleads with one Lord to have mercy on them, begs interpreta-tion, and the principal source of numerological wisdom in late antiquity was Pythagoras, interest in whom grew in late antiquity—manifest in Porphyry's life and Iamblichos' treatment of the 'Pythagorean' life—such interest add-ing fuel to the 'inclination towards the One,' that I have already mentioned. The account in Genesis is very open to such numerological interpretation: God appears as one to Abraham, manifest both in his addressing the three in the singular and his pleading with God as the one Lord to show his love and mercy towards the cities of the plain; the 'three' is the first manifestation of God; while the two, called angels, represent God's wrath, administered through the two angels.

Philo's discussion of this episode at the Oak of Mamre is to be found in *De Abrahamo* 119–123:

> When, then, as at noon-tide God shines around the soul, and the light of the mind fills it through and through and the shadows are driven from it by the rays which pour all around it, the single object presents to it a triple vision, one representing reality (or being), the other two the shadows reflected from it . . . No one, however, should think that the shadows can be properly spoken of as God . . . Rather, as anyone who has approached nearest to the truth would say, the central place is held by the Father of the Universe, who in the sacred scriptures is called 'he who is' as his proper name, while on either side of him are the senior powers, the nearest to him, the creative and the royal: the creative power is called God (*theos*), since it made and ordered the All; the royal power Lord (*kyrios*), since it is his right to rule and control what has come into being. So the central being flanked by each of the powers presents to the seeing mind the appearance sometimes of one, sometimes of three: of one, when that mind is highly purified and, passing beyond not merely the multiplicity of numbers, but even the dyad which next to the monad, presses on to the ideal form which is free from mixture and complexity, and being self-contained needs nothing more; of three, when, as yet uninitiated into the highest mysteries, it is still a votary only of the minor rites and unable to apprehend the one who is alone by itself and apart from all else, but only through its actions, as either creative or ruling. This is, as they say, a 'second best voyage' [proverbial, popularized by Plato in a philosophical context: e.g., *Phaedo* 99D]; yet all the same there is in it an element of a way of thinking such as God approves. But the former state of mind has not merely an element; it is in itself the divinely-approved way, or rather it is the truth, higher than a way of thinking, more precious than anything that is merely thought. (Translation by F.H. Colson (somewhat modified) in Philo VI, 63–5)

There is—no surprise—nothing 'Trinitarian' about Philo's interpretation of this episode. There is only *one* God; God's two companions are called 'shadows,' who cannot properly be spoken of as God. The figures—one and three—do not directly apply to anything in God's being, but rather to *our* conception of God: a lower, more accessible apprehension of God beholds him as three, where human apprehension is still caught up in lower levels of multiplicity, while a higher contemplation of God passes to unity, indeed beyond number altogether. In all this Philo draws on Pythagorean numerological wisdom, contrasting the One with the 'multitudes of numbers,' speaking of it as transcending the dyad which is 'neighbor to the monad.'

The Christian interpretation of the episode at the Oak of Mamre is indebted to Philo (often directly), but is quite different: the one and the three refer not to different stages in human apprehension of God, but to different ways of apprehending God—as one and as three—both, paradoxically, true. This way of interpreting the episode at the Oak of Mamre was to have a long history and takes two forms: on the one hand, a tradition of literary commentary on the passage, and on the other hand, a tradition of visual interpretation—both traditions are fully and accessibly set out in a book by the one-time monk of Chevetogne, now a Russian Orthodox archimandrite, Gabriel Bunge, called in English *The Rublev Trinity* (but in the original German, *Der andere Paraklet*, 'The Other Paraclete' [Bunge 2007]). The tradition of commentary is fairly consistent, the heart of which is summed up in Ambrose's remark: *tres vidit, unum adoravit*—'he saw three, he worshipped one' (Ambrose, as is well known, was a reader of Philo). The iconic tradition is also extensive, in its origins possibly pre-Christian, even pagan, as there is dispute over the provenance of an early pilgrim token associated with the Oak of Mamre (Bunge 2007: 113–14). To begin with—however interpreted—the depiction of the episode at the Oak of Mamre is called *Philoxenia tou Abraam*, 'The Hospitality of Abraham'; which is the inscription on most icons in the first millennium. In the second millennium, attention is more and more directed to the three figures, interpreted in ways that underline their equality, either my placing them side-by-side with no distinguishing features, or—more subtly—by enclosing them in an aureole, in that way emphasizing their equality, though allowing for their distinctness; both these forms of the icon are inscribed 'The Trinity,' *Trias*, *Troitsa*. The most famous icon of this scene, almost certainly inscribed *Troitsa* (no longer visible owing to its cleaning), is the fifteenth-century Russian icon, painted by Andrey Rublev—indeed, not just the most famous Trinity icon, but the most famous icon of all. The slowness with which the title 'The Trinity' was accepted may have something to do the reluctance to accept any depiction of the Uncreated Trinity, the uncreated being, by definition, beyond circumscription.

In the Greek tradition, as already noted, there emerges by the fourth century a Christian understanding of the Godhead as *monas kai trias*, 'monad and triad,' which I want to explore a little and suggest what motives lay behind such a paradoxical formula. It is a tangled story, and for the purposes of this chapter I only want to draw out the different way in which what one might call the 'yearning for the One' (title of Ramfos 2000) is represented in Philo and Christians.

To speak of God as *monas kai trias* has a distinguished lineage, finding its origins (so far as I can tell) in Gregory of Nazianzus ('the Theologian'; *c.* 329–*c.* 390), and picked up from Gregory in Dionysios the Areopagite (writing at the beginning of the sixth century) and occupying a prominent place

in the Emperor Justinian's *Edictum rectae fidei* (dated to 551) which, as an
imperial edict, had the force of law throughout the Byzantine Empire (on a
par with the decisions of Ecumenical Councils), and then—inevitably, given
its authority—taken as a starting point for expressions of Trinitarian theology
by later Christian theologians such as Maximos the Confessor (*c.* 580–662)
and John Damascene (*c.* 675–c. 750). The trinitarian section of Justinian's
edict begins with a citation of Gregory the Theologian:

> For we worship monad in triad and triad in monad, holding in paradox the
> distinction and the union (*Or.* 25.17), the monad in accordance with the prin-
> ciple of being or the godhead, the triad in accordance with the distinguishing
> characteristics, or *hypostases* or persons (for it is divided without division, so to
> speak, and united in separation; for the godhead is one in three and the three in
> which the godhead is, or rather to speak more precisely, which the godhead is,
> are one), each one God, yet only beheld by the intellect which separates what is
> inseparable, God conceived of as three together with one another by identity of
> movement and being, since it is necessary to confess the one God and proclaim
> the three *hypostases*, or three persons, each with its distinguishing characteristic.
> (Justinian, *Edictum*, in Schwartz 1939: 72)

There are two other places in Gregory's orations in which he speaks of *monad*
and *triad* in strikingly similar ways. In *Oration* 23.8 on Peace, he remarks,
'The monad is moved because of its abundance, the dyad is surpassed (for it
is beyond matter and form, which determine bodies), and the triad is defined
because of perfection'; and in the second theological oration (*Or.* 29.2) he
says that 'Therefore, the monad from the beginning [or, eternally: *ap'archēs*]
moved to the dyad, rests in the triad; and this is for us Father, Son, and Holy
Spirit.' What Gregory himself meant is quite unclear; the second remark suggests to my ear that Gregory is quoting from a non-Christian (presumably
Pythagorean) philosophical source, as he contrasts whatever meaning the
clause had originally with what is means for us—Christians presumably—
for whom it means that God, *monas kai trias*, is the Father, Son, and Holy
Spirit. Similarly, in the passage, quoted above, from the Oration on Peace,
the dyad is surpassed and we are left with *monas kai trias*. Why? It seems to
me that Gregory is engaging with Pythagorean number theory, but wanting to
make a distinctively Christian point, while remaining still in thrall, to some
extent, to the 'yearning for the One.' The Pythagoreans made a distinction
in the meaning of the one: one as the first number, and one as the source of
number. We have seen something of this already in Philo's interpretation of
the episode of the Oak of Mamre: Abraham's apprehension of God as one is
seen as an apprehension of God in his unknowable unity, a unity that passes
beyond any human conception of what is meant by 'one.' This is why Philo
contrasts, as we have seen, the One with the 'multitudes of numbers,' and sees

it as transcending the dyad which is 'neighbor to the monad.' 'Transcending the dyad'—this recalls what Gregory says in *Or*. 22 about the monad moving and passing beyond—transcending—the dyad, while the triad is defined because of perfection. *Monas kai trias* passes over the dyad, *dyas*, combining oneness and threeness. What may lie behind Gregory's thought here is the way the evolution of number could be conceived in Pythagorean terms thus: the beginning of number is the one, but one, by itself, cannot generate the manifold, the multiple, without which there is no number at all: hence the distinction between 'the One,' and one, the first number. But one, the first number, needs some way of advancing into the manifold, which is provided by the dyad, which introduces division, separation—itself a bad thing, as it takes one away from the One—but without which there is nothing to be numbered. Two, itself, is not properly a number, in this respect like one, which is only number if conceived as the first, which itself entails a sequence, a series, to which there is no final term, as for any term there is always the next one. So three? Dependent on one, the beginning of any series, and two, the principle of division and therefore of negative valence, three is the first 'proper' number, the first number that possesses completion, 'perfection' (as number), the first number that can be regarded as 'perfect' or 'complete,' *teleios*, as opposed to the one, difficult to detach from the One, and the dyad, which is only incipiently a number. That could be what Gregory took the saying of 'them,' cited in *Or*. 29, to mean: the *monad*, as the unit, moves towards the dyad, but passes beyond it to rest in the triad, the first complete number—but, for us, *monas kai trias* means 'Father, Son, and Holy Spirit,' God, one and three, lying behind and beyond the whole created order, characterized by multiplicity. Confirmation for this perhaps lies in a remark of John Damascene's in his letter on the *Trisagion* hymn:

> The monad is without quantity, the dyad is the beginning of number, and the triad a complete [perfect or whole: *teleios*] number. But it is not because of number that the Godhead is in a triad, but because the Godhead is in a triad that the number three is complete. For 'the monad is moved from the beginning towards the dyad until it reaches the triad.' (*Trisagion* 28; ed. Kotter 1981: 331)

Yearning for the One—the nondual, 'advaitist' tendency in late antique philosophical thought—opposes the One to the manifold and sees the One, not as the first, which is already part of the manifold, but as transcending the multiplicities of number. Christians are not unaffected by this 'yearning for the One,' but place the Godhead beyond the manifold in a different way—by seeing the doctrine of God as Father, Son, and Holy Spirit as qualifying *altogether* the transcendence of the nonmultiple. What is truly ultimate is the one and three, the *monas kai trias*, a paradox that lies beyond the reach of number.

If my line of reasoning is valid, then the Christian confession of God as *monas kai trias* is not to be understood as, or suspected of being, a denial, or at least qualification, of a monotheistic faith in God as one, but as a way of expressing an intuition that the oneness of God means not just that there is only one of them (that is, gods), but that God transcends the unit or monad, being something beyond (though not contradicting) unity or oneness—expressed by the paradoxical affirmation of God as *monas kai trias*.

BIBLIOGRAPHY

Primary Sources

Philo, vol. 6, 1935. London/Cambridge, MA.
John Damascene, *Epistula de Hymno Triasgio*, in Kotter 1981: 304–32.
Justinian, *Edictum rectae fidei*, in Schwartz 1939, 71–111.
Leontios of Neapolis, fragments *Contra Iudaeos*, in Thümmel 1992: 340–53.

Secondary Literature

Athanassiadi P. & M. Frede, eds. 1999. *Pagan Monotheism in Late Antiquity*. Oxford.
Bunge G. 2007. *The Rublev Trinity*. Crestwood, NY.
Louth A. 2002. *St John Damascene: Tradition and Originality in Byzantine Theology*. Oxford.
Kotter B., ed. 1981. *Die Schriften des Johannes von Damaskos*, vol. 4. Berlin.
Peterson E. 1951. *Theologische Traktate*. Munich.
Ramfos S. 2000. *Ho Kaemos tou Henos*. Athens; Eng. tr. by N. Russell 2011. *Yearning for the One*, Brookline, MA.
Schwartz Eduard, ed. 1939. *Drei dogmatische Schriften Iustinians*. Munich.
Thümmel H. G. 1992. *Die Frühgeschichte des ostkirchlichen Bilderlehre: Texte und Untersuchungen zur Zeit vor dem Bilderstreit* (Texte und Untersuchungen 139). Berlin.
Witt R. E. 1971. *Albinus and the History of Middle Platonism*. Amsterdam.

Chapter 4

Law and Love in Judaism

Norman Solomon

Love is about the quality of relationships; law is about the ordering of society. Both are fundamental to Torah and fundamental to life. For the most part they work together harmoniously, but occasionally they conflict, as in Shakespeare's story of Romeo and Juliet, where the 'star-crossed lovers' fall foul of the unjust law of the Montagues and Capulets.

Several words are used in the Hebrew scriptures to convey loving relationships of one sort and another. The root *ahav* is used for love between people, including parental love, love of a sexual nature, or 'Platonic' friendships: Ahasuerus loved Esther more than any other woman (Esther 2:17); David loved Jonathan with a love 'surpassing the love of women' (2 Sam 1:26); Rebecca loved her son Jacob (Gen 25:28); Michal loved David (1 Sam 18:28). It can be used also of illegitimate love, such as the incestuous passion of Amnon for his half-sister Tamar (2 Sam 13:4). It is commonly used for love of or by God.

Biblical writers use a wide range of terms to indicate aspects of love, both good and bad, but precise equivalents in other languages are not available. So, for instance, *hesed*, often translated as 'loving kindness' or 'compassion,' *rahamim* 'mercy,' *habab* 'endearment' and other words indicate positive aspects of an event or relationship, whereas *hamad* 'covet' or *ta'av* 'desire' are more likely to be used negatively. To equate specific Hebrew terms with, for example, a later Greek distinction between *agapē*, *philia*, *philautia* and *eros* is as misleading as it is to read into the Hebrew scriptures a sharp division between love of God as 'spiritual' and love between the sexes as 'carnal'; the one root *ahav* applies to both equally and the Septuagint, as illustrated below, translates with *agapē* and derivatives in both contexts.

The Deuteronomic Code prescribes love: 'You shall love the Lord your God with all your heart, with all your soul and with all your might' (Deut

6:5) (LXX *agapēseis*). God loves you too, at least for the sake of your fathers: 'Because he loved your fathers, He chose their heirs after them . . . led you out of Egypt' (Deut 4:37). You are 'Israel, my servant, whom I have chosen, the seed of Abraham whom I loved' (Is 41:8); because He loved you, he changed Balaam's curse to a blessing (Num 23:6). Reproaching Israel for infidelity, the prophet Jeremiah, speaking in God's voice, recalls: 'I remember the affection of your youth, the love of your espousals, how you followed me through the wilderness' (Jer 2:2); promising redemption he proclaims, 'I loved you with eternal love' (Jer 31:2). The prophet Hosea dwells on the love between God and Israel that arises within their covenantal relationship; God and Israel are pictured respectively as a loving, forgiving husband and errant wife.

The command to love God is not the only one to govern our relationship with Him; indeed, it can only take effect once we become aware of His presence, and this will first of all inspire awe, or fear. So we are also told to fear and obey Him. He will not stand for unfaithfulness: 'For the Lord your God is a zealous God—lest the anger of your God blaze forth . . . ' (Deut 6:15). No single image covers the relationship between God and people; as well as lover and beloved we have king and subject (Judg 8:23), shepherd and flock (Ps 23), owner and possession (Exod 19:5), doctor and patient (Exod 15:26; Ps 147:3), father and child (Deut 14:1), judge and plaintiff (Job 9:15) and others.

The Code of Holiness, framed in the language of law, prescribes love of neighbor: 'You shall love your neighbor as yourself' (Lev 19:18) (LXX *agapēseis*). Deuteronomy extends the commandment beyond your 'neighbor': 'You shall love the stranger, for you were strangers in the land of Egypt' (Deut 10:19) (LXX *agapēsete ton prosēluton*). The Psalmist calls on men to 'shout with joy' to the Lord because He 'loves what is right and just; the earth is full of the Lord's faithful care' (Ps 33:3–5); 'The Lord loves what is right, He does not abandon His faithful ones' (Ps 37:28); and 'The Lord preserves all those who love Him' (Ps 145:20). Conversely, the Lord hates seven kinds of evil (Prov 6:16 f.), but is not said to hate people, though he might punish those who hate Him. Wisdom personified, as in *Proverbs*, commends love: 'A man who loves wisdom will bring joy to his father' (Prov 29:3); love brings peace and harmony: 'Hatred stirs up strife, but love overcomes offense' (Prov 10:12). Even Kohelet, for whom 'all is vanity,' concedes that love—human love, between man and woman—makes the world bearable: 'See life with a woman whom you love' (Eccl 9:9).

The *Song of Songs* is the book of love *par excellence*. But of what love does it speak? Superficially, it speaks of human love and no other; there is no unequivocal reference to God. But as Naftali Rothenberg has argued, it is incorrect to categorize the work for that reason as secular:

The dichotomous approach reached its apex in the early Middle Ages . . . The ultimate expression of this approach is the idea of human love as a material, rather than a spiritual phenomenon. Although such a view may have existed on the margins of ancient society, it was by no means a dominant cultural force. *Song of Songs* was no more 'secular' in their eyes than agriculture or natural phenomena. Spirituality and longing for God could be expressed in every area of life, while continuing to relate to life itself, to the passions and aspirations that are an essential part of human nature. (Rothenberg 2017: 95)

We shall see below how the Rabbis read the book, but at the very least its presence in scripture indicates that love, including among humans and between the sexes as well as of and by God, is a good thing, to strive for.

We now turn to law. Hebrew *Torah* and English 'law' have overlapping, but different semantic fields. *Torah*, from a root meaning to teach or instruct, may be used in any of the following senses:

1. Occasionally, it refers to a law, group of laws, or instructions relating to a specific topic (e.g. Lev 6:2; Ezek 43:12; Hag 2:11).
2. It may denote the way of life revealed by God through a prophet: 'Remember the Torah of Moses my servant' (Mal 3:22).
3. When the Pentateuch (Genesis, Exodus, Leviticus, Numbers, Deuteronomy) came to be accepted as a whole possessing unique authority it was known as The Torah.
4. In later Jewish parlance, it may refer to scripture and tradition as a whole.

In most contexts 'teaching' or 'way' would be a closer rendering than 'law,' since *Torah* suggests helpful guidance rather than compulsive legislation, let alone burden.

Hebrew *mitzvah* is awkwardly rendered 'commandment,' since it derives from a root meaning command. Unfortunately, English commandment implies something you have to do against your will just because it is ordered by a person in a position of seniority. *Mitzvah* does not sound like that. A *mitzvah* is not so much an order as a privilege; I am glad to have the opportunity to do 'the good deed.' I visit the sick or donate to charity (two common *mitzvot*) not because I am ordered to do so by a powerful Being, but because that Being has graciously revealed to me the best and happiest way to live and I am now in a position to put it into practice. Or I may learn that some religious observance, say presenting first-fruits in the Temple, is a *mitzvah*, and I will perform it with joy and satisfaction.

Torah and *mitzvah* are nicely combined in *Proverbs* (6:1 and 23): 'My son, keep to the *mitzvot* of your father and the *Torah* of your mother . . . *Mitzvah* is a lamp, *Torah* a light.'

Mishpat is appropriately translated 'judgement.' It is a narrow term, indicating 'correct decision in a particular case.' Abraham requested it from God on behalf of the people of Sodom (Gen 18:24); Solomon established his reputation for it through his decision in the case of the two prostitutes (1 Kgs 3:28); the plural *mishpatim* heads a collection of specific laws in Exodus 21–23.

In the post-Biblical period the term *halakhah* came into use to denote specific rules within the system. It is of wider application than English 'law' or Hebrew *mishpat*, since it covers not only civil and criminal law, but ethics and religious observance.

The Hebrew scriptures consistently regard the *mitzvot* as God's gift to humankind, the token of His love, the means by which, with His help, people may avoid sin and enjoy life. Psalm 19, with the aid of four different terms for 'law,' expresses this perfectly. Its opening declaration of the wonder of creation of heaven and earth is paralleled by this fulsome affirmation of the wonder of the law: The teaching (*Torah*) of the Lord is perfect, renewing life; the decrees (*'edut* 'testimony') of the Lord are enduring, making the simple wise; the precepts (*piqudim*) of the Lord are just, rejoicing the heart; the instruction (*mitzvah*) of the Lord is lucid, making the eyes light up (Ps 18:8–9 JPS). Love and law work in unison; there is no dichotomy.

Nor did the Sages of the Talmud, who defined subsequent Judaism, set up any dichotomy between love and law. One of their most lasting achievements was the consolidation of the forms of daily prayer which remain to this day the basis Jewish worship. The set morning and evening prayers are built around two elements, recital of the Shema, containing the declaration of God's unity and the command to love Him 'with all your heart, soul and strength,' and the silently recited *tefillah* (prayer), a compilation of praise, petition and thanksgiving. Prior to the Shema two blessings are recited, the first praising God for bringing the day (or night, as the case may be), and the second, known as *ahavah* (love) invoking His love for the people Israel. Here is J. Sacks' translation of the evening *ahavah* as in the Orthodox Ashkenazic rite:

> With everlasting love You loved Your people, the House of Israel. You have taught us Torah and commandments, decrees and laws of justice. Therefore, Lord our God, when we lie down and when we rise up we will speak of Your decrees, rejoicing in the words of Your Torah and Your commandments for ever. For they are our life and the length of our days; on them we will meditate day and night. May you never take away Your love from us. Blessed are You, Lord, who loves His people Israel. (*Authorised Daily Prayer Book*)

Torah, that is, the law, is received as the expression of God's love.

Debate as to the canonical status of the *Song of Songs* is attributed to second-century rabbis. A brief report in the Mishnah (*Yadayim* 3:5) ends with this outburst:

> Heaven forbid! declared Rabbi Akiva. No Israelite [sage] ever suggested that the Song would not defile the hands! The whole world was never as worthy as on the day on which the Song was revealed to Israel! All scripture is holy, but the Song is holy of holies! If there was any disagreement, it could only have been about Kohelet (Ecclesiastes).

('Defile the hands' here indicates sanctity of the text.)

Rabbinic interpreters read the Song metaphorically: the beloved is God, the bride is the Congregation of Israel, the marriage took place at Sinai and the bride seeking her beloved is Israel in exile seeking God and looking to her restoration. So a simple verse, 'He brought me to the banquet room, and his banner of love was over me' (Song 2:4 JPS), is paraphrased in Aramaic as: Said the congregation of Israel: "He brought me to the study house of Sinai to learn the Torah from Moses the great scribe and I received the text of his commandments with love, saying, 'Whatever you command I shall hear and obey'." Far-fetched as this interpretation is, two things are clear. Love (between God and Israel) is central to the relationship, and this love is articulated through the words and commands of Torah.

This does not imply that mere human love is to be despised. As Rothenberg (2017: 96) has written,

> We must come to the conclusion that [the *Song*] is a semiallegorical work. In Song of Songs, love itself is an exalted end—the harmony of emotional longing and physical union. There is no distinction between the ideal of love, in all its purity, and religious-spiritual elation. The latter cannot be understood without the experience of love. Uniting in love (two that become one)—the 'knowledge' between man and woman—embodies the idea of universal unity, and serves as the conventional allegory of the bond between man and God.

Allegorical interpretation of the Song remains a major inspiration for Jewish religious poetry and mysticism. The lover seeks to do what will please the beloved. How do you know what will please him/her? Israel's answer is straightforward: God, the beloved, will be pleased if you live by the rules of his Torah.

Perhaps observing throngs filling the towns to hear the rabbis expound the Torah, Rav Ḥisda (third-century Babylonian) observed: 'God loves the gates of Zion more than all the tents of Jacob (Ps 87:2)': God loves the gates festooned with *halakhah* more than all the synagogues and study-houses (Babylonian Talmud, *Berakhot* 8a).

The very clothing and homes of Israel are reminders of God's love: Israel are loved [by God, for] the Holy One, blessed be He, has surrounded them with *mitzvot*: tefillin on their heads and arms, fringes on their garments, mezuzahs on their doors (Babylonian Talmud, *Menaḥot* 43b). More than anything, God loves the restrained, temperate, congenial person: The Holy One, blessed be He, loves three: one who doesn't get angry, one who doesn't get drunk, and one who doesn't insist on his opinion (Babylonian Talmud, *Pesachim* 113b).

Ideally, one should serve God out of love. But even to serve out of fear of the consequences of disobedience carries reward: What is the difference between one who acts from love and one who acts out of fear? It is as it was taught: Rabbi Simeon ben Eleazar says: Who acts out of love is greater than who acts out of fear, for [the reward for the latter] extends to a thousand generations (Ex 20:6), [for the former,] to two thousand (Dt 7:9) (Babylonian Talmud, *Sota* 31a).

The fear of God, as *Proverbs* repeatedly tells us, is at least the *beginning* of wisdom. The fourth-century teacher Abbaye called on his disciples always to act in such a way as to lead others to the love of God, but may not have felt confident that they were able to maintain that elevated level; he is said to have remarked to them frequently: 'Always be resourceful in the fear of God' (Babylonian Talmud, *Yoma* 86a).

At the extreme, the lover is ready to sacrifice all for the sake of the beloved. In relation to God, this may culminate in martyrdom. In Rabbinic Judaism the classic illustration is the martyrdom of Rabbi Akiva, who fell victim at the time of the Bar Kochba Revolt in the 130s. His martyrdom, allegedly for teaching Torah in defiance of a Roman edict, is graphically described, if with variations, in both the Palestinian (Jerusalem Talmud, *Berakhot* 9:5, 14b) and Babylonian Talmudim and further elaborated in Midrashim. Here is part of the Babylonian account:

> One should bless God for bad things as one blesses Him for good, as it is said: 'You shall love the Lord your God with all your heart etc.'—'With all your heart' [means] with both inclinations, the good inclination and the bad inclination; 'with all your soul' means even if He takes your life; 'with all your strength' means with all your possessions or, alternatively, for whatever he 'measures out' to you, render thanks to Him. (Babylonian Talmud, *Berakhot* 54a)
> . . . When they brought Rabbi Akiva out for his execution it was time to recite the Shema, and they were combing his flesh with iron combs. As he took upon himself the yoke of heaven his disciples asked, 'Master! Thus far?' He replied, 'Throughout my life I was troubled by this verse, '[Love God] with all your soul,' [meaning,] even if He takes your life; now that the opportunity has come should I not fulfil it?' He lingered at the word 'One' until his soul departed. A heavenly voice issued forth and proclaimed, 'Happy are you, Akiva, for

your soul departed at 'One'!' The ministering angels then asked the Holy One, blessed be He, "Is this the Torah, and this its reward? 'Arise, O Lord, deliver my life . . . from men'." He replied 'Their portion is in life!' (Ps 17:13–14). The heavenly voice then proclaimed, 'Happy are you, Akiva, for you are ready for the World to Come!' (Babylonian Talmud, *Berakhot* 61b)

The precise wording of the report, 'Throughout my life I was troubled . . . ,' indicates that martyrdom is not, in the view of the Rabbis, something to be *actively* sought, though it must be courageously accepted if and when the occasion arises.

For most people love of God is not expressed through martyrdom but through steadfastly adopting a pattern of life in tune with God and His universe. The Rabbis, when they developed, on the basis of biblical text and living tradition, the comprehensive system of *halakhah* presented in the Talmud and subsequent legal codes, were aiming to give clarity and precision to this vision.

Any system is vulnerable to hypocrisy. Some, by outward observance, may establish an unjustified reputation for piety and bring the Torah itself into disrepute:

As it is taught: 'You shall love the Lord your God'—[this means,] the Name of Heaven should be loved on your account. [For if] you read Torah, learn Mishnah and wait upon the Sages, and deal calmly with people, people will say, 'Happy is his father who taught him Torah, happy his teacher who taught him Torah! Woe to those who have not learned Torah! See how pleasant are his ways and how correct his dealings!' Of such a one scripture says, 'You are my servant, Israel, in whom I glory!' (Isa 49:3). But if someone reads Torah, learns Mishnah and waits upon the Sages, but does not speak calmly with people, people will say, 'Woe to his father who taught him Torah, woe to his teacher who taught him Torah! This man who has learned Torah, see how unpleasant his ways are and how nasty his dealings!' Of such a one scripture says, 'These are the people of the Lord, who have gone forth out of His land!' (Ez 36:20). (Babylonian Talmud, *Yoma* 86a)

Love cannot prevail where there is injustice, so much of the law is concerned with mundane matters such as commercial dealings, marriage settlements, and damage accidental or otherwise. A perhaps surprising amount of attention was devoted by the rabbis of the Talmud to the sacrificial system, no longer in operation; it remained as the paradigm for the economy of sin and forgiveness and for relationships with God, and its restoration was eagerly anticipated.

Laws concerning duties of care of the poor, the sick, the dead and the bereaved are clearly concerned with the practicalities of love of neighbor. The extent to which the duty of love extends is most sharply demonstrated by a less obvious, extreme example. The capital punishments mandated by the Bible for certain offenses were no longer in operation in the rabbinic period, but the theoretical question was posed as to what form of execution should be applied if an individual was sentenced for two offenses carrying different death penalties. The unequivocal answer is, 'Choose the more lenient [form of death], for [scripture teaches,] 'love your neighbor as yourself' (Babylonian Talmud, *Sanhedrin* 52 and parallels). That is, the call to love of neighbor applies *even if your neighbor is guilty of a capital offense.*

Rabbinic Judaism matured in the Middle Ages in areas dominated by Christianity, both Eastern and Western, and Islam. It found expression not only in commentaries and codes of law, but through liturgical composition, poetry, philosophy and mysticism.

Baḥya Ibn Paquda (1973), in Saragossa in Muslim Spain, composed c. 1080 his 'Guide to the Duties of the Heart,' still popular devotional reading among Orthodox Jews. Baḥya, a Neoplatonist influenced by Sufi mysticism, held that the soul, which was divine in origin, was confined by God in a material body where it was in danger of forgetting its own spiritual nature. Spiritual perfection and communion with God could only be achieved through a combination of exercise of the rational faculty together with the fulfillment of the revealed *mitzvot* (commandments). This, said Baḥya, calls for special attention to the 'duties of the heart,' that is, the *mitzvot* that relate to the emotions and intellect. Foremost among these are the belief in and love of God, which can only be achieved through the full exercise of the God-given intellect; the soul thirsts for closeness to the Divine Light, if not for actual *unio mystica.*

Moses Maimonides (1138–1204) stressed the intellectual and emotional aspects of the love of God, arising from contemplation on the wonders of Creation. In the opening section of *Mishneh Torah*, his great code of law, he writes:

> What is the path by which one comes to love and fear Him? When a person reflects on His deeds and His wonderful creatures and discerns His infinite wisdom within them he will immediately love and praise, glorify and greatly desire knowledge of this great Being, as David said, 'My soul thirsts for God, for the living God' (Ps 42:3) . . . When anyone reflects on these matters and is aware of all that has been created, from the angels and heavenly spheres to human beings like himself, his love of God will increase and he will be filled with awe and dread on account of his own lowliness and insignificance when he measures himself against any of those great and holy beings. (Maimonides, *Yesodei Hatorah* 2:2, 4:12)

For Maimonides, *halakhah* is the preparatory discipline that conditions the individual to ascend the spiritual heights culminating in the love of God.

Hebrew poets transcended the prose of the philosophers, few more succinctly than the kabbalist Eliezer Azikri (sixteenth-century Safed), probable author of *Yedid Nefesh*, a hymn recently introduced into the Friday evening synagogue service welcoming the Sabbath:

> Beloved of the soul, Father of compassion, draw Your servant to
> Your will;
> Like a deer will Your servant run and fall prostrate before
> Your beauty;
> To him Your love is sweeter than the honeycomb, than any taste.
> Glorious, beautiful, radiance of the world, my soul is sick with love
> for you . . .
> Ancient of days, let your mercy be aroused and have pity on Your
> beloved child.
> How long have I yearned to see the glory of Your strength . . .
> Reveal yourself, my beloved, and spread over me the tabernacle of
> Your peace.
> Let the earth shine with Your glory, Let us be overjoyed and rejoice
> in You . . .
> (*The Authorised Daily Prayer Book* 2007: 257, tr. J. Sacks)

Modernity profoundly impacted the religious thought of Jews, leading in the early nineteenth century to a major rupture between Reformists and traditional Orthodox, as well as fragmentation within each group and eventually the secularization of some sections of Jewry.

Liberal/Reform and Orthodox continue to speak of the love of God, if with much leeway in interpretation. They differ profoundly, however, in their understanding of *halakhah* (the law) and its role in contemporary Judaism. Reform apologists emphasize the centrality of ethics rather than law in Judaism. However, the centrality of ethics is not in dispute; what is in dispute is the Orthodox claim that ethics is most perfectly expressed in traditional *halakhah* which they recognize as the authoritative interpretation of scripture, the Word of God.

Here is a brief look at what three leading Jewish thinkers of the early twentieth century had to say on law and love.

For Martin Buber (1878–1965), on the Liberal wing of Judaism, 'the law,' in the traditional Jewish sense, is dysfunctional: 'Every great culture . . . rests on an original relational incident,' he writes (Buber 1958: 54), hinting rather than stating clearly that, in the case of Judaism, he has in mind the meeting with God that was the formative experience of the people of Israel. He continues in poetic vein:

> Where hitherto a heaven was established in a law, manifest to the senses, rais-
> ing its light arch from which the spindle of necessity hangs, the wandering stars
> now rule in senseless and oppressive might . . . we are laden with the whole
> burden of the dead weight of the world, with fate that does not know spirit.
> (Buber 1958: 55)

Buber is writing here of religions in general, targeting the rational systems
devised in consequence of their institutionalization. So far as Judaism is concerned, he has in his sights the system of *halakhah* which, he insists, reduces
the seminal 'I–Thou' meeting with God, the 'eternal Thou,' to the level of an
'I–it' relationship with an inert object:

> Everything that has ever been devised and contrived in the time of the human
> spirit as precept, alleged preparation, practice, or meditation, has nothing to do
> with the prime, simple fact of the meeting. (Buber 1958: 77)

Our direct 'I–Thou' relationship with people affords an entry to the encounter
with God and somehow involves love: " . . . our life with men . . . is the main
portal: 'When a man is together with his wife the longing of the eternal hills
blows round about them.' The relation with man is the real simile of the relation with God; in it true address receives true response; except that in God's
response everything, the universe, is made manifest as language" (Buber
1958: 103).

Buber's friend Franz Rosenzweig (1886–1929) wrote more straightfor-
wardly on the role of love in God's revelation: 'It is love which meets all
the demands here made on the concept of the revealer, the love of the lover,
not of the beloved. Only the love of a lover is such a continually renewed
self-sacrifice ' (Rosenzweig 1971: 162).

Rosenzweig does not take the traditional account of God dictating the
Torah, written and oral, to Moses, in a literal sense; he fully accepts the find-
ings of historical criticism. Even so, contrary to Buber, he adopts a positive
attitude towards the law (*halakhah*) and its fulfillment. In a letter to his close
associate Nahum Glatzer, who had said that only the election of Israel came
from God, but the details of the law were from man alone, he questioned
whether one could draw so rigid a boundary between what was divine and
what was human. True observance of the law could not, in the light of modern scholarship, be based on historical claims about its revelation at Sinai.
Only in doing, i.e., in actually performing the *mitzvot*, do we come to perceive the law as articulating the revelation of God: you cannot appreciate the
God-given nature of the Sabbath until you commit yourself to its observance.

Glatzer writes of Rosenzweig that he 'found his peace in the practice of
Halachah where the enthusiasm of Divine love is translated into the word

of daily prayer, the longing for salvation is resolved in the sober conformation to the *mitzvot* and the ecstasy of religious experience is silenced by the commanding word at Sinai and the scrupulous interpretations of the sages' (Rosenzweig 1965: 24).

At the Orthodox end of the religious spectrum stands Abraham Isaac Hacohen Kook (1865–1935). Rav Kook, as he is generally known, was born in Latvia; in 1904 he emigrated to Jaffa, Palestine, and after WWI was appointed Chief Rabbi of Mandatory Palestine. An ardent follower of the Lurianic kabbalah, he engaged in spiritual exercises with the aim of attaining mystical ecstasy; his literary genius expressed, in poetry as well as prose, the thirst for God's 'lights of holiness,' the experience of the divine light and the burning desire to share it with others.

Creation is driven by two currents, one emanating from the love and creative power of God and reaching even to the lowliest creature (Kook was a vegetarian), the other being the redemptive flow of the reflected light as it ascends toward its creator. Kook expressed sympathy with the concept of evolution, but what he had in mind was not a Darwinian process of natural selection but rather, like Teilhard de Chardin, a purposeful, redemptive process by which creation evolves toward its creator.

He universalizes 'Love your neighbor *as yourself*' (Lev 19:18). Only if we can achieve true self-love, by discovering the divine spark within ourselves, can we love our neighbor; from this we proceed to love of fellow Israelites and thence to love of all humanity and beyond to all creation.

As to law, the gift of God's love, for Kook every one of the *mitzvot*, however apparently obscure, was endowed with spiritual energy that issued forth from the great Revelation at Sinai at which the soul of every Jew, even those yet to be born, had been and was eternally present.

BIBLIOGRAPHY

The Authorised Daily Prayer Book 2007. 4th ed. London.

Bahya ibn Paquda 1973. *The Book of Direction to Duties of the Heart*, tr. M. Mansoor, S. Arenson & S. Dannhauser. Oxford.

Buber M. 1958. *I and Thou* tr. R. G. Smith. Edinburgh.

Rosenzweig F. 1971. *The Star of Redemption*, tr. W. W. Hallo. London.

Rosenzweig F. 1965. *On Jewish Learning* ed. N. N. Glatzer. New York.

Rothenberg N. 2017. *Rabbi Akiva's Philosophy of Love*. Jerusalem.

Solomon N. 2009. *The Talmud: A Selection*. London.

Norman Solomon

SUGGESTION FOR FURTHER READING

Shatz D. & L. Kaplan, eds. 1995. *Rabbi Abraham Isaac Kook and Jewish Spirituality*. New York.

Chapter 5

Love

An Orthodox Perspective

Andrew Louth

Christians, at least, often say that Christianity is a religion of love, as opposed to Judaism which is a religion of the law. The origins of this seem to lie in a hasty and somewhat ill-informed reading of the Apostle Paul's epistle to the Romans, and some other of the apostle's letters. Nevertheless, it is worth noting that the twofold command to love (God and one's neighbor) is not only drawn from the Hebrew Bible (Deut. 6:4–5; Lev. 19:18), but, in Luke's account, is presented as the *lawyer*'s answer to Jesus' response to his question about what one needs to do to inherit eternal life: 'What is written in the Law? How do you read it?' (Luke 10:25–8; the 'parallel' accounts in Mark 12:28–31 and Matt. 22:34–40 place the twofold command on Jesus' lips, though in Mark's account, Jesus' summing up the Law in the twofold command is greeted with enthusiasm by the lawyer, who is himself praised by Jesus: Mark 12:32–4).

This seems to me to suggest that the centrality of love is something that Christianity shares with Judaism, rather than something that distinguishes between them. Moreover, this is borne out elsewhere in the New Testament where love is seen as the fulfillment of the Law or Torah: Paul, for instance, in Romans—'Owe no one anything except to love one another for he who loves the other has fulfilled the law,' repeated a few lines later: 'Love works no ill to the neighbor; therefore love is the fulfillment of the Law' (Rom. 13:8, 10). The same centrality of love is found in the other main NT tradition, the Johannine: see John 13:34—'A new commandment I give you that you love one another, even as I have loved you, that you also may love one another.' Elsewhere, however, there is an ambivalence about the newness of the commandment to love, for it is asserted that this commandment is not

new, but old: 'Beloved, it is not a new commandment that I am writing to
you, but an old commandment that you have had from eternity (*ap' archēs*);
the old commandment is the word that you have heard' (1 John 2:7). Perhaps
the 'newness' of the commandment lies in the fact that it is exemplified
in Christ—'Greater love has no one than this, to lay down his life for his
friends. You are my friends' (John 15:3–14)—and for John, Christ's love is
the love of God:

> Beloved, let us love one another, for love is of God, and he who loves is born
> of God and knows God. One who does not love does not know God; for God
> is love. In this the love of God was made manifest among us, because God sent
> his only Son into the world that we might live through him. In this is love, not
> that we loved God, but that he loved us and sent his Son to be the expiation of
> our sins (1 John 4:7–10).

This can be compared a verse from the Gospel: 'For God loved the world
in this way (*houtōs*—though St John Chrysostom says that the word is used
with an intensifying sense, that is, "so much"), that he gave his only Son,
that everyone who believes in him should not perish, but have eternal life'
(John 3:16).

The centrality of love is developed in different ways by Paul and by John
(or: in the Pauline and Johannine traditions), and yet they converge in the
centrality of Christ. John seems to start from there; Paul rather starts from
love as the fulfilling of the Law—though the goal or end (*telos*) of the Law is
Christ (Rom. 10:4)—and Paul has other ways of expressing the central role
of Christ: for example, 'For you know the grace of our Lord Jesus Christ,
that though he was rich, yet for our sake he became poor, so that by his pov-
erty you might become rich' (2 Cor. 8:9), which cannot refer to the *human*
example of Christ (who was no rich man who gave away his riches—like
St Francis of Assisi, for example), but what was involved in Christ as God
made human. Another example of Paul's expressing the centrality of Christ
is Philippians 2:5–11, which presents Christ as emptying himself, humbling
himself to the point of death, indeed death on the Cross, for which God has
exalted him beyond measure and given him the 'name above every name,'
namely 'Lord,' understood as the divine appellation, representing the divine
name, YHWH. But more commonly the centrality of Christ is *implicit*, rather
than explicit, in Paul's praise and commendation of love: so Paul's account
of the 'more excellent way' in 1 Cor. 13—Christian preachers often see in the
qualities of love listed by Paul the features of Christ, but there is nothing that
explicitly suggests this. Other traditions in the New Testament bear witness to
the centrality of love, though briefly or allusively: for instance, in the epistle
of James, the command to love one's neighbor as oneself is called the 'royal

law' (James 2:8) and the first of the Petrine epistles recommends above all 'fervent love,' 'because love covers a multitude of sins' (1 Peter 4:8).

That constitutes my exordium. I now want to address three questions: first, what is love? And secondly, how important is the twofold command to love in the teaching of the Fathers of the Church? And thirdly the question of self-love.

What is love? The first impression given by the New Testament is that love is something immediate and obvious, while at the same time indefinable. There is a reluctance to reduce love to a list of commands, though certain commands are entailed by love—those summed up in loving one's neighbor as oneself, the 'second table' of the ten commandments—and though John speaks of a '(new) commandment,' it is spelled out in terms of the relationship of discipleship to Christ. 'You are my friends, if you do what I command you' (John 15:14)—not a list of commandments, but obedience to Christ; that combined with the contrast Jesus introduces between 'servants' ('slaves,' *douloi*) and 'friends' (*philoi*)—between those who 'do not know what the master does' and those who are intimate to Jesus' relationship with the Father (cf. John 15:15–18). Or take the famous 'hymn to love' of 1 Cor. 13; there love is described as 'patient, kind, not jealous or boastful, not arrogant or rude' and so on: not a list of commands or things to do, but a list of attitudes that are to govern one's behavior. There is a similar, but significantly different list, in Galatians 5:22–3: 'love, joy, peace, patience, kindness, goodness, faithfulness, gentleness, self-control'—'against such there is no law.' The law is seen as forbidding certain actions, but no acts or behavior inspired by these qualities could possibly be condemned. The list that Paul commends, however, are called the 'fruit of the Spirit,' not virtuous achievements or habits, but blossoms or fruit, that can certainly be cultivated, but not are to be regarded as achievements. Perhaps one can bring in another term used by Paul, and more generally other Christians, especially later, and that is the 'heart' (*kardia*), the innermost part of the human person, the source of feelings and emotions, but also of thoughts and plans: a deep center to the individual person, where—paradoxically—one finds oneself not separated, or closed off, from others, but united with them, barriers of separation having been broken down. In a slightly surprising metaphor, Paul speaks of the Christians he is writing to—Christians converted by his teaching—as 'our [systatic] letter [or letter of recommendation], engraved on your hearts, known and read by everyone . . . written (or engraved) not in ink but by the Spirit of the living God, not on tablets of stone but in tablets of living (lit: fleshly) hearts' (2 Cor. 3:2–3). Paul goes on to develop this contrast, speaking of a 'new covenant,' not of the letter but of the Spirit, 'for the letter kills, but the spirit gives life' (2 Cor. 3:6) . . . and the chapter concludes with his vision—in essence, it seems to me, a vision of the transforming power of love, or the love of Christ—'The Lord is the Spirit; where the Spirit of the Lord is, there is freedom. We all, with unveiled face, reflecting the glory of the Lord, are transformed from glory into glory, as by the Lord the Spirit' (2 Cor. 3:18). This notion of the transforming effect of love is given succinct expression in John's first epistle: 'Beloved, now we are the children of God, and it is not yet apparent what we shall be. We know that when he appears we shall be like him, for we shall see him as he is' (1 John 3: 2). There is no explicit mention of love here, but such mention is found in abundance both in the rest of the epistle and in John's Gospel: 'No one has ever seen God; if we love one another, God dwells in us and his love is perfected in us . . . God is love, and one who abides in love abides in God and God abides him. In this love is perfected in us' (1 John 4:12, 16–17a). This notion of a unitive love—a love that unites us to God and therefore to one another—builds on what is presented more discursively and in narrative form in John's Gospel, especially in the Last Discourses (John 13–16) and in Jesus' 'high priestly prayer' to the Father, which replaces the prayer of Gethsemane, found in the other Gospels (John 17).

I have dwelt on the unitive nature of love as we find it in the New Testament, as it is often overlooked when love, as *agapē*, is reduced to the practice of beneficence—which takes us to the controversy that, for nearly a century now, has dogged discussion of the nature of Christian love. That is the controversy sparked off by Anders Nygren's book, known in English as *Agape and Eros* (Nygren 1953), called, as I notice in the new fourth edition of the *Oxford Dictionary of the Christian Church* (Cross et al. 2022), 'the biggest theological red herring of the century.' The opposition of *agape* and *eros*—whatever lexical justification it may have—as fundamental, and fundamentally opposed, *Motiven* runs counter to the way these terms were used by the Greek Fathers (who, after all, were native speakers of the Greek of that period), but more basically to the evidently unitive understanding of love (for which, in the New Testament, the Greek word is *agape*), that seems to me the clear connotation of the word in the New Testament. Nygren's straitjacket seems also to make it impossible for him to take seriously the close similarity of meaning of the two words *agape* and *philia* in the Johannine tradition, where it is difficult to separate them systematically. For the Jesus of the Fourth Gospel, 'greater love (*agape*) has no one than this, than to give his life for his friends (*philōn*)' (John 15:13). As striking is the conversation between the risen Jesus and the apostle Peter:

> When therefore they had eaten, Jesus says to Simon [son] of John, Do you love (*agapas*) me more than these? He says to him, Yes, Lord, you know that I love (*philō*) you. He says to him, Graze my lambs (*arnia*). He says to him again a second time, Simon [son] of John, Do you love (*agapas*) me? He says to him,

Yes, Lord, you know that I love (*philō*) you. He says to him, Guard my sheep (*probatia*). A third time he says to him, Simon [son] of John, Do you love (*phileis*) me? Peter was grieved that he said to him a third time, Do you love (*phileis*) me? And he said to him, Lord, you know everything, you know that I love (*philō*) you. Jesus says to him, Graze my sheep (*probatia*) (John 21:15–17).

I find it then hardly surprising that when we come to look at the treatment of love in Christian history, love seems to be treated as unitive: love joins together—human beings one to another and to God. This love flows from God (for 'God is love') and draws all to himself. Such an approach to love had already developed within the Platonic tradition, which is therefore eagerly embraced and developed among the Fathers—and along with it the sense that love is the fruit of an ascetic struggle that frees the center of human being—*nous* (mind) or *kardia* (heart)—to cleave to God. Another aspect of this affinity between Christian and Platonic insights is the notion that love draws us to our center—the center of our being, and to God as the center of all being: an idea important to Augustine, summed up in two quotations from his *Confessions*: *pondus meum amor meus* (my love is my weight: *Conf.* XIII. 9.10); *fecisti nos ad te, et inquietum est cor nostrum, donec requiescat in te* (you have made us for yourself, and our heart is restless until it rests in you: *Conf.* I.1.1).

The prominence of the twofold command to love as summing up the Law, the Torah, seems so prominent in the Synoptic Gospels that it might seem otiose to ask who first saw the significance of this twofold command. But it has been claimed by Oliver O'Donovan that it is to Augustine that we owe the emphasis on the twofold commandment to love as summing up the essence of the Christian life (O'Donovan 1980: 4). I wonder: there seem to me to be two Greek Fathers who make such a claim—Clement of Alexandria and St Maximos the Confessor; Maximos is, of course, a couple of centuries later than Augustine, but O'Donovan's claim is not that Augustine was the first, but that it is to Augustine that we owe the emphasis on the twofold command as summing up the essence of the Christian life. That is a stronger claim, but there is no secure evidence that Maximos had any notion of Augustine and his theology (various articles have claimed to demonstrate this in one context or another, but without any real success). Clement, however, is about two centuries earlier than Augustine, so if we can demonstrate that Clement also sees the significance of the twofold command to love, our objection to O'Donovan's claim is substantiated. (I sought to substantiate this as one strand in the Augustine Lecture I gave at Villanova University in 2001, on which I am drawing in this chapter: Louth 2002.) First, it seems to me that Clement makes a great deal of the twofold command to love: he frequently returns to it in his discussions of the perfect Christian life in his *Stromateis*, and yet more frequently the notion of the twofold nature of love guides his reflections, even when the Dominical commandment is not explicitly cited. But it is more than a matter of mention. For the twofold commandment has for Clement, it seems to me, something of the same pivotal significance that it has for Augustine. Let me take a couple of examples. First, from the second book of *Stromateis*. One of Clement's ways of proceeding in this work is to discuss gnomic sayings from both the classical and the Biblical traditions. Here is an example:

> A little more mysterious is the sentence, 'Know yourself.' It comes from the text, 'You have seen your brother, you have seen your God.' In this way I suppose we must take 'You shall love the Lord your God with your whole heart and your neighbor as yourself.' He says that the whole of the Law and the Prophets depends on these commandments. This matches the others: 'I have spoken thus to you so that my joy may be made full. This is my commandment, that you love one another as I have loved you.' 'For the Lord is full of mercy and pity,' and 'The Lord is good to all.' Moses, transmitting 'Know yourself' with greater clarity, often says, 'Take heed' [*prosekhe seautōi*, common in Deuteronomy]. 'By acts of mercy and faith are sins cleansed; by the fear of the Lord everyone is turned away from sin.' 'The fear of the Lord is education and wisdom.' [These last two citations from Proverbs] (*Strom.* II.70. 5–71.4, Ferguson 1991: 205–6)

Here the apocryphal Dominical saying—'You have seen your brother, you have seen your God'—is used to link the Delphic saying, 'Know yourself,' with the commandment to love (which suggests an attention to the qualification 'as yourself' in the second part of the twofold commandment, that O'Donovan also denies before Augustine).

The other passage of Clement I want to look at briefly in this connection is the passage that O'Donovan cites in support of his claim: from *Quis dives salvetur* (Butterworth 1968). This is the passage where it is claimed that by loving one's neighbor, Clement means loving Christ (the implication being that this robs the command of its function as a basis for human morality). He, of course, does say this, but this is because in the passage (*Quis dives* 27: Butterworth 1968: 327–57) Clement is not just discussing the twofold commandment on its own, but in its context in St Luke's Gospel, where Jesus' answer to the lawyer's query as to the identity of the neighbor we are to love is the parable of the Good Samaritan. Clement reads this parable with more care than some exegetes. It seems to me that he sees it functioning on two levels: the Lord's final words, 'Go and do likewise' subvert the lawyer's question to limit the commandment to the 'neighbor,' for, as Clement comments, Jesus' words show that 'love bursts out in good works.' The neighbor then is the one whom we are to love, and it is these good works (*eupoiia*) that are important rather than the identity of the neighbor. This is the usual way in which the parable is taken. But Clement is conscious that the parable is meant to *answer* the lawyer's question. Taken like that, it is the good Samaritan who is the neighbor: he is the one who is to be loved. That is, it seems to me, a more profound suggestion: that we are to love the one who shows us pity, for only in that way will we open ourselves to the One whose pity we desperately need, namely Christ himself. But even that interpretation does not frustrate the commandment in the way O'Donovan feared, for Clement goes on to say that he who loves Christ will obey his commandments, and as an example quotes Matt. 25.34–40, the Lord's words to the sheep in the parable of the sheep and the goats, a demanding account of neighborly love. Before Clement reaches this point he argues that such love on our part will not be possible unless we are freed from the wounds visited upon us by the 'world rulers of darkness': 'fears, lusts, wraths, griefs, deceits and pleasures.' 'Of these wounds,' he says,

> Jesus is the only healer, by cutting out the passions absolutely and from the very root. He does not deal with the bare results, the fruits of bad plants, as the law did, but brings his ax to the roots of evil. This is he who poured over our wounded souls the wine, the blood of David's vine; this is he who has brought and is lavishing on us the oil, the oil of pity from the Father's heart; this is he who has shown us the unbreakable bands of health and salvation, love, faith and hope; this is he who has ordered angels and principalities and powers to serve us for great reward, because they too shall be freed from the vanity of the world at the revelation of the glory of the sons of God. (*Quis dives* 29: Butterworth 331–3)

A little later on in this treatise, or homily, there is another striking passage that leads up to an affirmation of the twofold commandment to love:

> Behold the mysteries of love, and then you will have a vision of the bosom of the Father, whom the only-begotten God [*monogenēs theos* is a variant reading for the more usual *ho monogenēs huios* in John 1:18 'No one has ever seen God; the only-begotten God who is in the bosom of the Father, he has declared him,' which is all but quoted here] alone declared. God himself is love, and for love's sake he manifested himself to us. And while the ineffable part of him is Father, the part that has sympathy with us became Mother. By his loving, the Father became female, a great sign of which is he whom he begat from himself; and the fruit that is born of love is love. For this reason he himself descended, for this reason he clothed himself in humanity, for this reason he willingly suffered the human lot, so that, having been measured to the weakness of us whom he loved, he might measure to us his own power. And when he was about to be offered and give himself as a ransom, he leaves us a new covenant: 'I give you my love.' What love is this, and how great? For each of us he lays down his life,

equal to that of the whole world. In return he asks this from us for each other (*Quis dives* 37: Butterworth 347).

This passage is perhaps best known for its reference, unusual in the Fathers, to God's motherhood. But it is not that I wish to pursue now. What we have in this passage is a remarkable account of the manifestation of God's love for us, through the Son, in incarnation and redemption: a love that manifests God to us and through that manifestation calls from us love on our part, a love for God, but primarily manifest in our love for one another, for the twofold command is to characterize the life of those who have responded to God's gift of himself to us in love.

We should, too, mention Maximos, though more briefly. In his beautiful letter on love (*ep.* 2), which is really a lengthy encomium of love, Maximos says:

> For nothing is more truly godlike than divine love, nothing more mysterious, nothing more apt to raise up human beings to deification. For it has gathered together in itself all things that are recounted by the understanding of truth in the form of virtue, and it has absolutely no relation to anything that has the form of wickedness, since it is the fulfillment of the law and the prophets. For they were succeeded by the mystery of love, which out of human beings makes us gods, and reduces the individual commandments to a universal meaning. Everything is circumscribed by love according to God's good pleasure in a single form, and love is dispensed in many forms in accordance with God's economy (Maximos the Confessor, *ep.* 2 (PG 91.393BC); Louth 1996: 85–6).

Even though Maximos speaks (like Clement) of divine love, he means God's love towards us and the love he inspires in us, a love manifest both in our longing for God, and also in our love for our fellows. Like Clement, and Augustine, the twofold commandment constantly guides Maximos' reflections on love; Maximos even concurs with Augustine in finding in the two pence the Good Samaritan leaves with the innkeeper an allusion to the twofold commandment (*Centuries on Love* IV.75; cf. Augustine, *Qu. Evang.* II.19; *En. Psa.* 125.15; Dekkers-Fraipont 1956: 8855–6).

Let us now turn to the question of self-love. The 'second like [the first]' of the twofold commandment is: You shall love your neighbor as yourself—*hōs seauton—sicut teipsum*. What does this mean? Does it mean that there is a proper love of oneself? I think there may be some support for this in Clement of Alexandria, but there is not much support elsewhere in the Fathers for the notion that the second part of the Dominical command to love entails that we are commanded to love ourselves, that there is a proper *amor sui*, a proper *philautia*. I fear this will be disappointing, even annoying, to those influenced by modern psychotherapeutic notions of proper self-esteem.

The usual interpretation we find among the Fathers is that we naturally love ourselves, so that we can take this as a benchmark for the minimum requirement of love of others: we are to love others at least as much as we (naturally) love ourselves (one might derive this principle, or something like it, from the remark, maybe Paul's, in the letter to the Ephesians, where, discussing a husband's love for his wife, he says that 'he who loves his own wife loves himself; for no one ever hated his own flesh, but nurtures and cares for it . . . : Eph. 5:28b–29). Even when there is some sort of recognition of the value of loving oneself—as Augustine occasionally does, when he regards loving oneself as proper, for we are created by God in his image, and that image/likeness in ourselves is to be cherished—we need to note that the regard for oneself is expressed in verbal form ('loving oneself'); the substantive form—*amor sui*—is always used in a negative way, as of something to be avoided or fought against; similarly for the Greek Fathers, in whom I have not detected even neutral use of the verbal form. This is strikingly true of Maximos the Confessor for whom self-love, *philautia*, is regarded as the 'mother of all wickedness,' to be resolutely rooted out (e.g., *Centuries on Love* II.59; Ceresa-Gastaldo 1963: 122).

BIBLIOGRAPHY

Primary Sources

(translations my own, except where a translation is given below, though with Butterworth I have often corrected extensively)

Augustine 1934. *Confessiones*, ed. M. Skutella, Stuttgart. (Eng. tr. H. Chadwick 1991).

Augustine 1956. *Enarrationes in Psalmos* CI–CL, ed. D. E. Dekkers and I. Fraipont, *CCSL* 40.

Augustine 1980. *Quaestiones Evangeliorum*, ed. A. Mutzenbecher, *CCSL* 44B, 1–118.

Clement of Alexandria 1906. *Stromata* Buch I–VI, ed. Otto Stählen, GCS 15. Leipzig. (Eng. tr. J. Ferguson 1991).

Clement of Alexandria 1968. *Quis Dives Salvetur*, in Butterworth 1968, 270–367.

Maximos the Confessor, *ep.* 2 (PG 91. 392D–408B). (Eng. tr. A. Louth 1996, 84–93).

Maximos the Confessor 1963: *Capitoli sulla Carità*, ed. A. Ceresa-Gastaldo. Rome.

Secondary Literature

Butterworth G. W. 1968. *Clement of Alexandria*. Cambridge, MA/London.

Chadwick H., tr., 1991: Saint Augustine, *Confessions*, Oxford.

Cross F. L., with E. A. Livingstone and A. Louth. 2022. *The Oxford Dictionary of the Christian Church*, 4th edn, Oxford.

Ferguson J. 1991. Clement of Alexandria, *Stromateis, Books One to Three* (Fathers of the Church 85). Washington DC.

Louth A. 1996. *Maximus the Confessor*. London.

Louth A. 2002. 'Love and the Trinity: Saint Augustine and the Greek Fathers' (2001 St Augustine Lecture), *Augustinian Studies* 33 (2002), 1–16.

Nygren A. 1953. *Agape and Eros*, tr. P. S. Watson. London.

O'Donovan O. 1980. *The Problem of Self-Love in St. Augustine*. New Haven and London.

Chapter 6

The Christian Church
as the New Israel

Andrew Louth

When given this title for one of the contributions to our Jewish–Orthodox colloquy, it seemed to me that it would be straightforward—just a matter of looking at the way the Christian Church came to be spoken of and thought of by Christians as the 'New Israel.' Very quickly I discovered that, as such, it is an elusive notion in early Christianity and the thought of the Christian Fathers, indeed so elusive as to be most likely nonexistent (one cannot be sure, but it seems that no instances of the expression survive). It is well known that in the New Testament there is no idea as such of the 'new Israel,' applied to the Church, but the same is true, so far as I can see, for the patristic period. Whether *ho neos Israel* or *ho kainos Israel*, Lampe's *A Patristic Greek Lexicon* records nothing, and although Lampe is not infrequently lacunose, my own further searches have come up with nothing (word searches online are beyond my competence, so all that follows might prove nugatory). What we do find in the Fathers are claims that the Christian Church is Israel, as such, or the true Israel, *ho alethinos Israel*—both of which could be (and probably should be) construed as making a more radical claim than calling the Church the 'New Israel,' for the implication of the Church's being Israel or the True Israel is not that the Jews, the people of Israel of the Old Testament, are the 'old Israel,' but that they are not to be thought of as Israel at all, or as the 'false Israel.'

The contrast old/new is found in the New Testament (and the Fathers) in relation to the Christian understanding of the relationship of the Christians to the Jews, but it is not applied, explicitly, to the notion of Israel: it is applied in the context of Jerusalem, to the Covenant or Testament (in Greek: *diatheke*); Jesus is said, in the Fourth Gospel, to give his disciples a 'new commandment,' *entole kaine*, 'that you love one another' (John 13: 34)—in contrast, presumably, to the old commandment. Although the author of the first letter of John is at pains to make clear that that there is no 'new commandment,' other than the 'one you have had from the beginning,' nevertheless in some way there is a new commandment, 'which is true in him and in you, for the darkness is being dispersed and the true light is already shining' (1 John 2:7–8).

My task, however, is to address the question of the Church as the New Israel; and this I propose to approach in three sections: first, the New Testament; secondly, the Christian Fathers; and then thirdly a particular example which, I think, brings out different valences in the attitude of Christians to the Jews.

It is not just that references to the New Israel are not to be found in the New Testament, references to Israel at all are seldom found, and rarely developed. Even the Apostle Paul's long discussion of the relationship between Jews who belong to the people of the (old) Covenant and those—Jews who have accepted Christ—who put their faith in Jesus as the Messiah, the Christ (Rom 9–11), makes few references to Israel, and can hardly be said to develop them (he refers to his kinsfolk after the flesh, 'who are Israelites, to whom belong the adoption and the glory, the covenants and the giving of the Law, whose are the Fathers, and from them the Christ according to the flesh, who is God above all, blessed to the ages, Amen': Rom 9:4–5); a little later he remarks that 'not all those from Israel are Israel' (Rom 9:6b). Other references to Israel in Paul's letters are few and undeveloped: he refers to 'Israel after the flesh' in 1 Cor 10:18, a fugitive reference in the context of arguing that participation in pagan sacrifices involves being involved in all that paganism represents—this was true of participation in the sacrifices of the Jewish Temple, and is true of participation in the Christian Eucharist; and to the 'Israel of God' in Gal 6:16, 'Grace and mercy be on them [who form the new creation, which embraces both circumcised and uncircumcised], and on the Israel of God,' that is, the Christian Church. One might say that we find here in Paul's thought a distinction between 'Israel after the flesh' and the 'Israel of God,' but that would be an unwarranted extrapolation, for the two expressions are embedded in their very different contexts.

There are two rhetorical contrasts—the old *versus* the new, and flesh *versus* spirit—that often allude to a passage in Jeremiah (31:31–4), where the prophet speaks of a new covenant, which will be written on the heart, not on tablets of stone. The whole passage is quoted at length in Heb 8, where a contrast is made between the first covenant and a new and better covenant that God will make in 'days to come,' when God will make a 'new covenant' with the 'house of Israel, and the house of Judah,' instead of the covenant, 'that he made with their fathers at the time when he led them by hand out of the land of Egypt' (Heb 8:8–9), because they did not abide by that covenant: "this is the covenant that I will make with the house of Israel, after those days, giving them my laws in their understanding, and writing them on their hearts, and I will be their God and they shall be my people; and no one will teach his fellow citizen or brother, saying, 'Know the Lord,' for they shall all know me from the least to the great among them, and I shall have mercy on their injustices and I shall remember their sins no longer" (Heb 8:10–12). The conclusion drawn by the author of the letter to the Hebrews is: 'in saying new, he makes the first old, and what has become old, showing its age, is already passing away' (Heb 8:13—an interesting comment, as the culture of Late Antiquity tended to prize antiquity and regard what is new as untried and trivial: 'innovation' was not term of praise). The 'new covenant'—which is bound up with (if not actually identified with) the Christian Eucharist, celebrated 'in memory of [Christ]'—is something written on the heart, not merely recorded on tablets of stone, or written in ink; these contrasts—old/new, written on the heart/written on stone or in ink—seem frequently to underlie Paul's train of thought. They inform Paul's witness to the tradition of the Eucharist, which "I received from the Lord and have passed on to you, that the Lord Jesus in the night in which he was handed over took bread, gave thanks, and broke it, saying, 'This is my body, which is for your sake; do this in memory of me.' And so with the cup after the meal, saying 'This cup is the new covenant in my blood; this do, as often as you drink it, in memory of me'" (1 Cor 11:23–5). Similar rhetorical contrasts are made, quite in passing, in the second letter to the Corinthians, where he says, 'You are our letter [a systatic letter, that is, a letter of recommendation], written in your hearts, known and read by everyone, making clear that you are Christ's letter, delivered by us, written not in ink, but by the Spirit of the living God, not on tablets of stone, but in tablets of your hearts of flesh' (2 Cor 3:2–3). Paul goes on to develop these contrasts, speaking of the new covenant (of which he is the servant), which is not of the letter, but of the spirit; for, he comments, 'the letter kills, but the spirit gives life' (2 Cor 3:6), and there follows a long (and famous) contrast between the covenant given to Moses and the new covenant of which Paul is the servant—a contrast symbolized in the veil with which Moses covered his face after being with God face-to-face—a contrast that remains, for when Moses is read 'today' (in the synagogue?) there is a veil over the hearts of those that listen, which is only taken away by turning to the Spirit, who is the Lord, so that 'we all, with unveiled faces, reflect the glory of the Lord, transformed in this very image, from glory to glory, as by the Lord, the Spirit' (2 Cor 3:18). Similarly in Galatians 4:21–31, Paul makes a contrast between the 'two covenants,' symbolized by the two sons of Abraham, one born of a slave, Hagar, the other by his freeborn wife, Sarah—a contrast interpreted as between Sinai and Jerusalem, the former a 'mountain in Arabia' (such a demeaning description of Sinai would not be characteristic of the later Christian tradition), consisting of Jerusalem as it now is, the latter 'the Jerusalem above, [which is] free, the mother of us all'— a contrast further developed by the opposition of flesh and spirit (flesh with a negative valence in this context, in contrast to the positive valence it has when contrasted with stone), referenced by the persecution by the one born of the flesh of those born of the Spirit—'as now' (Gal 4:29)—and concluding with Paul's triumphant 'Therefore, brothers, we are not children of the slave girl, but of the free woman.'

All of this, however, prescinds from the topic I am meant to be addressing: the idea of the Christian Church as the 'New Israel,' though the themes I have developed are pertinent to it.

If we turn to the early Christian Fathers, we find no mention of a 'new Israel,' but rather a sense that the 'scripture/s' belonged to the Christian Church: it was *their* 'scripture/s' as Christians (only in the late second century were these 'scriptures' called the 'Old Testament,' at the same time as the Gospels and other apostolic writings were gathered together as the 'New Testament'). So Clement of Rome, 'bishop' of Rome (whatever that meant at the end of the first century), who was certainly a Gentile Christian, rather than a converted Jew, refers quite unselfconsciously to the figures of the Old Testament—the patriarchs and the prophets—as 'our fathers' (*1 Clement* 62.2). This is sometimes developed in terms of the 'newness' of Christianity, but the epithet 'new' is applied, not to Israel, but to people, as in the Epistle of Barnabas (*Barnabas* 5.7, 7.5), or in the Letter to Diognetos, to race (*Diognetos* 1.1). For the letter to Diognetos, this is part of his presentation of Christianity as a 'new race' alongside the Greek and the Jews. Barnabas' use of 'new' in relation to people is intended to convey the idea of the religion of the Christians being newly revealed, but what has been revealed is the real meaning of the Scripture, which had been utterly misunderstood by the Jews. The contrast is between newly revealed truth, to be found in the Christian Church, and ancient error, based on misunderstanding, found among the Jews; but this truth is the real meaning of Scripture, as Barnabas refers to it, for the later Christian designation of the Hebrew Scriptures as the 'Old Testament' Barnabas would not have understood. The Jews had misunderstood their Scriptures, the real meaning of which is to be found in the Apostolic teaching, eventually (though after Barnabas' time) gathered together as the New Testament—the Gospels and other apostolic writings. Barnabas' understanding of the Hebrew Scriptures (in fact, for him, the Greek Septuagint) was that they were old—older than any other religious traditions—and because the oldest, the truth, the pristine truth. And this was the predominant way in which defenders of Christianity (the 'Apologists') represented their faith, not as something new (that was a mistake, though understandable as the Christians themselves knew that the term Christian was recent: see Acts 11:26), but as old, as the oldest, the aboriginal faith, written into creation itself. In arguing thus, they were responding to the settled conviction of their time (already referred to) that the truth was old; what was new was untried, and doubtless unsound, innovation. Christians were, of course, not the only claimants to the Hebrew Scriptures; there were, quite evidently, the Jews, whose claim must have seemed more plausible, as their Scriptures were in the original Hebrew, read in Hebrew in their worship in the synagogue, whereas the Christians, once they became convinced that the Christian Gospel was universal, not limited to a Jewish Messianic sect, found themselves predominantly Greek-speaking, with Greek scriptures, first the Septuagint, supplemented by the 'New Testament,' also, written in Greek, in contrast to which the Septuagint received the title of the Old Testament.

Mention of the Jewish synagogue reminds me of a lecture I heard Rabbi Norman Solomon give (to a study weekend for my then students at Goldsmiths, London, enrolled for a part-time course in Religious Studies), when he told us that we were not to think of Judaism and Christianity related as mother and (wayward) daughter, but as siblings, both trying to make sense of the Hebrew Scriptures in the aftermath of the fall of the Temple in Jerusalem and the end of sacrifice—rival attempts to make sense of the same heritage, both of them developing in the first millennium, both producing a parallel literature: the New Testament corresponding to the Mishnah, and the writings of the Fathers (an indeterminate term) corresponding to the Talmud and the Midrash. 'Rivalry' was, as it were, inherent in the development of both faiths: the two successful faiths based on the heritage of the Hebrew Scriptures. Christians will surely say that I am failing to mention the most important difference: namely Christ, his ministry of teaching and healing, his death on the Cross and the Resurrection. That is certainly true, but it is also worth observing that the fall of the Temple and the end of sacrifice is rarely absent from the background of the Gospel accounts of Christ. His claim to be able to destroy the Temple and rebuild it in three days lies behind any attempt to reconstruct the meaning of his teaching and his death and resurrection—for Christians, the Paschal mystery, the mystery of the Christian Passover.

In Christian engagement with the Jews, there seem to me (no expert in the field) two fundamental arguments: one, what one might call the 'Apostasy of Israel' argument; the other the argument from the universalism of the New Covenant—they are there from the very beginning and are to be found in virtually every stratum of the New Testament. The apostasy of Israel argument regards the Jews as failing to accept the claim made for Christ (or even by Christ) that he is the Messiah promised in the Hebrew Scriptures; the fall of the Temple and the destruction of the 'old Jewish religion' is retribution for failure to confess Christ. The old religion is to be replaced by the new religion that confesses Christ. The universalism of the New Covenant, on the other hand, argues that God's covenant is no longer restricted to the Jews, the descendants of Abraham, or Isaac, or Jacob/Israel, or of those to whom God made a covenant through Moses, but open to all: as the words of Jesus at the Last Supper make clear, as he gave the cup of wine to his disciples, 'This is my blood of the covenant, poured out for many, for the forgiveness of sins' (Matt 26:28), or as it is rendered in the Divine Liturgy of St John Chrysostom: 'This is my blood of the new covenant, poured out for you and for many for the forgiveness of sins' (assimilating Luke 22:20). Virtually all Christian commentators, from the Fathers to the present day, make the point that 'for you and for many' means 'for all,' both Jews and, along with them, non-Jews, 'Gentiles'—both included in the new covenant.

It is very often not at all clear whether the Christian Fathers are speaking of exclusion of Israel, to be replaced by the Christians, or a fulfillment of the old covenant in the new, whereby the Jews are included in the new and all-embracing covenant. See, for instance, Justin Martyr's summary of his position in the *Dialogue with Trypho the Jew*:

> This is the new law and the new covenant and the expectation of those from all nations to await good things from God . . . We are the true and spiritual nation of Israel, the race of Judah and of Jacob and Isaac and Abraham, who when he was still uncircumcised received witness from God for his faith, and was blessed, and was called father of many nations—we, I say, are all this, who were brought nigh to God by him who was crucified, even Christ (*Dialogue* 11.5).

Another example of this sense of identity with Israel—of broader significance than theological arguments—is to be found in the Byzantine chronicles or chronographies, which, as a rule, give an account, in principle year by year, from the foundation of the world. They start with the six-day creation of the world in Genesis and continue with the history of Israel up to the Exile (with sometimes, cross-references to the history of other, mostly Near-Eastern and Mediterranean, peoples); they then switch to the histories of empires up to the Roman Empire, and thereafter follow the history of the Roman Empire, which continued up to, in principle, 1453. This is intended as a history of the ancestors of the people who finally came to form the Roman Empire—the Old Testament histories are embedded into it.

It would be interesting to trace the controversy between Jew and Christian over how their shared heritage was to be interpreted, but this is no easy task, for the Jewish side of the story is, for the most part, only to be gleaned from the way in which the Christians responded to Jewish argument—at least until relatively modern times. There is, however, one episode where we can glimpse something of the differing ways in which Christians represented their relationship with the Jews, and that is in the polemic over icons in the eighth and ninth centuries. One of the results of this polemic was attempts, on both sides of the iconoclast controversy, to draw up arguments from the Christian tradition on the question of the legitimacy of icons and their veneration. The controversy emerged in the seventh century and the most notable defender of the icons was John Damascene, writing from Jerusalem, where he was a monk, but a Jerusalem which, by then, had been a part of the Arab Umayyad Empire for nearly a century. Reflection on icons was not very prominent in the early centuries, which had the effect of making both sides treasure what they could find, and indeed make a great deal of what little they could find, quarrying for arguments that could be used to defend (or attack) icons and their veneration—arguments that originally had quite a different antagonist and another purpose altogether.

Some of the most interesting extracts included by John in his florilegia to his defenses of icons against the iconoclasts come from a sixth-century bishop of Neapolis in Cyprus, Leontios. Traces, sometimes more, of many of his writings have survived, notably his hagiographical works—he composed *vitae* of John the Merciful, Patriarch of Alexandria, to whose circle he probably had belonged, of Symeon the Fool for Christ, and of a earlier Cypriote bishop, the renowned Spyridon, bishop of Trimuthis—but nothing more than extracts survive of book V of a treatise *Against the Jews*, concerning the veneration of the Cross of Christ and the images of the saints and their relics (the other books, which are quite lost, presumably concerned other issues at stake between Christians and Jews, for example, the doctrine of the Trinity). These extracts, concerning his defense of images of saints, survive in iconodule florilegia. As he is arguing against Jews, who had (presumably) accused the Christians of idolatry for venerating the Cross of Christ and images and relics of the saints, he takes as the basis of his arguments something they both accepted, namely the Hebrew Scriptures (in, of course, the form they take in the Septuagint). Examples from the Old Testament demonstrating that veneration of people and places was not thought of as idolatry, but is recorded without comment (e.g., Abraham bowing before those from whom he bought the cave for a sepulcher: Gen 23:7, 12; Jacob bowing to Esau: Gen 33:3); evidence that God works miracles through matter (e.g., Elisha's staff, Moses' staff, Aaron's rod), and reference to the material accouterments of the tabernacle, on which such devotion was lavished; the importance of visible memorials for recalling the mighty deeds of God in the past; and that there is evidence in the Old Testament for a distinction between veneration (*proskynesis*) as a way of showing honor, and veneration of God, entailing worship (*latreia*). All these arguments are incorporated by John Damascene into his first treatise against the iconoclasts. There is, however, a striking difference of context, for while Leontios was arguing against (or with) Jews, the Damascene's primary opponents are the iconoclasts, who are Christians. There are elements of John's arguments quite foreign to the way Leontios argues: John argues, for example, that the Incarnation makes all the difference; before the Incarnation depicting God was impossible, and indeed, the proscription of idols in the second commandment was, John suggests, to prevent Jews from idolatry to which they were prone. He also suggests that the iconoclasts, in appealing to second commandment, are, in effect, Judaizers. There is none of this in Leontios, for the simple reason that Leontios wants to keep the Jews in his argument; he wants to show them that, on the basis of their Scriptures, Christian veneration of the Cross, icons, and relics is not ruled out. John has a different target and, given that, it is worthy of note that John endorses so much from Leontios. Or least he did to begin with, for it is in the first treatise that John makes so much of the arguments he had found in Leontios, arguments that draw on the Old Testament, and John is happy to go along with these arguments that argue for the Jewish roots of Christian veneration of icons by grounding icons and their veneration in passages from the Hebrew Bible. A little later (maybe five years later) John composed a second treatise against the iconoclasts. In his introduction he says that there had been complaints about the complexity of his argument in the first treatise. So he will simplify, and indeed he does. The first ten chapters (after the introduction) develop a single argument: that idolatry is the work of the devil, who was especially successful with the Jews, leading to Moses' prohibition of the making of images. However, with Christians it is different, for they are grown up, unlike the childish Jews, and may make images without the danger of idolatry; iconoclasm is a further ruse by the devil to undermine the Christian faith in the Incarnation. Even the key argument in the first treatise, that in the Incarnation God made himself visible, is only mentioned in passing. The supersession of the Old Testament by the New is affirmed uncompromisingly.

There is, then, I argue, a striking contrast between John Damascene's first defense of icons, which, by relying on Leontios, emphasizes the extent to which the Old Testament itself, despite the commandment forbidding idolatry, endorses devotion expressed in bodily gestures, directed towards creatures, both human beings and human artifacts, such as pictures. His second treatise abandons all this and represents the iconoclast appeal to the second commandment as evidence of a Judaizing tendency, backing this up with an emphatically supersessionist account of Judaism, the religion of those who rejected Christ and the Incarnation, which is the ultimate justification for icons and their veneration.

I find this a melancholy example of different attitudes on the part of Christians towards the Jews, often enough not at all clearly distinguished by Christians themselves: on the one hand, a sense of fulfillment of authentically Jewish insights in Christian faith, devotion, and worship, which can still be deepened by an appreciation of the Church's Semitic past; on the other hand, a dismissal of the Jews as mistaken and uncomprehending, who have been superseded by the truth of the Gospel. The notion of the Church as the New Israel is so rare, not because of any respect for Jewish sensibilities, but because the Church saw itself as the True Israel, in contrast with the religion of the Jews which was not so much old, as false.

RECOMMENDED READING

For a recent presentation and analysis of the eighth-century arguments about icons, including those by John Damascene, see: Andrew Louth, 'The Theological Argument about Images in the 8th Century,' in *A Companion to Byzantine Iconoclasm*, ed. M. Humphreys. Leiden 2021, 401–24.

Chapter 7

The Journey to Oneself

Anti-Judaism in the Search for Christian Identity

Elena Narinskaya

Once in Oxford I got myself an audience with the Professor of the Study of the Abrahamic Religions, Guy Stroumsa, to ask him a question about Islam, the latest religion of the Abrahamic family. I was embarking on my academic journey from Judaism and Christianity to Islam, and I was contemplating various opinions about Islam not being an *original religion*. Professor Stroumsa's answer brought my thinking process to the next level. He answered with the question: Is any religion original? This question leads me into the current chapter.

This world's religious history often demonstrates to us that every subsequent religion builds itself on the foundation of the previous one, and then tries its hardest to disengage from it to form its own independent identity and tradition. The complexity of religious development could be compared to a child's development. Young children are totally dependent on their parents, while in their teenage years they go through the process of adolescent rebellion as a necessary phase of their search for self-identity and as part of their process of building character. As an unfortunate and extreme side effect of this process children may even reject their parents or distance themselves from them. As children develop further, and as a sign of maturity, they grow into appreciating their parents, learn to make amends and show gratitude. Further along children might even start caring for their parents and switch the roles by adopting parenting roles themselves, not only to their growing children, but also to their aging parents. And so, the circle of life continues.

In my online article 'What does it take to be anti-Jewish?' I have tried to identify the problem of a snowball effect in relation to the early Christian sources and their interpretation. While preparing for the article, and also when reading through the works of St Ephrem the Syrian and also the secondary literature about him for my PhD at Durham University I noticed one interesting nuance in the secondary literature. Edmund Beck could be considered the earliest academic author who revived Syriac studies in general, and the study of Ephrem the Syrian in particular, in academia. He produced a number of books and articles translating Ephrem, and also analyzing his writing. I noticed that certain trends in scholarly opinions about Ephrem's writings originating with Beck were repeated by the majority of other scholars. What I found puzzling is that for a number of decades after Beck's argument, scholars were relying on his assumptions without bothering to go back to Ephrem and revisit his writings.

When I started to work on St Ephrem, my supervisor, Professor Robert Hayward, encouraged me to read Ephrem in the original language and to form my own opinions about his writings, not influenced by the secondary literature. When the time came for me to pay attention to secondary writings I was surprised to find that most of the writers consider Ephrem's theology to be nonsystematic and not very elaborate, and also assume that Ephrem was an antisemite or an anti-Jewish writer. Imagine my amusement at these discoveries in the secondary literature when I had been marvelling at Ephrem's theology and biblical exegesis for a couple of years and was astounded how close his exegetical writings were to the rabbinical and targumic literature.

I rigorously protected St Ephrem in my PhD and went out of my way to present him as an original thinker who was deeply rooted in Jewish exegesis. I also argued that one cannot possibly call Ephrem an antisemite, because this was a twentieth-century concept, and the fourth-century writer could not possibly adhere to it. I also protected Ephrem against the charge of being an anti-Jewish writer, arguing that his particularly highly colored hymns were not addressed to a Jewish audience, but to a Christian one, and were only expressing his disappointment with the Jews' not recognizing Christ. My goal in this study is to revisit Ephrem's verses with a hopefully more experienced look, and to try to reach a more general conclusion about what was happening in Ephrem's church then, and how it affects my church now.

Antisemitism is a well-known concept now, but it still lacks clarity in definition and in the boundaries of its application. It is probably agreed that demonizing and denigrating remarks against Jews as a nation clearly fall under the definition of antisemitism, but what about the so-called 'innocent' joke-like and often casual remarks that one hears every so often: how does one classify them? What if these remarks are extremely subtle, for example, when someone comments that such and such a person has a Jewish surname:

can this be considered antisemitic? Casual antisemitism could often be heard as a passing remark, which an untrained ear might not detect. In that case, the question to ask is: if it is no longer detected as antisemitism, does it stop being antisemitic? Another, more complex, example: if one criticizes the state of Israel for its external politics, is this antisemitic? When does a critical remark cross the line of constructive criticism and step into the realm of racism? I am afraid there is no black-and-white border: it all depends on the context.

The context is something that is essential to consider in assessing other people's remarks and verses, and there are many books that emphasize that early Christian writers, for example, with their critical remarks were targeting not Jews as such, but Judaizing Christians, as in the case of St John Chrysostom and others. This may be so, but what is important to consider is the implications that such critical remarks had for the future of Jewish–Christian relationship. More so, it is crucial to reconsider these writings at the time when history witnessed the atrocities of the Holocaust.

Reading particular hymns of St Ephrem the Syrian or certain homilies of St John Chrysostom which have been carefully selected by contemporary scholars, or a few particular passages from St Justin's *Dialogue with Trypho*, the idea of charging these authors with anti-Judaism becomes very attractive. And, indeed, there is no point denying or being shy about the existence of particular writings that show rather sharp criticism of Jews as a people, Jewish laws and practices, and so on. However, in scrutinizing the anti-Jewish writings of some early Christian authors as such, one has to be acutely aware of how these writings were perceived by people at the time. If one is disturbed by these writings today one has to bear in mind that they were specifically formulated for the sensitivities of the audiences of the early centuries, and take this into account when reading them. One can do a great injustice to the early fathers in reading them as if they are blogging today. In approaching the early sources one has to develop a certain skill, and the ability to look through the external phraseology in order to find an inner didactic meaning, often hidden underneath the surface.

If not read skillfully, misunderstanding their writings could cast a shadow on the legacy of the church fathers as such, and distort people's understanding of their religious tradition. In considering a sanctified person as a whole one has to bear in mind that there were instances in their lives when they made mistakes. If one looks at the life of St Mary of Egypt, for example, one cannot ignore the fact that at some period of her life she was a prostitute and a nymphomaniac. One can argue that this was before she became a saint, but one cannot argue that it was not part of her life. The important lesson here is to accept the saints, and to allow them their mistakes. Some say that to recognize holiness one has to have it in the first place. Hence, it is much easier to recognize the more mundane realities and raw emotions in others by virtue or by misfortune of having them in ourselves. The process of maturity and wisdom allows one to learn about one's own shortcomings, work on them, and appreciate others having their own struggles as well. Often, judging the other is a way of covering one's own mistakes or shortcomings, or even a more elaborate way of allowing oneself the exact thing one judges the other for.

There is a danger in misunderstanding the fathers, which could be seen in singling out anti-Jewish remarks. Often this method of reading the Christian scriptures allowed anti-Jewish interpretations into the church, casting a shadow on Jews as the ones who criticized Jesus, even persecuted him, and ultimately crucified him. Twentieth-century academics have dealt with this problem, but has it reached the level of popular belief yet?

Changing one's mind and even one's belief could be a sign of maturity and growth. One tends to forget that one of Jesus' followers, the apostle Paul, was the one who first persecuted Jesus but then followed him and even died for him. The example of Paul shows an early church leader making mistakes and changing his mind drastically. One can certainly add to it that even as committed Christians they were entitled to their own opinion which could be considered questionable (for example, Paul's remark that women should keep silent in the church, 1 Cor 14:34). In this matter, one has to appreciate the complexity of Paul's character. He was a man of strong convictions, some of which he was able to change throughout his life, while others he chose not to.

There were many other Jews who played a crucial role in forming Christianity. Are they also considered as targets of anti-Jewish sentiment? One should not forget that the two foundational figures of Orthodox Christianity, Jesus and his mother, were Jews. One essential characteristic of antisemitic, anti-Jewish or other racist or antireligious remarks is their blunt generalization. Any generalizing of people or their writings deprives them of their complexity and even perhaps undermines their lives by stripping them of their colors. For example, taking some characters hostile to Jesus in the Gospel and projecting their opposition and hostility onto the whole nation is misleading and wrong. One cannot forget that it is not just Jews who do not accept Christ in our world, but in this secular age most nominal Christians would have some sort of hostility if not to Jesus then to his church.

In order to avoid the common mistake of generalization leading to misunderstanding and confusion, I propose a tedious process of focused and detailed study of each individual author prior to the process of applying any sort of definitions to their writings. I am particularly concerned with the term 'anti-Jewish,' precisely because it is increasingly commonly used without much knowledge and understanding of what it actually means.

The next step of this presentation is to find as clear a definition of the term 'anti-Jewish' as possible. By doing so one becomes equipped to deal with the secondary task, which allows one to critically approach and deconstruct the arguments of some scholars who pursue certain early Christian writings as anti-Jewish. I am mostly equipped to talk about Ephrem the Syrian, but I also have a few other names in mind. The earliest Christian source is the New Testament itself. In addition we have: the *Epistle to Barnabas*, possibly written by an Alexandrian Jew (between 70 CE, the destruction of the Temple, and 131, the Bar Kokhba revolt), Justin Martyr and his *Dialogue with Trypho* (second century, Palestine), St John Chrysostom (fourth century, Antioch), St Ephrem the Syrian (fourth century, Syriac Christianity).

If we look for anti-Jewish remarks in these writings we will find plenty. What we do with these remarks is up to the discretion of each individual. What is important to bear in mind is whether we pursue our own agenda or try to understand the intentions of the author.

As an example, Kuhlmann depicts Ephrem within the tradition of anti-Jewish polemic and as the one who dominated it (Kuhlmann 2004:179). There was an anti-Jewish polemic at the time, and with some of his writings Ephrem gets himself involved with it, while with others he does not. However, when Kuhlmann presents Ephrem as an author who detests Jews (Kuhlmann 2004: 180) this may be considered as stepping a bit too far. What is important is the fact that Ephrem's and other early church fathers' anti-Jewish remarks were possibly used later as a way of feeding antisemitic tendencies. There is a very important development, which needs to be accentuated here. Once again, it is about taking certain remarks out of context and using them for one's own social or political agenda. How much blame can one put on early church fathers for the Holocaust? One could answer this by looking closely into the primary sources and highlighting a certain rhetoric there that could ignite hostility towards Jews. Indeed, reading passages or sentences, or even singular out-of-context remarks, as sharp criticism of Jews as a people opens possibilities for further interpretations of these remarks. But then we have to admit that we are stepping outside the original intention of the author and allowing ourselves to follow our own intentions.

As stated before, Christian identity in the first few centuries was still in a formative period, insecure and threatened by virtue of being in a minority. The ties with Judaism were very strong and often confusing. Early church fathers occasionally used anti-Jewish remarks as a way of winning newly converted Christians to the church. This was, perhaps, an unfortunate strategy, which clearly indicate the feeling of insecurity within Christian communities. What is even more unfortunate is to notice tendencies in the church to elaborate on its anti-Jewish sentiment during the time of Christian dominance. It is important to point out that further use of anti-Jewish elements outside the writings of the early church fathers to build up an anti-Jewish ethos in the church is the responsibility of those who are interested in building up this ethos.

Early Christian writers used language rather freely. Twenty-first-century sensitivities can no longer afford such freedom of literary expression. One should not forget that the unbounded comments of the church fathers were precisely because they did not have two centuries of Jewish–Christian mis-understandings on their shoulders. Hence, they had fewer concerns about their allusions and felt much more relaxed with their language. They had the luxury of not being acquainted with the deliberate extermination of world Jewry. Additionally, some of their contemporaries quite possibly did not even clearly differentiate between Christians and Jews. One has to consider all the above while looking closely at the particular writings of the early fathers.

Often, one finds an alternative explanation for apparently anti-Jewish con-notations in Ephrem. Kuhlmann writes about 'the gratuitousness of Ephrem's anti-Judaism' (Kuhlmann 2004: 180) commenting on Ephrem's verse from *Hymns on the Faith* 82.2: 'Your symbol rebukes the Jewish girls when they wear you.' The context of the *Hymn* is nature testifying to God's greatness and witnessing divine presence in this world, which, as an idea, represents one of the major pillars of Ephrem's theology. Hence, the pearls as the sym-bols of Christ threaded into the jewelry on the necks of the Jewish girls testify to them about Christ.

About another hymn Kuhlmann states the following: 'Ephrem's personal bitter animosity towards the Jews is nowhere revealed more clearly than in the 67th Nisibene Hymn. Here his anti-Jewish rhetoric sinks almost as low as anything produced by modern antisemites when he openly admits how much he hates the Jews' (Kuhlmann 2004: 180). Kuhlmann does not, however, present a balanced argument. He makes several mistakes. He places Ephrem in the field of anti-Jewish and antisemitic polemic, when this was never an agenda for Ephrem. Kuhlmann draws his conclusions out of the context of the overall scope of Ephrem's work. His references are predominantly from Ephrem's hymnology, which limits the author's presentation of the whole range of Ephrem's writings. There is no reference to Ephrem's exegesis, which contains highly laudatory and appreciative remarks about Jews. Kuhlmann makes no effort to reflect on Ephrem's connection to Judaism as such. Not many of the authors ascribing anti-Judaism to Ephrem notice that Ephrem borrowed much from the Jewish tradition.

A glaring example is the writings of Deschner, which define Ephrem as 'one of the wildest enemies of Jews not only in his time' (Deschner 1986: 131–2), and present an apocryphal narrative of Ephrem being raised as an antisemite from his childhood. Emphasizing a consistency in Ephrem's hatred of Jews, and extrapolating this attitude into Ephrem's theology and even into the definition of the church, Deschner states: 'The saint is confronting the radiant purity of the church with the madness and the stink and with the killing of the Jewish people. For St. Ephrem the Church is free from the stink of the stinking Jews who want to hand over their earlier sickness to the healthy' (Deschner 1986: 132). Deschner's approach to Ephrem's writings is somewhat misleading. Even Kuhlmann admits that Ephrem is taken out of context by Deschner (Kuhlmann 2004: 182). However, similar thoughts are expressed by many other scholars. Not all of them are so extreme in presenting their argument, but quite a few, for example, state that Ephrem is anti-Jewish in his theology.

Ephrem's Semitic background and closeness to Judaism may play a factor in his critique. A number of scholars have noticed the rather sharp and intense criticism of Jews as a people in his hymns, and have described this as a theological position. One of the reasons for his criticism of Jews could be his attempt to distance himself from Judaism and 'the people,' i.e., the Jews, in order to develop a theology of 'the peoples,' i.e., the gentiles. Jansma points out the problem that Ephrem had to solve within himself, namely, dependency on Judaism. Jansma writes: 'The extent of Ephraem's indebtedness to rabbinic fundamental concepts, so it seems, is directly proportioned to the intensity of the invectives directed by him to the people of the crucifiers' (Jansma 1973: 13).

The distinctive feature of Ephrem's creative approach to Judaism is that he introduced Christ into the very core of some of the Jewish concepts, ideas, and practices, for example, the Passover celebration or the concept of the merits of the fathers. Ephrem allowed himself great freedom in working with the Jewish tradition of exegesis, developing it further with his Christological perspective. However, even when Ephrem disagreed with the Jewish argument, he composed his exegetical writings in close collaboration with the Jewish exegetical tradition.

Even some eminent scholars in the earlier editions of their books express regret about Ephrem's writings. For example, Robert Murray: 'It must be confessed with sorrow that Ephrem hated Jews. It is sad that the man who could write the magisterial Commentary on Genesis, with the command it shows of the tradition which still to a great extent united Christians and Jews, could sink to writing *Carmina Nisibena* 67' (Murray 1975: 68). Another statement suggests that with his theology Ephrem was 'happily moderating the hatred of which he was capable' (Murray 1975: 60).

It seems natural at this point to look closely at selected examples from Ephrem's writings in order to illustrate both sides of the argument, i.e., Ephrem's critical remarks and negative imagery of the Jews as well as his appreciation of Jews as a people.

One has to admit that it is not easy to read the *Hymn on Nisibis* 67: it is the most difficult and suggestive one. At first reading, and even reading it for the second and third times, one cannot help accepting that Ephrem was anti-Jewish. There is no doubt that (like Chrysostom) he uses rather sharp and

uncompromising language. One must wonder whether this language is appropriate in the current times. However, one should not forget that these lines
were produced when the Holocaust had not yet happened. The most important
question is whether these words and images contributed to the Holocaust.

Reading the most suggestive lines from this hymn, verses 16 and 17 (in the
Nicene and Post Nicene Fathers translation), disturbs one's modern sensitivities with its racist sentiment: 'I wonder at the Holy Spirit, that He thus dwelt:
in the midst of a People whose savor stank, as their conversation. Onions and
garlic *are* the heralds of their doings: as is the food so is the understanding,
of this defiled people.'

When taken out of the context the two verses sound anti-Jewish, and even
antisemitic, as they evoke antisemitic folkloric sentiment of a rather low
caliber. However, if one looks at the overall idea of the hymn, it becomes
clear that it is constructed on the basis of using examples of negative imagery
for the purpose of discouraging certain practices, scandalizing insincerity
and deceit.

It is important to notice that there are five examples of negative types
in the Hymn:

1. Sheol
2. Death
3. Jezebel
4. The People
5. Ephrem using himself as a negative example.

Ephrem deconstructs the dominance of negative types in the hymn by
emphasizing the redeeming sacrifice of Jesus. This reveals his goal: glorifica-
tion of Christ. He achieves this by depicting Christ as triumphant over Death
and Sheol, putting to shame the Jews who did not accept Him and whose
deeds are an abomination, and even shaming himself, the author, whom
he considers the 'unworthy' Christian. Thus, Ephrem negates and rejects
everything, including his own self, in order to paint the darkness on which
he enthrones Christ in his shining glory. This is Ephrem's choice of creative
literary form.

Most of the imagery in the hymn is biblical, making it a poetic version of
a number of Old Testament themes. Some scholars who read these verses as
antisemitic did not trouble themselves with the broader context of the hymn,
for example, misinterpreting verse 17 as referring to the 'stink of the stinking Jews,' which seems to be a further elaboration on Ephrem's allusion. It
is more appropriate to understand this verse within the biblical imagery of
Peshitta, Num 11:5, when writing about the smell of the garlic and onions
as 'the heralds of people's doings.'

The aim of this part is to highlight the difference between Ephrem's use of the exegetical and literary tools of antithesis, polarization and apology in relation to the Jews, and his so-called 'theology of anti-Judaism.' Ephrem does allow a figurative approach to the Jews as the daughter of Zion, who killed the Watcher, Christ (*Hymns on Nisibis; Hymns on Nativity* 6.23–4). There is a personification of Israel as a whore in Ephrem, but there are also biblical examples of the personification of Israel as a whore in Hosea 2:5, 3:3, 4:10–15, 5:3, 9:1. Old Testament narrative is a part of the common tradition to which both Jewish and Christian writers had access (Narinskaya 2011). When Ephrem is critical of Jews he is sharp, but he also relies on the examples of the merits of the Jewish fathers through the figures of Moses, David, and Abraham; and he brings the figures of Elijah, Elisha and Melchizedek into the picture, further diluting suspicions of his anti-Judaic inclinations. More so, Ephrem affords high regard to Jews as a chosen nation. Further on in this study there will be examples demonstrating that Ephrem's presentation of Israel in his writings amounts to a very special treatment of 'the people,' i.e., as the people of God, and as the chosen nation.

In his commentaries on Exodus Ephrem twice mentions occasions when Israel was able to see God (Commentary on Exodus 24.2, 4 in Salvesen 1995: 60, see Exod 24:9–10, 13–17). By showing that there was a time when Israel was able to see God, Ephrem explores further the tragedy of Israel losing the ability of capturing the sight of God. Ephrem emphasizes the exclusive relationship that Israel has with God. His additional commentary on Moses' song of praise is a good illustration of this. Moses' words according to the Bible were 'The Lord will reign over us forever' (Exod 15:18; Narinskaya 2011), and Ephrem adds to this 'and not other nations' (Commentary on Exodus 15.1 in Salvesen 1995: 48). Ephrem would not make such an exclusive remark unless he accepts the divine choice of the people of Israel. Thus, Ephrem describes the exclusive and privileged relationship that Israel had with God at the time of Moses and calls Israel 'the People' (Commentary on Exodus 15.3 in Salvesen 1995: 49), while all other nations he styles differently. There are multiple examples showing a different Ephrem to the one of the Hymn of Nisibis, one who is focused on praising the Jews rather than criticizing them.

The language of the early Christian Fathers often sounds bluntly anti-Jewish to a modern ear. But was it so to the audience that these verses were actually addressed to? Disregarding the context underestimates historical, religious and cultural situation in which these writings were produced.

Anti-Jewish sentiments in relation to Ephrem are misleading, because they link the actual writings of a particular author with anti-Jewish tendencies in the church throughout the following centuries. The question that is important to pose here is why the church in its later development was so prone to anti-Judaism and later on to antisemitism? Why the church continued to persecute Jews when it gained power and became a majority religion? Why the church chose to emphasize the negative remarks towards Jews in the early writers and act on them with rigor, hatred and hostility through later centuries? Who is to be held responsible for bringing negative literary remarks to the next level by taking the battle from the epistemological genre and into the streets? Whose initiative was it to proceed beyond the literary genre of negative imagery and into the deliberate and intentional denigration or demonization of the Jews as a people and Judaism as a whole?

I remember when I was reading certain verses from Ephrem's hymns I was cringing and needed to have a break from them, as they were very sharp and did exhibit anti-Jewish elements. But I was on a mission to prove those who called St Ephrem anti-Jewish wrong, so I was searching for all the reasons behind such sharp words. Now, a couple of decades later, I am getting ready to share some new insights about his verses. I am perhaps more accepting towards Ephrem's anti-Jewish remarks. In doing so I try to remind myself that he was writing them at a time when Christianity was very much dependent on Judaism, and trying its hardest to disengage from it. It was a time when Christianity was not sure of itself, and chose the policy of defending itself from Judaism by attacking it. There are plenty of excuses that I can still find for Ephrem's writings being a little non-PC for the twenty-first-century sensitivities. Even the fact that he was working in the pre-Holocaust era could be enough of an excuse, as he could not have possibly imagined all the atrocities that so-called Christian citizens would inflict on their Jewish neighbors. The reason that I am confident that Ephrem was not capable of imagining the Holocaust is because no one in their right mind could, ever. Therefore, I am still not short of excuses for Ephrem, but what I am struggling to find an excuse for is the church accepting its anti-Jewish legacy, elaborating on it and going so much further with its antisemitic sentiment, and shamelessly bringing it into the twenty-first century.

A certain, unfortunate, process in Christian development was highlighted at the start of this chapter: anti-Judaism was an expression of Christian uncertainty at the very beginning of the path to being an independent religious tradition. Orthodox Christianity perhaps always was and still is the closest to Judaism in its biblical, theological and liturgical expressions. This closeness in the early days perhaps determined the appearance of anti-Jewish tendencies. However, there is no explanation or justification for the church keeping its anti-Jewish remarks in the liturgical cycle without revision until today. There is no reason for the church withholding its continuous repentance and apologies for the Holocaust, for the painful history which took place within the Christian era and in Christian Europe. The fact that anti-Jewish elements in the liturgy and antisemitism in popular expressions remain permissible is a clear sign of stagnation. Rejection of the previously existing religion is regrettably understandable at the early stages of religious development. However, when the rejection and nonappreciation of the previous religion continue through the centuries, then it is a worrying sign which needs immediate attention and work.

BIBLIOGRAPHY

Deschner K. 1986. *Kriminalgeschichte des Christentums*, Bd.1. Reinbek.

Hayman A.P. 1985. 'The Image of the Jew in the Syriac Anti-Jewish Polemical Literature,' in *To See Ourselves as Others See Us*, eds J. Neusner & E. S. Frerichs, 423–41. Chicago.

Kuhlmann K. H. 2004. 'The Harp out of Tune: The Anti-Judaism/Antisemitism of St. Ephrem,' *The Harp* 27, 177–83.

Murray R. 1975. *Symbols of Church and Kingdom. A Study in Early Syriac Tradition*. Cambridge

Narinskaya E. 29 Dec 2011. 'What does it take to be anti-Jewish? A deconstruction of statements held to be anti-Jewish in early Christian writers' http://www.bogoslov.ru/text/2333542.html

Narinskaya E. 2010. *Ephrem, a 'Jewish' Sage: A Comparison of the Exegetical Writings of St Ephrem the Syrian and Jewish Traditions*. Turnhout.

Salvesen A. 1995. *The Exodus Commentary of St Ephrem*. Kottayam, Kerala.

SUGGESTED READING

McVey, Kathleen E. 1990 'The Anti-Judaic Polemic of Ephrem Syrus's Hymns on the Nativity,' in *Of Scribes and Scrolls: Studies on the Hebrew Bible, Intertestamental Judaism, and Christian Origins Presented to John Strugnell on the Occasion of His Sixtieth Birthday*, ed. H. W. Attridge, J. J. Collins & T. H. Tobin, 229–40. Lanham, MD.

Chapter 8

Idolatry, Veneration of Icons and Worshiping God in Orthodox Christianity

Elena Narinskaya

This article addresses two questions. The first is about the significance of icons in Orthodox Christianity; the second aims to reflect an Orthodox understanding of the Old Testament prohibition of reproducing the image of God. First of all, the Old Testament prohibitions will be addressed to understand the nature of the commandment and its context. This will be followed by a discussion of the theological significance of icons. I shall end with a compilation of discoveries and some overall conclusions.

Exodus 20:4–6 and Deuteronomy 4:13 prohibit any images of the divine. The meaning behind the commandment is to eliminate idolatrous tendencies in Israel. The attention to images and idols in these Old Testament verses clearly indicate that at the time there were prominent religious practices in the surrounding areas using graven images and pictures of the divine for the purpose of worship. The biblical account of Israel wandering in the desert testifies that the people were very much influenced by the idea of worshiping idols. Hence, Israel was directed to stay away from these practices and to worship one God. And to this day Judaism prohibits any religious images and pictures.

Orthodox churches, on the other hand, are filled with iconographic images both inside and outside. These images are at the very essence of Orthodox ecclesiastical aesthetics. Moreover, these images are at the center of the Orthodox Christian worship and veneration. One observes Orthodox Christians bowing down in front of icons, kneeling and often kissing them.

On the surface it looks as though Orthodox Christianity has totally turned its face away from the Old Testament prohibition.

Orthodox Christian understanding of the Old Testament points to manufactured images which were permissible and were produced by God's command, such as the image of the Bronze Snake used by Moses, which had the power to heal (Numbers 21:9), or the Ark of the Covenant. Such images were taken into account in developing the Orthodox Christian tradition of icons and their veneration.

Over several centuries, Orthodox Christianity developed an iconographic tradition of religious imagery of Christ, the Son of God, the second person of the divine Trinity, his mother, biblical scenery, memorable feasts, and the numerous saints. The question is how such a leap was possible, from the Old Testament prohibition of divine images to the long-standing and well established iconographic tradition of religious imagery and art. It is even more surprising when one finds that in the New Testament there are also prohibitions of idol worship. The apostle Paul, in his letter to the Romans 1:22–9, identifies the worship of created things rather than the Creator as the cause of the disintegration of sexual and social morality (Dunn 1998: 33–4). According to the book of Acts 17:16, Paul tells the Athenians that though their city is full of idols, the true God is represented by none of them and requires them to turn away from idols.

It is important to notice that both Judaism and Christianity objected to any form of worship of matter. The practice of worship itself was encouraged, but a very clear line was drawn as to the object of that worship. People always recognized and acknowledged something which is beyond their created world, and paid to that something all due respect, veneration and worship. What unites the Old Testament and New Testament commandments in prohibiting the worship of idols is the attempt to train people in monotheism, that is keeping their worship directed exclusively to one God and away from other deities, idols, and objects.

Orthodox Christianity did not always appreciate icons. It had an iconoclastic crisis in the eighth century CE when iconographic images of God, or any kind of imagery or representation of God, were seriously challenged. It resulted in many icons being destroyed and theology prohibiting veneration of icons was developed. The Orthodox church survived the iconoclastic controversy and refined its theology of icons and their veneration. A number of Greek words and their theological significance should be identified in this respect. In Orthodox Christianity there is a distinction between *latria, dulia* and *proskynesis,* which are often used interchangeably. One clear meaning of these words is worship, and the theological understanding of the reality of this worship is that it is due to God alone. Therefore, the worship of anyone or anything other than God is forbidden by the Orthodox church. However, veneration is another reality, which is distinguished from worship, and is accepted, allowed and often expected for religious images, statues or icons. Veneration of icons was codified in 787 CE by the Seventh Ecumenical Council. This was triggered by the iconoclastic controversy that followed Christian–Muslim wars and a period of iconoclasm in West Asia. The defense of images by the Syrian scholar John of Damascus was pivotal during this period. The Orthodox church has ever since celebrated the use of icons and images.

The subject of veneration of icons and sacred objects remains as controversial in Christianity today as it was in earlier periods. One may hear arguments from Protestant circles about the redundancy of the tradition and all its heritage, including veneration of sacred images; about the commandments of the Old Testament against producing any sort of images; and also the fear of idolatry, which is closely associated with the tradition of veneration of icons. One still rather popular iconoclastic argument states that there is no need to venerate anything but God, because venerating God is in itself more than enough.

There are no clear indications of what caused the iconoclastic controversy in the eighth century. There were various political, religious and ecclesiastical movements in and around the church that could have encouraged iconoclastic arguments, but it is still rather difficult to single out a particular event that brought the whole iconoclastic movement to life. Of course, no one would deny that the decrees of iconoclastic emperors and the decisions of iconoclastic councils of the early church were of great influence and importance. However, they were only symptomatic, and could by no means be seen as indicative of the fundamental basis for the initiation of iconoclasm at that particular time and place in history. One could also talk about the rising influence of Islam and its dislike of images, or one could draw parallels with iconoclastic tendencies in Judaism at the time. However, neither of these phenomena could be conclusively presented as the trigger for iconoclasm in eighth century history. It is indeed the fact that iconoclasm was imposed by imperial edict, and therefore was primarily political. However, politics was not separated from religion in Byzantium. There is no direct evidence for the reasons behind the imperial edict. Therefore, the question of the initial reasons for the rise of iconoclasm will be left open here.

In contemplating the potential reasons for iconoclasm, however, it is useful to look at the theological highlights of the seven ecumenical councils of the church. Each of them was stimulated by one or another controversy rooted in the essentials of Christian identity, such as christology, ecclesiology, trinity, or pneumatology. It almost looks as though by the seventh century the church had covered the basics of its identity and reached a time of revision. Hence, it turned back to the first council, that of Nicea, and christology, in order to reconsider through the light of the incarnation the importance of the existing practice of veneration of sacred images and objects.

The actual tradition of veneration, by the eighth century, already existed independently in the church, and was developing in random fashion. As will be demonstrated later, the defenders of icons located the origins of veneration of sacred images and objects in the Old Testament, in the times of the Tabernacle and Solomon's Temple. As for the Christian era, the tradition of venerating icons was also traced to the very emergence of Christianity in the time of the apostles. Did the apostles venerate Christ as their beloved teacher and leader? Did they venerate each other? They were certainly encouraged to do so by Christ himself (See Mat 20:26–7, 23:11–12, also Luke 7:38, 44–5, John 13:5–14). Veneration of people and objects is still relevant in some cultures in the contemporary world, and is often firmly grounded in the religious practices of contemporary times as well as in the practice of the earliest recorded accounts of biblical narratives of both Old and New Testaments.

Coming back to the church of the eighth century and its particular attention to the veneration of icons, one may suggest that it must have felt like the time for the Church to approve officially of the long-existing practice of venerating icons. Consequently, it received the veneration of icons and sacred images through the process of dealing theologically with all the controversies around the practice, and bringing the matter for discussion at the Seventh Ecumenical Council.

It is fitting at this point to talk about the phenomenon of veneration as such, in order to disclose the problem with people's attitude to veneration. In order to do so it is fitting to go to the original sources in the writer who could be introduced as an ultimate apologist against iconoclasm. St John Damascene produced *Three Treatises on the Divine Images* at the very beginning of the first wave of iconoclasm. He was writing his treatises geographically well away from the epicenter of iconoclasm in the Byzantine Empire, so he was able to exercise theological freedom in his writings without experiencing the danger of being persecuted for it. He wrote partly in response to iconoclastic arguments, i.e., polemically; but mostly to advocate and theologically explain the practice of veneration of sacred images and objects.

Moreover, St John was based in a Muslim society, which he could not openly criticize. In 'safely' criticizing iconoclasm in Byzantium, he was probably criticizing iconoclasm in the newly and powerfully flourishing Muslim religion around him.

St John presents two senses of the word veneration (*proskynesis*). On the one hand, he talks about the notion of respect that is revealed through veneration of 'things, places and people associated with God, as a way of showing respect to what belongs to God' (St John of Damascus 2003: 11). Veneration by association can include almost anything even remotely connected to God.

St John also presents another component or expression of the practice of veneration best captured in English by the sense of the word worship (*latria*), which is addressed exclusively to God, and attributed to God alone.

St John describes different forms of veneration, namely veneration as honor, and veneration as worship (St John of Damascus 2003: 24). Quoting from the narrative of the Old Testament, the author recollects that the veneration of honor was acceptable towards anyone, even towards one's enemy, as in the case when 'Abraham venerated the sons of Emmor, godless men suffering from ignorance of God' (St John of Damascus 2003: 24–5). St John also mentions Jacob venerating Esau, his brother, and the Egyptian Pharaoh, or venerating objects, as in the case of bowing down his head to the staff (St John of Damascus 2003: 25; see also Gen 33:3, 47:7–10, Heb 11:21, Gen 47:31). What is important in these instances is the fact that veneration does not necessarily mean worship. Hence, the question again is about the possibility of a nonidolatrous form of veneration, in the sense of honor, which can be offered to anybody and anything.

In addressing the concrete forms of expression of veneration one has to mention that the Greek word *proskynesis* assumes the physical act bowing oneself to the ground. St John writes about the process of bowing down and its symbolic meaning as an expression of respect and honor. What the writer differentiates here is the *proskynesis* of worship, only due to God, and the *proskynesis* of respect. Varying veneration to different causes and objects, St John indicates that veneration of worship points to God as the only God by nature worthy of such veneration (cf. Gal 4:8). As a second type of veneration, St John writes about 'veneration offered, on account of God who is naturally venerated, to his friends and servants' (St John of Damascus 2003: 27), thus broadly expanding the framework of such veneration to include the veneration of the angels, the places of God, and the things sacred to him, such as the Tabernacle and the Temple, and even veneration through bowing to the rulers ordained by God (St John of Damascus 2003: 27–8), which further expands the applicability of veneration beyond the religious sphere into the political one.

From St John's definition of *proskynesis* it is possible to assume that it is an act of veneration, which is directed to the so-called divine entourage or divine associations or attributes. The offering of veneration therefore is possible to people and objects, which are a part of life, even life outside religious context. However, worship as such, that is, *latria*, is indeed exclusive to God. By diverting *latria* away from God one steps right into idolatry. But with *proskynesis* idolatry does not seem to be possible, because of the broad nature of the term and the large range of appropriate objects for veneration. It seems that the only instance, according to St John, that *proskynesis* can be idolatrous is when it expresses *latria*, which in its turn is redirected away from God.

However, on its own, as an act of veneration, that is a sign of respect and honor, *proskynesis* ceases to be idolatrous.

It is important to notice here that the idea that the very act of *proskynesis* does not necessarily constitute idolatry could have been unfamiliar to the Christian martyrs or their executors. However, to the contemporary era of pluralism, and further contextualizing St John's theology, one can treat another's objects of belief and worship with respect without offering one's own worship to that deity, object, or an idol. There is no clear boundary where veneration stops and worship starts, and it is not the purpose of this essay to determine one. The most important question for both Jews and Christians, then and now, is what is the object of one's worship. The answer that Jews, Christians and Muslims give is that this object is God and God alone.

Returning to St John, he chooses the examples from the Old Testament in order to demonstrate the legitimacy of veneration of religious objects as a long-standing religious practice. The reason for such an in-depth excursus into the scriptural narrative of the Old Testament seems to be obvious, namely, to counter the arguments of iconoclasts, whoever they were: Christians, Jews and Muslims selectively use Old Testament law in support of their claim against the practice of veneration of images, saints and sacred objects. As a response to such arguments St John simply states the following: 'Such veneration is offered to others as a mark of honor. Either, therefore, reject all veneration or accept all of these forms with its proper reason and manner' (St John of Damascus 2003: 28). In other words, if veneration as such is a legitimate exercise then it should be accepted in all its appropriate forms of expression. And the criterion for discerning which form of veneration is proper to which subject is twofold: it is based both on the scriptural narrative and on the living tradition of the faithful.

The pre-Christian era faced people with a very big gap between the created material world and the Creator of that material world. The idea of venerating the creation could only have worked as an offering of thanksgiving to the Creator for the gift of life and the possibility of procreation in the world. However, even in the pre-Christian era, created matter could acquire respect and honor as a means by which the Creator expressed his love for creation. This is an idea that St John expresses when he states that matter, simply because it is a product of creation, cannot be despised (St John of Damascus 2003: 11). From St John's response one can extract the argument of the iconoclasts, which must have been leaning towards disregard of created matter.

St John's builds up towards the 'fact that the Son of God himself assumed a material form in the Incarnation.' This is indeed the key answer of iconophiles to iconoclasts. The main reason and the only possibility for the fundamental transformation of one's attitude to matter is the incarnation of God, and his descent into the created world as a human being. Through the incarnation not only did God assume material human nature, but also material human nature was able to contain God. This twofold New Testament revelation unveils the mystery of matter and reveals to humanity a mystery about the created material world which was unknown before the experience of incarnation.

The very fact of incarnation, therefore, gives enough reason for veneration, respect and appreciation of matter. Matter after the incarnation revealed its capacity to contain the divine presence in its fullness without being destroyed by it, as was implied in the preincarnation religious history of humanity. According to the Old Testament narrative matter was only able to contain memories of experiences of the divine presence, but was not able to behold or contain God. We can see examples in the stories of Moses and others illustrating the concept of sacred space in the biblical narrative. Orthodox theology insists that it is only through the New Testament revelation that people were granted the experience and knowledge of deification. Deification became a possibility even for the human body, through experiencing the fullness of divine presence and remaining unbroken by it.

The act of incarnation brought the awareness of the human body into a completely new dimension, which was neither comprehensible nor approachable to the human race before. The human material body did not break under the circumstance of a divine being born from a human mother. This very instance revealed the possibility of the human body partaking in the fullness of the divine presence. Afterwards, in the liturgical context, through partaking of the body and blood of Christ during the celebration of the eucharist, the people are not only partaking in Christ's divinity on a spiritual and mystagogical level but also on the physical level by eating the bread and drinking the wine. The material human body, therefore, becomes transformed by deification. This extraordinary leap of the understanding of matter through incarnation presents matter in a completely new light, which was hidden from the understanding of people before God revealed himself on earth in a human body. Through incarnation, matter acquired the possibility of being transubstantiated in the framework of one's own life, and in the much broader context of life everlasting.

The fact that God revealed himself in the incarnation, as a man, allowed the depiction of him in images, be it from the memory or from the accounts of witnesses. Created material icons acquired two important capacities or functions in the life of the church. Firstly, icons are used as witnesses to the material world about the divine revelation of God. Icons synergize the product of the material world with the world of art, while also reflecting theology while pointing to the incarnation of Christ. Secondly, icons reflect the process of transformation by deification, which is also the result of the incarnation.

Summarizing the effects of the iconoclastic controversy on the life of the church one can see a number of important outcomes. Theological debates with iconoclasts encouraged early church thinkers to formulate the church's teaching about icons and their veneration. Iconology, as theology of the icons, together with iconography, entered the living Christian tradition, while ultimately being strengthened by iconoclasm. Iconoclasm allowed the church to refine its theological appreciation of matter and the deification of it through the incarnation. Ultimately, the debates with iconoclasts contributed to the formation of the church's teaching about the images of Christ, the Mother of God, and the saints, and determined their place in the living tradition of the church.

The first Sunday of the Great Lent before Easter is celebrated as the Sunday of the Triumph of Orthodoxy, in commemoration of the Seventh Ecumenical Council reinstating iconography and the tradition of venerating the icons in church practice. The Orthodox church reveals the theology of icons and explains the practice of their veneration. Orthodox iconology demonstrates the seriousness with which the church took and understood the meaning of icons in Christian life. Through liturgical texts, as well as through the writings of theologians, the church advocates the necessity of venerating icons for the spiritual life of the faithful. Thus, iconographic tradition penetrated the theological, liturgical, and practical levels of the life of the church.

The phenomenon of an icon, as a product of incarnation, has two elements to it, a human and divine. An icon could be viewed as a human response to incarnation, to the divine revelation, and the human-divine relationship that it created. The iconographic image as such is also a continuous expression of that relationship. Apart from being an *aide mémoire* of the divine physical presence on earth, icons also contribute to the continuation of Christian history. Icons of Christ, of significant events in his life and in the life of his mother, icons of the disciples and followers allow the succession and passing on of divine experience in life, in theology, and in human history. Icons link the past, the present and the future; they link earthly and heavenly realities. They are the door, and the pillow, the reflection and the projection, they are art and liturgy, human prayer and divine response.

Icons are a product of the synergetic relationship between God and people. By maintaining an iconographic tradition and developing it accordingly people keep the tradition alive and hold on to the newness of understanding of the divine realities in the world. Through iconography, as well as through scripture, people feel and revisit their relationship with God. Icons, as well as scripture, teach people about their identity, remind them about God's promises and revelations, and encourage them to follow in the steps of the fathers of the faith. The parallel between icons and scriptures is not random here, as in early times, with a lack of printed scriptural sources, as well as the illiteracy of the people, iconography narrated the scripture to the people through the art of the ecclesiastical interior.

The lack of icons would deprive the church of fuller human understanding of the New Testament relationship with God. Incarnation itself cannot be fully revealed without iconography. If the church loses the capacity to depict Christ, his mother or the saints then it loses its understanding of incarnation. The christology of the iconoclastic church could no longer contain the uniqueness of the Christian understanding of the newness of its relationship with God becoming flesh and descending to earth as a man.

Empty walls in the church represent the stripping of the Christian tradition from its identity of continuation and apostolic succession. It is not the icons that are being neglected in some churches today, it is human collaboration with the divine that is being wiped out and deserted. The results of such negligence are clearly seen in the lack of human understanding of incarnation and christology. By neglecting iconography, theology itself is wiped of its expression and understanding.

Icons penetrate and represent the very essence of Orthodox Christian identity. They reveal God's revelation on the personal level, through the personal inspiration of the iconographer. But icons also have a public function. They are a testimony of the church and its place in the synergetic collaboration with the divine. The church charges iconography with a liturgical context, which reveals the mediatory or transitional stage of the church itself, being, on the one hand, the body of people, and, on the other hand, the body of Christ. Iconology and ecclesiology, therefore, are two sides of the same coin. Through ecclesiology, iconology is revealed in the living tradition of the church, and through iconology, ecclesiology, as well as christology, gains the fullness of its understanding as God's revelation to humankind.

The presence of icons in the Orthodox Christian church can be seen as an aid for the people. Icons bridge the connection between the material world and divine realities. Icons reflect on and depict the human ability to be transformed by deification. Through the depictions of the lives of the saints, icons point to the incarnation of Christ and to the outcomes of such an event for humanity. The services of celebrating icons in the church offer the teaching of and the explanation of the practice of venerating icons.

The outcome of the iconoclastic controversy completes the process of appropriation of New Testament revelation, the incarnation, on every level of Christian tradition, i.e., in the theology of the church, in its liturgy and in practice. Theologically, the teaching of the church about icons is expressed through scriptural and patristic writings. Liturgically, the practice of icon veneration is secured and further explained through a number of services, such as the blessing of the icon services written in the Book of Needs of the Orthodox church, and the Triumph of Orthodoxy Feast in the Lenten Triodion. Practically, the tradition of iconography, as the art of icon painting, accommodated itself under the umbrella of sacred art. Additionally, the practical use of icons in its turn unites all of these theological and liturgical levels of the church.

On the theological level, through the theology of the icon, one can learn and appreciate the christology of the church just by looking at the icon and discovering the story of Christ's incarnation in it. Liturgically, through emphasizing the importance of icons in the interior expression of the Orthodox church, icons surround the people with their symbolic imagery. The icons in the church not only secure the boundaries of Orthodox Christian identity, but also expand these boundaries by pointing towards an ongoing divine revelation in the life of the church. The significance of icons is emphasized by the fact that they occupy a prominent place in the liturgical assemblies of Orthodox Christians and in their private homes.

Practically, mystically, and spiritually, therefore, icons represent a unique collaboration of the material world and the world of divine realities. The material world is enclosed in matter being used to create sacred art, while divine realities are expressed through icons by means of divine grace, divine glory, and divine presence through the name and participation of the subjects of the icons. Many fathers of the church, starting from St John of Damascus, followed by St Theodore of Studios the eighth–ninth century CE, commented on the relationship between the icon and its prototype. Their theology was followed through the centuries by other church writers, such as St Gregory Palamas in the fourteenth century, and until modern times, e.g., Leonid Ouspenskiy.

The study of iconology, therefore, can only be seen as part of an ongoing living tradition of the church. The icons are there in the churches as silent witnesses of the divine love, grace, and beauty. They contain within their sacred images the richness of Christian theology and the mystery of divine revelation of the New Testament church of Christ.

As a concluding remark, one has to highlight that all veneration, worship, and respect are directed to the one and only prototype of every icon. All iconographic images are directed to the prototype, God, and God alone. The divine is expressed in every scene and every saint. In that sense there is no contradiction between the Old Testament prohibition, the contemporary Protestant arguments about worshiping one God, and the Orthodox Christian expression through icon veneration. Orthodox Christian tradition is a tradition of mystery, of symbolism, which is deeply rooted in its christology. However, both for Orthodox Christians and for outsiders, it is crucial that every ritual is done with full appreciation of its theological significance. In a nutshell, everything in the Orthodox church points to Christ, and all its worship, pomp, and glory are directed to God, the creator of heaven and earth, and with the appreciation of the inspiration of the Holy Spirit.

BIBLIOGRAPHY

St John of Damascus 2003. *Three Treatises on the Divine Images*, tr. A. Louth. New York.

Dunn J. D. J. 1998, *Theology of Paul the Apostle*. Grand Rapids.

Florensky, P. 1996. *Iconostasis*. New York.

Lossky V. 2002. *The Mystical Tradition of the Eastern Church*. New York.

Louth A. 2002. *St. John Damascene: Tradition and Originality in Byzantine Theology*. Oxford.

Ouspenskiy L. 1978. *Theology of the Icon*. New York.

Chapter 9

Iconic Theology in Classical Rabbinic Literature and Orthodox Christianity

Daniel H. Weiss

At first glance, one might think that rabbinic Judaism stands very far away from the theology of icons in the Orthodox Christian tradition. It is certainly true that on a practical, legal level, rabbinic tradition forbids both the making and engagement with any images of divine beings. However, upon closer inspection it turns out that the texts of classical rabbinic Judaism contain a strongly 'iconic' understanding of the human being's relation to God, which parallels many of the theological dynamics put forth by Orthodox writers in their arguments against iconoclasts. Exploration of this rabbinic theological understanding can contribute to new paths of Jewish–Orthodox dialogue in the present. Likewise, engagement with Orthodox theologies of icons can help Jews today to reengage with classical rabbinic traditions that have sometimes been overshadowed by later anti-iconic streams of medieval Jewish thought.

We will first engage with classical rabbinic texts that illustrate this iconic understanding, and this engagement will then enable comparison and contrast with Orthodox understandings. By 'classical rabbinic texts' I refer to collections from the period bounded by the Mishnah on the one end and the Babylonian Talmud on the other, with an historical time span from around 200 until around 600 CE. These texts have continued to play a central role in medieval, modern, and contemporary Judaism. For our purposes, although the texts were written in Hebrew, they notably use terms derived from the Greek *eikon* to describe the human being's relation to God. Although *eikon* is a normal Greek term for images—and the Septuagint uses *eikona theou* for *tselem elohim,* 'image of God,' in Gen 1:27—it stands out more strikingly in the context of the Hebrew-based rabbinic passages.

We begin with a text from Leviticus Rabbah, in which Hillel the Elder casts physical care for the human body as a form of reverence and respect for God's 'icon.' (For more on this and the following three examples, see Lorberbaum 2015: 174, 181, 171, 161, 208.)

> 'The pious man does good to his own soul/self [*nafsho*]' (Prov 11:17). This is Hillel the Elder, for when he would take leave of his students he would start walking and he would walk with them.
>   His students said to him: Where are you going?
>   He said to them: To carry out a commandment [*la'asot mitzvah*].
>   They said to him: And what is this commandment?
>   He said to them: To wash in the bathhouse.
>   They said to him: This is a commandment?
>   He said to them: Yes! If it is the case that for icons/images [*iqonin*] of kings that they place in their theaters and their circuses, one who is appointed over them polishes them and washes them, and they even pay him a salary for doing so, and not only that, but they exalt him among the great ones of the realm—how much more in the case of me, for I was created in the image and likeness [of God], as it is written, 'For in the image of God He made the human being' (Gen 9:6). (Leviticus Rabbah 34:3)

Set in the context of the Roman Empire, Hillel's explanation asserts that the relation between a human being (as image of God) and God parallels the relation between icons/images of Roman emperors and the emperors themselves. Because imperial portraits were understood as making present, in a real and numinous manner, the power and authority of the emperor, those portraits were treated with great respect and reverence, as one would give to the emperor himself, and were guarded from dirt and degradation (cf. Ando 2000: 232–9, 369). Hillel implies that the embodied human being should likewise be conceived in terms of an 'icon' of God, and therefore a person should similarly clean and attend to his or her own body. In keeping with a broader pattern of classical rabbinic understanding, the visual and material dimensions of each human being are part of the 'image of God,' which does not just consist of mind or rational intellect, but is constituted holistically of the dynamic, living combination of body and soul together (see Weiss 2013; Goshen-Gottstein 1994: 176–8; Boyarin 1993: 31–5).

The next example recasts each human being as part of a regal-celestial visual display. "Rabbi Joshua ben Levi said: When a person walks on the highway, a procession [*iqonia*] of angels goes before him, proclaiming: 'Make way for the icon/image [*iqoniah*] of the Holy One, blessed be He'" (Midrash Tehillim 17:8).

Here, Rabbi Joshua ben Levi also draws on imperial practices, specifically the ritual of procession, in which images of the emperor are ceremonially paraded, with imperial messengers leading the procession and announcing the images' arrival to onlookers (see Ando 2000: 207, 232–3; Elsner 1998:42–44). Importantly, such processions of images often took place precisely in times and places when the emperor himself was not visually present. In this passage, the 'procession' is headed by angels announcing the progress of the human pedestrian, who constitutes the 'icon' of the Holy One, blessed be He. The implication seems to be that just as onlookers should treat the imperial images with the respect due to the emperor, so too each human being, as the image of God, should be accorded the honor and respect that befit God's icon. (The rabbinic concept of *kevod habriyot*, respecting/honoring all human beings and according dignity to every human being, is relevant in this regard; see, e.g., Babylonian Talmud, *Berakhot* 19b.)

Similarly, a passage from the Mekhilta de-Rabbi Ishmael (to Ex 20:13) proposes, in reference to the Ten Commandments inscribed on the two tablets given to Moses, that the top line on the first tablet ('I am the Lord your God') stands in parallel to the top line on the second tablet ('Thou shalt not kill'). The midrashist notes that in the case of human emperors, when people wish to negate the past honor of a despised former emperor, they will overturn his icons/portraits (*iqonot*) and break his images (*tselamim*), thus 'diminishing the image of the king.' The midrashist states that, likewise, when someone kills a human being, Scripture accounts it to him as though he had 'diminished the image of the (divine) king [*mema'et demut ha-melekh*].' The midrashist cites Gen 9:6 in connection with this assertion, a verse which is often translated as 'Whoever sheds the blood of a human being, by a human being his blood shall be shed, for in the image of God He made the human being.' Yair Loberbaum (2015: 208) argues, however, that by citing the verse in connection with this parable the midrashist may be interpreting the verse as meaning, 'When anyone sheds the blood of a human being—in the human being [that is killed], His [i.e., God's!] blood is shed, for in the image of God He made the human being.' In other words, the assault on the human being, who constitutes God's image, is also an assault on God, just as an assault on an icon of the emperor would be understood as 'an assault on the emperor' (on this latter practice, see Stewart 1999).

To take one final example, Tosefta *Sanhedrin* 9:7 presents a surprising interpretation of Deut 21:23. While many could read 'a hung person is a curse of God' as indicating that an executed person is cursed *by* God, here Rabbi Meir reads it as indicating that to hang or crucify a human being is to direct a curse *at* God.

Rabbi Meir said: What does scripture mean when it says, 'For a hung person [*talui*] is a curse of God' (Deut 21:23)? A parable: it is like a case of two twin brothers who were alike in appearance. One was king over the whole world, and the other took to banditry. After some time, the one who took to banditry was arrested, and they crucified him on the cross [*vehayu tsolvin oto al ha-tsaluv*]. Everyone who passed by would say, 'It seems like the king has been crucified!' Therefore is said [in the verse], 'For a hung person is a curse of God.'

Here, the visual aspects of the way that the human being 'mirrors' God are emphasized. Just as viewing the one brother who is hung on the cross calls to mind the other brother, so too the visual display of a human being who is executed and hung constitutes a degradation of God's icon/image, and thus directs the mind of any onlookers to view it as though *God* has been insulted and degraded. To visually display the body of an executed human being is thereby to direct a curse at God. This sensitivity for the dignity and bodily integrity even of a convicted criminal, on theological grounds, may have connections with the strong trend in classical rabbinic law of making capital punishment extremely difficult, if not impossible, to carry out in practice.

These examples appear to reflect a broader 'iconic' understanding of each human being as the 'image of God.' According respect and honor to each human being thereby constitutes an act of showing respect and honor for God, and conversely, causing physical harm to any human being constitutes an act of insult and attack upon God. Moreover, visually beholding a human being—and noting the respect or disrespect given to her or him—should direct the observer's mind to think of the attitude toward God that is entailed in the treatment of God's 'icon.' Far from opposing the notion of a material, visual 'portrait' of God, the classical rabbinic texts appear to view every human being, precisely in his or her living and physically embodied status, as 'standing in' for God, as the icons of the Roman emperor 'stood in' for the emperor.

In order to fully appreciate this iconic understanding, it is helpful to contrast it to 'anti-iconic' modes of understanding that arose in some streams of medieval Jewish thought. To take a prominent example, Maimonides, unlike classical rabbinic texts, associated the idea of 'image of God' with the rational intellect, rather than with the dynamically embodied union of body and soul. For Maimonides, a person's status as image of God has nothing to do with visual appearance or bodily form, particularly since Maimonides understands God as having no connection to corporeality or visibility. Instead, the invisible rational intellect constitutes the 'image' of the invisible and incorporeal God (see Lorberbaum 1999; Lorberbaum 2001: 69–72). By contrast, the classical rabbinic texts do not treat God as invisible, and affirm that God has revealed Godself visually in history—for example, to all the Israelites at the Red Sea (see Boyarin 2003). While such visual manifestations on God's part may be relatively rare occurrences in history, the classical rabbinic texts do not rule out such occurrences categorically, and they are therefore much more open to treating the living and embodied human being as a visible 'icon' of God.

Likewise, for the classical rabbinic texts, every human being constitutes the image of God, regardless of that person's intellectual capacities. By contrast, Maimonides holds that a person properly constitutes the image of God only insofar as that person has developed and actualized their rational intellect. Thus, while the classical rabbinic texts seek to uphold bodily integrity and respect even for criminals and transgressors, Maimonides holds that executing a criminal does not in fact impinge on the image of God, since criminals have shown themselves not to constitute the image of God, by virtue of their departure from 'rational intellect' via their criminal actions (see Lorberbaum 1999).

Thus, within the broader Jewish tradition, there are both 'iconic' and 'anti-iconic' understandings of the human being as image of God. If one were to compare Maimonides' understanding to Orthodox Christian theological understandings of icons, the result would likely consist of more differences than similarities. However, if one compares the classical rabbinic understanding to Orthodox understandings, a wider range of parallels can be brought to light.

As the Orthodox interlocutor for the classical rabbinic iconic dynamics, I focus on John of Damascus's *Three Treatises on the Divine Images*. Composed in the eighth century, they were written with keen awareness of competing Christian anti-iconic movements and have been influential on subsequent Orthodox theologies of icons down to the present day. In addition, John's texts extensively cite previous Christian writers on icons and images, enabling the reader to engage with earlier Christian dynamics of thought as well. While present space is limited, the comparisons between John and classical rabbinic texts here can set the stage for future studies that bring in comparisons with other Orthodox thinkers from later centuries, as well as with iconic modes of thought in later Jewish tradition (see, e.g., Wolfson 1994 on iconic thinking in kabbalistic texts).

John argues against those who say that the reverencing of icons should be rejected because icons are material objects. He points to the doctrine of the incarnation. Because God made Godself visible in material form, this provides justification for making materially visible icons of Christ: 'Now that God has been seen in the flesh and has associated with human kind, I depict what I have seen of God.' He holds that God 'became matter for my sake and accepted to dwell in matter, and through matter worked my salvation.' Therefore, he says, 'I will not cease from reverencing matter, through which my salvation was worked' (John of Damascus 2003: 29). Thus, in relation both to the incarnation and to humanly-made icons, John holds that God can be 'imaged' in visible matter. The classical rabbinic understanding of the human being as the 'icon' of God similarly holds that God is visibly 'imaged' in the material body of the living human being. Both frameworks therefore oppose the idea that material form is incompatible with imaging God.

John also draws upon the analogy of the emperor and images of the emperor in order to support his ideas of imaging God. He cites Basil of Caesarea, who noted that 'the image of the emperor is called the emperor' and that 'the honor offered to the image passes to the archetype' (42, 48) so that when people show honor to the image of the emperor, they are thereby showing honor to the emperor. Likewise, John argues, showing honor to an icon of Christ, to an 'image of God made flesh,' is a way of showing honor to Christ (48). Similarly, in the context of disrespecting images, he cites John Chrysostom, who wrote, 'Do you not know that if you insult the image of the Emperor, you carry your insult to the archetype of this image?'(78) John also cites Athanasius, who—in explicating Jesus' assertion in the Gospel of John (14:9) that 'one who has seen me has seen the father'—states, '[O]ne who has seen the Son has seen the Father; for the divinity of the Father is seen in the Son. One might understand this more closely from the example of the image of the Emperor; for the form and shape is in the image of the Emperor, and the form in the image is in the Emperor. The likeness in the image of the Emperor is exact, so that one who sees the image sees the Emperor in it and again one who sees the Emperor understands that this is in the image' (147). As we saw above, the classical rabbinic texts also draw upon the analogy of imperial images and icons, both in terms of insisting that showing respect toward each human being is simultaneously an act of piety toward God, and in terms of declaring disrespect to the embodied human being to be an act of disrespect toward God. Thus, both streams of tradition draw upon, while reworking, prevalent imperial understandings of the relation between the emperor and his material images.

Once we are attuned to these noteworthy similarities, we can also note certain differences between the two traditions. For instance, while John does refer generally to the idea of humanity as made in the image of God (60, 75, 109), he also asserts God's 'invisibility' prior to the incarnation, so that until that time there was no visible 'imaging' of God, and it is only in Christ's incarnation that the 'invisible becomes visible in the flesh' (24). Similarly, John cites Col 1:15, which states that Christ 'is the image of the invisible God' (34; cf. also 2 Cor 4:4). By contrast, the classical rabbinic understanding insists that God has been and continues to be materially and visibly 'imaged' and made present in every embodied human individual, including both saints and sinners, from the first creation down to the present day—and in a manner that has significant practical implications for matters such as capital punishment. The question of precisely who, and to what extent, constitutes a visible imaging of God, would thus be a fruitful topic for Orthodox–Jewish dialogue and conversation.

Another point of difference is whether the visible imaging of God in a human being constitutes a justification for human beings to reverence humanly-made images or icons. John holds that God originally prohibited Jews from making or reverencing images, because God had not yet been made visible in the world (as well as because of the Jews' propensity towards idolatry)—but now that God has been made visible in the incarnation, Christians are authorized to make and reverence visible icons (24; see also 29, 41, 61). From the rabbinic perspective, by contrast, although God brought a visible imaging of God into the world through the creation of human beings, who are to be accorded honor and respect as 'pointing to' God, this does not authorize human beings themselves to fashion or reverence visible images. The rabbinic objection to humanly-made icons does not lie in the basic idea of relating to God through a visible image, but rather from the conviction that this can properly be enacted only in relation to living human beings—the work of God's hands, as it were—and not in relation to the inanimate work of human hands. While one can relate to God through relating to human beings as icons of God, humanly-made 'icons of those icons' do not properly bear the same status of God's living presence, and therefore are not appropriate for relating to God. Thus, while the two traditions share the idea of relating to God via a visible 'icon,' their differences regarding *what kind* of icon is legitimate and *who can craft* a legitimate icon can provide grounds for further discussion.

A related point of conversation between the two traditions lies in John's repeated appeal to the cherubim in his arguments against those who reject icons. John notes that God commanded the Israelites to forge two golden cherubim and place them on the cover of the ark of the covenant (Ex 25:18–22), and that these humanly-crafted images therefore formed part of Israel's worship. As such, those who claim that 'the law' categorically forbids the use of humanly-made images in worship are mistaken (28–9, 31, 33, 65, 70, 101, 109). A rabbinic passage from the Mekhilta de-Rabbi Ishmael (to Ex 20:19) also engages this line of thought:

> 'Gods of silver and gods of gold [you shall not make for yourselves]' (Ex 20:19). Why is this said? Because [scripture] says, 'And you shall make two golden cherubs' (Ex 25:18), [one should not therefore say] I shall make four. Scripture says 'gods of gold'—if you make more than two, then they are considered gods of gold . . . 'You shall not make for yourselves'—so that you do not say, 'Because the Torah permitted making [these] in the Temple, therefore

I shall do likewise in the synagogues and the study-houses. Scripture therefore
says: 'You shall not *make for yourselves*.'

The rabbinic text agrees that humanly-made objects are not categorically
forbidden in Israel's worship—but says that the two cherubim are permitted
only because God explicitly commanded them (cf. Faur 1978: 1–2, 15–16).
However, apart from God's specific command, human beings 'on their own'
are not authorized to make such images or to employ them in worship. The
text also emphasizes that alongside being God's specific command, such
humanly-made objects were legitimate *only* in the Temple, on the ark of the
covenant itself, and not in other places of worship, prayer, or study. From the
rabbinic perspective, now that the Temple has been destroyed, it is only the
embodied human being that legitimately images the divine presence. Thus,
the rabbis could agree with John that the cherubim constitute a use of images
in worship (cf. Neis 2013: 82–112), but they would say that this example
(and that of material objects in the Tabernacle or Temple more broadly) do
not grant human beings in the post-Temple era the authority to 'reverence'
similar representational objects in worship. While John holds that the coming
of Christ provides *increased* authorization to employ material images as compared to the past, the rabbis hold that the destruction of the Temple means that
there is a *decreased* authorization to employ material images as compared to
the past. While both traditions work with the idea that materiality can legitimately intersect with reverence and worship, their different understandings
of sacred history and human authorization lead to differing accounts of the
'what,' the 'where,' and the 'when' of such worship (cf. Weiss 2018).

Other questions that could also be explored include: if for John God the
Father is eternally and inherently invisible, while God the Son became visible
and enfleshed at the incarnation, while for the rabbinic framework God has
visibly revealed Godself at various (though not many) points in history and
so is not inherently invisible but rather 'seldom seen,' does this theological
difference contribute to a difference in iconology? Likewise, what specific
behaviors and attitudes correspond to the types of 'respect,' 'honor,' or 'reverence' that are appropriate for an image of God?

Despite the differences discussed above, the classical rabbinic and
Orthodox understandings can nevertheless be fruitfully understood as related
permutations of a shared 'iconic' mode of thought. They may thus have
more in common with one another than either has with anti-iconic modes of
thought within each of their 'own' (Jewish or Christian) traditions. As such,
dialogue between present-day rabbinic Jews and Orthodox Christians on
these topics can lead to deeper understandings, as each group can learn from
exploring precisely where and in what ways it differs from the other group,
and in what ways it is similar.

In particular, Jewish engagement with Orthodox Christians on the topic of iconic theologies can help Jews reconnect with streams of thought that are prominent in classical rabbinic literature, but which may have faded from view to a large extent in recent centuries. The various cultural, social, and political upheavals of modernity saw many Jews adopt a more 'anti-iconic' understanding of God that distanced God from ideas of visual imaging. While the texts of classical rabbinic Judaism have continued to play a key role in modern Judaism, the 'iconizing' mindset of the classical rabbinic texts has often been elided or explained away (see Lorberbaum 2015: 13–45; Neusner 1988: 5–6). Yet, as we have seen, these dimensions of the rabbinic texts hold rich theological possibilities, both in terms of how to understand embodied human beings' relation to God, as well as in terms of the ethical duties and restrictions toward other human beings when the latter are conceived of as material, visual 'icons' of God. For this reason, Jewish engagement with Orthodox Christians—who have preserved iconic theology to a greater degree even in the context of modernity—can provide a bridge for Jews to relearn the ways in which their own texts contain related theological dynamics.

In addition, the basic ways in which Jews and Orthodox Christians perceive the 'other' tradition can be reshaped by this type of dialogue. Even if the Orthodox practices involving icons differ from rabbinic practices, better awareness of the *shared conceptual dynamic* of iconic thinking can help Jews perceive Orthodox Christians as different from themselves in various ways, but not as operating with a categorically foreign theology. Conversely, Orthodox Christians may have tended to think of rabbinic Judaism as simply being an anti-iconic tradition, and greater Orthodox awareness of the classical rabbinic understandings can likewise help in reshaping those assumptions. In all, Orthodox and rabbinic traditions may have more in common than either tradition has previously realized. Even if circumstances in the past did not easily allow for mutual dialogue on the topic of iconic theology, the greater openness of present-day societies opens the door for carrying out such shared exploration today, to the benefit and enrichment of both traditions.

BIBLIOGRAPHY

Ando, C. 2000. *Imperial Ideology and Provincial Loyalty in the Roman Empire*. Berkeley.
Boyarin, D. 1993. *Carnal Israel: Reading Sex in Talmudic Culture*. Berkeley.
Boyarin, D. 2003. 'The Eye in the Torah: Ocular Desire in Midrashic Hermeneutic,' in D. Boyarin, *Sparks of the Logos: Essays in Rabbinic Hermeneutics*, 3–23. Leiden.
Elsner, J. 1998. *Imperial Rome and Christian Triumph: The Art of the Roman Empire AD 100–450*. Oxford.

Faur, J. 1978. 'The Biblical Idea of Idolatry.' *Jewish Quarterly Review* 69.1:1–15.

Goshen-Gottstein, A. 1994. 'The Body as Image of God in Rabbinic Literature.' *Harvard Theological Review* 87.2: 171–95.

John of Damascus 2003. *Three Treatises on the Divine Images*, translated by A. Louth. Crestwood, NY.

Lorberbaum, Y. 1999. 'Maimonides on Imago Dei: Law and Philosophy—Murder, Criminal Procedure, and Capital Punishment,' *Tarbiz* 68.4: 533–56 [Hebrew].

Lorberbaum, Y. 2001. 'Imago Dei in Judaism: Early Rabbinic Literature, Philosophy, and Kabbalah,' in *The Concept of God, the Origin of the World, and the Image of the Human in the World Religions*, ed. P. Koslowski, 57–74. Dordrecht.

Lorberbaum, Y. 2015. *In God's Image: Myth, Theology, and Law in Classical Judaism*. New York.

Neis, R. 2013. *The Sense of Sight in Rabbinic Culture: Jewish Ways of Seeing in Late Antiquity*. New York.

Neusner, J. 1988. *The Incarnation of God: The Character of Divinity in Formative Judaism*. Philadelphia.

Stewart, P. 1999. 'The Destruction of Statues in Late Antiquity,' in *Constructing Identities in Late Antiquity*, ed. R. Miles, 159–89. London.

Weiss, D. 2013. 'Embodied Cognition in Classical Rabbinic Literature.' *Zygon: Journal of Religion and Science* 48.3: 788–807.

Weiss, D. 2018. 'The Christianization of Rome and the Edomization of Christianity: *Avodah Zarah* and Political Power.' *Jewish Studies Quarterly* 25.4: 394–422.

Wolfson, E. R. 1994. *Through a Speculum that Shines: Vision and Imagination in Medieval Jewish Mysticism*. Princeton.

Chapter 10

The Concept of Tradition in Orthodox Worship

Kallistos (Timothy) Ware

According to Origen, there are two stages of the spiritual journey, symbolized by Martha and Mary. The former stands for *praxis*, the active stage of the Christian life and ascetic effort. The latter represents *theoria* or contemplation, the stage of insight and spiritual vision. *Theoria* is often equated with tradition, 'the life of the Holy Spirit in the Church' (Lossky 1974: 152). This kind of tradition, the only true tradition, is alive, immediate, dynamic and contemporary, loving and creative, informed by a vision of human freedom and the grace of the Holy Spirit. Stăniloae calls this 'lived experience,' 'the critical spirit of the church' (Stăniloae 1989: 47–50), not a mechanical repetition, but a constant reliving of the message of salvation. Florovsky emphasized that tradition is not only a protective, conservative principle, but primarily a principle of growth and regeneration. It is not a depository of doctrine, but a shared style of living and praying (Florovsky 1972: 112–13).

There is a difference between Tradition and traditions. The former is the uninterrupted life of the believing community; the latter, teachings and customs which are edifying but not an essential part of the faith. As one of the bishops present at the Council of Carthage in AD 257 said, "the Lord said, 'I am the Truth'; he did not say, 'I am custom.'" There is a need for a constant act of discernment or discrimination between Tradition and traditions, but the line of demarcation is not always obvious. Tradition is often used in a derogatory sense in the New Testament and the early church, to mean teachings and customs (e.g., Mark 7:5–13). They attempt to distinguish between the traditions of the Elders and the commands of God, implying that the Pharisees and scribes make void the word of God through the traditions which they handed on. In Col. 2:8, Paul contrasts the truth according to Christ with mere human traditions, which are to be discarded. 1 Cor. 11:2 and 5–6 talk of the practice by women of veiling the head during prayer as tradition in this sense, as does Gal 1:14 in relation to the traditions of the fathers. There is a respect for tradition, for Jewish observances, but it is obviously not considered obligatory.

1 Cor. 11:23 says, 'I received from the Lord what I also handed on to you,' namely, that Jesus, on the night he was betrayed, took the bread and the cup. In other words, the tradition here came direct from the Lord; it was not a set of doctrinal propositions, but an act of worship. The doxological context of the tradition was not a set of facts or assertions preserved orally or in writing, but action. This is a vital clue to understanding tradition in the Orthodox context.

1 Cor. 15:3–4 states, 'I handed on to you as of first importance what in turn I had received, i.e., that Christ died on the cross for our sins and that he later arose from the dead.' Here, tradition is not an act of worship, but the basic faith that Christ died and rose again.

Little use was made of unwritten traditions about Christ in the early church before the second century and they were not recorded in canonical scripture (the exception that proves the rule being Acts 20:35, where Paul cites an *agraphon* of Christ's: 'It is more blessed to give than to receive'). Papias and Hegesippus mention some, but they are not regarded as very important. The Gnostics of the second century refer to a secret tradition about Jesus, but they were strongly opposed by Irenaeus, who insisted that the truth was to be found in the canonical gospels, not in secret writings.

Clement of Alexandria, who died in AD 215, still made an appeal to a secret esoteric tradition, but he was not followed in this by his fellow 'Christian Platonist' Origen, who emphasized that all church traditions are based ultimately on the canonical Scriptures. St Basil of Caesarea, who died in 379, wrote in his treatise on the Holy Spirit that some things were to be handed down in writing, other things in a mystery from the tradition of the Apostles. Both traditions have the same force for piety (Basil, *On the Holy Spirit* 27. 66).

There therefore appears to be a two-source approach: scripture and oral tradition. What is handed down in mystery is not facts about Christ or doctrinal teaching, but various practices in Christian worship, e.g., the sign of the cross, the *epiclesis* in the Eucharist, turning towards the east in prayer, the three-fold immersion in baptism—these are all apostolic in origin, although they are not explicitly mentioned in the New Testament. Tradition is therefore linked with worship, as the traditions revealed in mystery teach us how to pray.

For the Greek Fathers, tradition was not a supplementary source of information about Christ additional to the Scriptures, but fundamentally the manner in which scripture is interpreted, prayed and lived by successive generations in the church.

In the agreed statement of the meeting of Anglicans and Orthodox held in Moscow in 1976, any disjunction between scripture and tradition was rejected; the two are correlative. Scripture is the main criterion by which the church tests tradition, and Holy Tradition completes scripture in that it safeguards the integrity of the Biblical message. Holy Tradition is equated to the entire life of the church in the Holy Spirit expressed in dogmatics, the liturgy, canonical discipline, and the spiritual life.

Praxis is the living, dynamic, creative face of tradition. In the Orthodox church today this is symbolized by its unity in diversity. Several major themes can be drawn out.

There has been a divergence in opinions in the twentieth-century Orthodox church about the use of *sacred time*. Until the First World War all Orthodox had followed the old, Julian calendar, but in 1923 some adopted a compromise calendar, called the 'New Julian Calendar,' which brings the calendar into line with the Gregorian calendar, but adopts a different and more accurate rule about leap years (so for the final years of each century there will be two every nine years, instead of every eight years, chosen so that the coincidence of the New Julian Calendar and the Gregorian Calendar will continue for a few centuries). This caused a schism which continues to this day: Greece, Turkey, Romania, and Bulgaria follow the New Julian Calendar, while Russia, Serbia, Mount Athos, and Jerusalem follow the 'old' Julian Calendar. They remain in communion, though many of those who follow the old calendar consider the new calendar a heresy. There is a failure here to distinguish between Tradition and traditions, and this can impose a grave disruption on the structure of time in Christian worship.

There is a question as to whether certain *languages* are intrinsically sacred and therefore the only ones which should be used in worship. Those who think so are vehemently opposed to the use of the modern vernacular. This is parallel to demands to use only Hebrew in some Jewish congregations.

In the ninth century, missionaries to the Slavs translated the Bible and the liturgy into Slavonic. Certain groups propagated the 'three language heresy,' i.e., that God may only be worshipped in Hebrew, Greek, and Latin, the three languages inscribed on the cross. But there were almost certainly other languages in use at the time, such as Armenian, Syriac, and Coptic among the non-Chalcedonian churches, and among the Chalcedonian churches, Georgian. The heresy was therefore rejected, but it reappears from time to time. This has nothing to do with Tradition. The real Orthodox tradition insists that worship should take place in the language of the people so that all can share in it.

No language is sacred in itself. All languages can be used to worship God, as all can be used to curse and blaspheme. The Law and the Prophets were written in Hebrew and the New Testament in Greek; both have their special place but there is no mystical significance to these languages.

What kind of English therefore may be used? All worship is sung, and the words are deepened and enlarged by so doing. What type of music should be used? Traditionally the words are chanted, but there are modern harmonized settings such as those composed by John Tavener, and both may be used in the same service

In the twentieth century the use of *space* has been a hotly debated issue. In the past, the main space was left empty, with perhaps a few stalls around the wall; everyone stood to pray. Now chairs and pews have been introduced, turning the congregation into spectators. We do not see the body in worship any longer; people cannot make prostrations, as was the Orthodox practice, or move about. Often a solid icon screen divides priests from people; an open one makes the clergy behave better for being on show.

Early Christian churches were built in an octagonal shape (eight representing eternity); modern church architects tend to favor a dome in the form of a cross.

From the seventeenth to nineteenth centuries *icons* were simply copied from western models, e.g., Murillo. We have now returned to the traditional, Byzantine, Slavic style of iconography. How narrowly should we define sacred art? Could we not use contemporary art in icons? Many modern iconographers make exact copies of Byzantine icons, which does not seem to show great creativity.

In the twentieth century the Orthodox have revived the practice of taking frequent *communion*, but this is often performed unequally: in a congregation of several hundred, only a few may actually communicate. Regular communion was part of the Tradition. However, there is a danger of neglecting preparation for communion and the practice of confession.

Many questions such as these arise in parallel with Judaism, and different groups have arisen in both religions with their differing viewpoints. Different local approaches to ritual have arisen in both.

Tradition should not be interpreted too broadly. Not everything can be included; diversity must be allowed for. We must struggle fiercely for what is best—and best for everyone.

BIBLIOGRAPHY

Florovsky G. 1972. *Bible, Church, Tradition: An Eastern Orthodox View*. Belmont, MA.
Lossky V. 1974. *In the Image and Likeness of God*, ed. J. H. Erickson and T. E. Bird. Crestwood NY.
Stăniloae D. 1989. *The Experience of God*. Brookline, MA.

Chapter 11

Tradition and Innovation in Contemporary Jewish Worship

Howard Cooper

'The true way leads along a tightrope, which is not stretched aloft but just above the ground. It seems designed more to trip one than to be walked along' (Franz Kafka).

Let me take you on a journey. It's *Rosh Hashanah* morning—the Jewish New Year—and people are gathering. They pass by the main synagogue service and find their way to a room with a note pinned on its door: 'Alternative Service.' Tentatively they poke their heads in. A few people are seated around the outside of the room, waiting. Some individuals are sitting quietly, immersed in, or flicking randomly through, their *machzor* (festival prayer book). Others are in family groups, or with friends, chatting quietly. The room is bare except for the sixty or so chairs hugging the four walls, and a small table on which a Torah scroll rests. The rabbi senses the hesitation of each newcomer and, as they arrive, welcomes each of them into this unfamiliar space. This service will depend upon each person who arrives.

It will be determined by who turns up, how they interact, how much they will share of themselves, how much they will be willing to be co-creators of the *tefillah* (prayer experience), how comfortable they are with a service that will not take a fixed route through the book, how tolerant they are of allowing the personal—the human spirit—to be at the heart of the religious occasion.

It will depend on how open they are to the notion that the divine Spirit uses the human spirit as its medium, that the Spirit of God, the *ruach Elohim*, seeks a conduit to make itself present and that the vehicle for divine self-disclosure is us: poor, fragile, human beings like me and you, with heart and soul atremble, uncertain what we believe, yet clinging to the hope that although we know how difficult the New Year themes of change and a return to goodness might be, such change, such returning, such goodness, might still be possible, even for us—whatever we believe, or don't believe, or can't believe. This service depends on each person who arrives—bearing their unique personal portmanteau of uncertainties, worries and hopes—and it depends on us finding a way to share what we all carry, and for the divine to be present through it and within it.

Each person—through their words when they speak, through their attentiveness when they listen, through their silence when they await what will happen next—is a living strand within the tapestry that we will weave together during our *tefillah*.

I try to approach these 'alternative' services with a trust in *Adonai* who says: *Ehyeh asher ehyeh*, I will be what I will be (Exodus 3:14)—which means that what this service 'will be' does not depend on me, certainly not me alone. It depends upon our capacity to be with one another, and with our own selves, and with that space between us in which we can listen in to the unfolding, moment by moment, of 'what I will be'; and listen in to how the *machzor*'s words resonate in our own lives, in our own hearts.

What unfolds as we spend the hours together cannot be planned—it is a tightrope act, for all of us. On the one hand there is the risk of the fall into the solipsistic, the narcissistic preoccupation with 'me, me, me: my life, my woes, my journey, my little dramas and sorrows.' The fall into the cul-de-sac of individualism. On the other side there is the fall into the familiar traditional words and tropes and certainties of the *machzor*, a book filled to the brim with a faith in a God who no longer exists for most of the community—at least not as the supernaturalist, anthropomorphized external deity that so much of the liturgy insists on us giving our devotions to.

This style of service attempts to shift the focus of our attention away from that 'vertical' model of external religious authority in which the traditional metaphors of the liturgy point to the divine as external to the human, towards a horizontal model of religiosity/spirituality, where the divine is encountered within our world, within ourselves and within our contact with each other. 'The sound of the *shofar* calls us to account, and Your still small voice speaks within us': the alternative service on the High Holy Days in the community to which I belong is an extended, innovative *midrashic* exegesis of, and response to, that sentence from the prayer book (Assembly of Rabbis 1985: 173).

The room is almost full. A few people look at their watches. A quiet descends—expectant, waiting, watching. I have no idea what will happen next.

I find myself welcoming everyone to our service. And—remembering that this High Holy Day service is not about me, it is not an opportunity for my ego to expand into the available space—I find myself speaking about what we are here to do, the work (*avodah*) we are here to do together, the work that is also (as the Hebrew word reminds us) service: *avodat ha-lev*—service of the heart, and *avodat hakodesh*—divine service.

I speak for some time, setting the scene, helping people feel able and willing to relax into the space, to open themselves to the experience of community. I mention that today we have space and time to do this work—and space to be ourselves—and that space (*ha-makom*) is one of the traditional names of God. I am speaking to establish a kind of trust in the process that will unfold, creating space for each person to feel a part of something larger than themselves, yet wholly including themselves. In truth I have no idea what I say. Each service I lead like this is different. But I know how important it is to set the right tone—of openness to the individual, of openness to the unknown, of openness to the divine 'I will be what I will be.'

In working in this way, I am trying to knit together the existential aliveness of Martin Buber's rubric 'All real living is meeting/encounter' (Buber 1987:11) with some of the traditional language and liturgy of our heritage. My hope is to be able to offer lines of continuity between how Jewish worship has been done over the generations and this new link in the chain of tradition that we are forging as the service unfolds. The tradition offers rich, fertile ground to explore—and working this ground as the service proceeds can help us feel that our own spiritual journey is rooted in something enduring, while remaining freshly minted as we open ourselves to what is unearthed moment by moment within ourselves and between us and the other members of the congregation.

Over the next hours, starting with what people have on their minds—divorce, illness, academic achievements, financial troubles, family conflicts, Israel, antisemitism, global concerns, health scares: an amalgam of sadness, hopes, fears, regrets, worries, gratitude—we move slowly, intuitively, zigzagging between the personal and the collective. I weave in some of the *machzor*'s prayers, songs, poetry, study material. The words of tradition act as springboards for personal reflections and associations. The thoughts people share lead me in turn, dialectically, to texts in the prayer book. Sometimes I add in liturgy I have written myself. The process is more akin to jazz improvisation or psychoanalytic free association than planned performance. We do some work in groups, or in pairs. There is space too for reflectiveness, silence, inwardness. This is *avodah*. People listen. People speak. This is conversation as a form of prayer. There is stillness, and space between the words. When the service ends we know that we have kept faith—in ways that we don't understand, and yet realize we don't have to understand—with the mystery of *Adonai*, the One who was and is and will be. It is, as I suggested, a tightrope act. It's easy to trip up—and it sometimes happens. But I try to keep my balance—and that of the assembled gathering—by reminding ourselves of Martin Buber's self-affirming, self-denying axiom: 'To begin with oneself, but not to end with oneself; to start from oneself but not to aim at oneself; to comprehend oneself, but not to be preoccupied with oneself' (Buber 1988:155).

I like to think that Buber's spirit is an animating presence within this form of innovative worship. His neo-Hasidic perception that divinity can be encountered within the realm of human engagement with the world is at the spiritual center of the approach to Jewish worship outlined here. This is not to deny the significance of transcendence for the religious imagination: indeed, experiences of awe, and an awareness of our insignificance in the scheme of things, are a crucial part of spiritual self-awareness and are often a significant element of what people speak about during these services. Nevertheless, the move towards a horizontal model of religiosity/spirituality, where the divine is encountered within our world and within our contact with each other, allows us to appreciate the radical immanence of the divine (Green 2010:59), incarnated within us and within the holiness of each moment.

Variations on this model of worship might be somewhat the exception in Europe but are now widely practiced in the United States, where the so-called Jewish Renewal movement emerged in the late 1960s and early 1970s as a countercultural force, the influence of which has subsequently penetrated other non-Orthodox denominations of Judaism around the world (Lerner 1995). To some extent, this creative approach to worship has de-centered the role of rabbinic expertise: although in the past any knowledgeable member of a community could lead prayer services, these newer ways of co-creating *tefillah* encourage religious leaders—clergy—to become fellow travelers on the religious journey, alongside their communities rather than set apart from them.

A service in which anyone can contribute their thoughts, share a reflection on the traditional liturgy, offer a sudden insight into what is unfolding, support a tearful neighbor, suggest a melody to a familiar text, is a service in which authority is horizontally distributed and spiritual perceptions are shared by laity and clergy alike. If a rabbi is a teacher—the traditional understanding of the title—rather than a consecrated individual, the role of the rabbi within contemporary innovative worship includes enabling each member of the community to give voice to their own inner rabbi, as it were: in an egalitarian spirit, we learn from and with each other as we journey together.

> '*Leopards break into the temple and drink to the dregs what is in the sacrificial pitchers; this is repeated over and over again; finally it can be calculated in advance, and it becomes part of the ceremony.*' (Franz Kafka)

To speak about tradition and innovation in *contemporary* Jewish worship entails an acknowledgment that the dialectical relationship between tradition and innovation has been a hallmark of Jewish worship throughout the ages. For the last two thousand years the fabric of liturgical texts has been woven out of a dazzlingly disparate array of poetic, literary and theological threads:

> Every stage of Jewish literary creativity contributed to the making of the current Siddur [prayer book] from the biblical, post-Biblical, rabbinic, payetanic, geonic, Sephardic, Ashkenazic, philosophical, kabbalistic, Hasidic, to the modern. There is hardly a century of the last two millennia that did not contribute to the ongoing formation of the Siddur, as there is hardly a country of Jewish cultural significance that did not contribute to the growth of the daily liturgy (Kimelman 2020:79).

Yet the catalyst for this liturgical creativity was an event that at the time was experienced as a disaster for Jewish connectivity with the divine: the Roman destruction of the Temple in Jerusalem in the year 70 CE. The elaborate sacrificial system—mediated through the priestly class—by means of which Jews were told that they could draw near to the God of Israel, was replaced over several generations by new modes of worship developed by the rabbis, who took up the mantle of spiritual leadership and established regular daily, weekly and annual rhythms of prayer services.

This process of replacing the old with the new included extensive debates over the nature of prayer itself: was it to remain an informal and spontaneous improvised act as had existed in parallel to the sacrificial rituals prior to the loss of the Temple? Or was it necessary to standardize and fix certain texts which could be recited, in community, by everyone? In an important sense this debate was never formally resolved: both elements—the formal and the informal—have remained in play since then. The development of printing meant that over the last five hundred years a certain liturgical standardization has tended to dominate the prayer life of Jewish communities, but the last two centuries have seen Jewish religious life split into several disparate strands and movements, each with its own idiosyncrasies of liturgical expression, reflecting different ideological and theological responses to modernity.

Nevertheless certain core texts, sanctified by tradition, appear in regular worship across the denominations, although minor revisions and reinterpretations proliferate. For example, non-Orthodox prayerbooks omit the traditional prayers asking for the restoration of the Temple and sacrifices; the traditional hope for a messianic redeemer may be replaced by the generalized hope for redemption; the statement that the dead shall be resurrected by God is replaced (either in the original Hebrew, or in the translation, or in both) by an acknowledgment of a God 'who brings death and life'; gender-neutral translations have been introduced, along with the inclusion of the matriarchs when the patriarchs are evoked; and so on. Technically speaking, all these textual emendations—and there are many dozens of them—are examples of innovation in Jewish worship.

However, all the different liturgies that exist are adhering to a time-honored principle: that prayer life requires the upholding of *keva*—that which is set, established. Jewish religious life has traditionally endorsed set times for communal prayer as well as a nucleus of long-established, officially sanctioned texts—although a surprisingly small number of prayers are legally mandated. Yet in tension with this institutionalization and regularization of worship there exists another time-honored principle aimed at adding vitality to an individual's prayer life: *kavanah*—to direct one's mind/heart/soul with purpose.

If *keva* speaks of the external content of worship, *kavanah* addresses the subjective experience of worship. *Keva* informs us about what is prayed; *kavanah* reminds us about how prayer might be offered. *Keva* locates us within a history; *kavanah* opens us up to the present moment. *Keva* helps keep our feet on the ground; *kavanah* allows the soul to fly.

Of course, *keva* can be combined with *kavanah*. But in a secularized era when many Jews have become disinclined to adhere to the strictures and patterns of earlier times—because of a lack of knowledge, or interest, or both—more creative approaches to worship have proved that a renewed emphasis on *kavanah* can reinvigorate Jewish connectivity to the divine. These more informal services, which often entail a deprioritizing of *keva*, allow contemporary Jews to discover (or rediscover) that eternal life belongs to those who live in the present. And that the God of tradition—the One who says 'I am what I am' (Exodus 3:14)—speaks not only through the texts of tradition but within the texts of our own lives.

> *Many people prowl around Mount Sinai. Their speech is blurred, either they are garrulous or they shout or they are taciturn. But none of them comes straight down a broad, newly made, smooth road that does its own part in making one's strides long and swifter (Franz Kafka).*

Along with his colleague Martin Buber, the German-Jewish philosopher and theologian Franz Rosenzweig sought to revivify European Jewish life in the first decades of the last century. Born into an assimilated Jewish family, Rosenzweig was preparing to convert to Christianity when a visit to a small, devoutly Orthodox, Eastern European-style synagogue in Berlin on Yom Kippur 1913 generated a numinous experience that changed the direction of his life. The piety he experienced there—the *kavanah*, as it were—engendered in him a new awareness of the richness of Jewish textual life and worship.

Thereafter he committed himself to the exploration of Judaism through a new model of open inquiry and egalitarian learning, becoming instrumental in the establishment of the *Freie Jüdische Lehrhaus* (Jewish House of Free Study) in Frankfurt in 1920 where teachers and students together sought to bring their secular intellectual life into animated engagement with Jewish sources.

In his opening Address at the *Lehrhaus*, Rosenzweig articulated his radical vision for a fresh approach to Jewish study, practice and devotion. He recognized that they were living in new times, when the old ways of connecting life and Judaism had either been sundered by circumstances, actively rejected through assimilation or conversion, or were no longer adequate to meet the intellectual challenges of modernity. In a world where the Jew 'finds his spiritual and intellectual home outside the Jewish world,' as he put it, a new way of learning was necessary:

> It is a learning in reverse order. A learning that no longer starts from the Torah and leads into life, but the other way round: from life, from a world that knows nothing of the Law, or pretends to know nothing, back to the Torah. That is the sign of the time . . . There is no one today who is not alienated, or who does not contain within himself some small fraction of alienation . . . [As a consequence, the work is to] lead everything back to Judaism. From the periphery back to the center; from the outside, in. This is a new sort of learning. A learning for which—in these days—he is the most apt who brings with him the maximum of what is alien . . . It is not a matter of apologetics, but rather of finding the way back into the heart of our life. And of being confident that this heart is a Jewish heart. (Glatzer ed. 1953: 231)

A century on from Rosenzweig's acute diagnosis of the diasporic Jewish condition in the contemporary world—a world in which for the majority of Jews the texts and ways of tradition are external to life rather than informing and regulating life—the liberating potential of his approach, bringing what we value and know from the intellectual disciples around us and allowing them to fertilize the spiritual resources of Judaism, is still bearing fruit within contemporary Jewish worship.

Take the liturgical work from the 1970s onwards of Rabbis Lionel Blue and Jonathan Magonet in the prayerbooks prepared for the Movement for Reform Judaism in the UK. Although all the denominations of non-Orthodox Judaism in the United States along with the Liberal Movement in the UK have their own liturgical creativity—with poetry and newly-written prayers assimilated into the standard framework of prayer services—modern Jewish-American scholarship has recognized the unique contribution of the Blue/Magonet liturgical innovations: 'they jointly revolutionized the way to do meaningful liturgical change and set the bar for Jewish literacy along with theological honesty. Their pivotal achievement was to revive the flagging Jewish spirit and let it take wing again' (Friedland 2013: 129).

This work—very much in the Rosenzweigian spirit—was spearheaded by Rabbi Lionel Blue's composition of new prayers, and reflections on prayer itself, texts written with 'engaging transparency and bracing lack of affectation' (Friedland 2013: 130). These are now integral to Reform Jews' experience of worship in the UK. The following piece forms part of the liturgy for the *Kol Nidrei* service for the evening of Yom Kippur—traditionally the most solemn and sacred service of the year:

> Perhaps God meets us and we do not recognize Him. He may speak to us in a chance remark we overhear, through a stray thought in our mind, or by a word from the prayerbook that resonates within us. Perhaps a side door is the only door we have left open to Him . . . Perhaps we do not like what he says, but are frightened to say so, and so pretend we never met Him, and indeed could not meet Him, for He is only an idea. The avoidance is natural because in the sight of God our success can seem failure, and our ambitions dust . . . Perhaps we are satisfied with our lives and do not want to meet Him. So we chant our prayers and sing our hymns to prevent a few moments' silence, for He speaks in the silence. (Assembly of Rabbis 1985: 311–12)

This is theology as a form of prayer: its hesitancy is integral to its truthfulness; its provisionality, which implicitly acknowledges that for the contemporary Jew uncertainty about matters of faith is now part of the fabric of our consciousness, channels a spiritual reflectiveness that is both down-to-earth and yet opens the reader to the presence of the divine.

Rabbi Jonathan Magonet's contribution to this liturgical creativity follows a different route. As well as being a liturgist of note, bringing a poet's sensibility to the task of crafting new ways of speaking about traditional themes: 'The sound of the *shofar* breaks into our lives. It shatters our illusions and we awake to truth. Our time on earth is short and we are forced to choose. Life and death have been set before us, good and evil, blessing and curse . . . The *shofar* sounds its warning, and calls us to account' (Assembly of Rabbis 1985: 217). The prayerbooks under his editorship now contain, running along the bottom of each page, his historical and theological commentary on the traditional liturgy. These prayerbooks thus act as both study guides to the liturgy, as well as containing the regular prayer services themselves. This reflects the Judaic view that study is a form of prayer, that one's connection to the divine can be through the mind and intellect as well as through the emotions and heart.

But perhaps the most significant innovation of his editorship is the expansion of study material into realms of Jewish thought far removed from those sanctified by tradition. Breaking down the traditional distinction between religious writing and secular thought, he has collected together a plethora of new material, gathered from multiple sources from every period of Jewish history from the Talmudic era to the present day. Poetry and parables rub shoulders with Hasidic wisdom; modern essayists, theologians and novelists are juxtaposed with songwriters, psychotherapists, scientists and philosophers; Anne Frank and Golda Meir appear alongside Jacques Derrida, Arnold Schoenberg and Philip Roth. These texts are strategically inserted into the regular services themselves, as well as being collected together thematically as a discrete anthology of material within each volume. Again, one might see this gathering of disparate cultural material as being done in the spirit of Rosenzweig's perceptions about bringing texts 'back to Judaism . . . from the outside, in.'

As Rabbi Magonet has put it:

> at a time when revelation is not immediately apparent, then at least we can try to go for an honest evaluation of our situation today. If a Kafka, a Freud, a Karl Kraus tell us the truth about ourselves, then theirs are the voices that should be added to a contemporary religious consciousness. (Magonet 1988: 190)

This all adds up to a quiet revolution in liturgical practice. Alongside the standard fixed prayer structures, the possibility of flexibility and choice within services enables congregations to mix the traditional and the innovative on a weekly basis. And with newly composed melodies now available for many traditional texts, no two services need ever be the same. One senses in these prayerbooks a larger project for contemporary Jewish religious renewal: 'the religious task is to find the synthesis that re-establishes the balance between intellect and emotion, between self-centeredness and altruism, between an anchoring in this world with its duties, responsibilities and enormous possibilities and a transcendent reality that gives perspective and meaning' (Magonet 1988: 190). This task, synthesizing tradition and innovation, is exemplified by—and finds its textual home in—the several prayerbooks published under Rabbi Jonathan Magonet's scholarly editorship over the last forty years or so.

> *'And so you know your destination?,' he asked. 'Yes,' I answered, 'didn't I say so? Away-From-Here, that is my destination.' 'You have no provisions with you,' he said. 'I need none,' I said, 'the journey is so long that I must die of hunger if I don't get anything on the way. No provisions can save me. For it is, fortunately, a truly immense journey'* (Franz Kafka).

In the eight centuries after the destruction of the Temple in Jerusalem, Jewish liturgy remained an oral tradition. A prayer leader would recite the prayers by heart and those gathered for prayer would either join in if they knew the liturgy, or respond with a brief 'Amen,' or the repetition of a line if they were unfamiliar with the set prayers. There were no written texts and indeed there was a strong injunction against producing them. 'Those who write down blessings are like those who burn the Torah' (Babylonian Talmud, *Shabbat* 115b).

It was not until the year 870 that, in response to a request from Jews in Barcelona who were confused about the order of prayers, the leader of world Jewry at that time, Rav Amram Gaon in Sura, Babylonia, wrote down the exact order of prayers for weekdays, Shabbat and festivals. This was the first *siddur*—prayerbook—the word itself meaning order—but was a guide for the community leaders rather than worshipers themselves (Millgram 1986: 386). Only copies of this *siddur* exist, and they demonstrate marked variations in the order and content of prayers, indicating that individual sages were already engaging in ad hoc innovations adapted to local congregational settings.

Over the next centuries various collections of prayers circulated in manuscript form—each with distinctive local elements along with standardized formulae for prayers—and, as mentioned earlier, it was not until the technological revolution brought in by printing that the various liturgies of Ashkenazi and Sephardi Jewry assumed a more regularly constant form. Yet new material has always been added: the mystics of sixteenth-century Safed created an outdoor ceremony to 'receive the Sabbath bride' with psalms and specially composed hymns, and eventually this became *keva*, a standard part of all synagogue liturgies.

So although the last fifty years have seen a profusion of innovations in both forms of worship and the content of texts, this is as it has always been: continuity over the centuries in a dialectical relationship with attempts to find new ways to encounter the One Who Is. Each generation seeks to overcome what Martin Buber described as 'the curse of fluency'—the rote recitation of familiar prayers—and find new ways to experience the cosmic pulse and collective meaning within the joys and vicissitudes of life.

There is, however, one recent development that might mark a fundamental change in this situation. The worldwide spread of COVID-19 could mark a historical moment in its implications for Jewish worship. At a stroke, worship was forced to move away from the immediacy of in-person community contact. And in many communities new technology—as revolutionary in their way as Gutenberg's printing press—opened up new ways of worship and prayer life. Suddenly, as the leading American liturgist Rabbi Lawrence Hoffman has put it, 'Covid has exposed the limits of print-based worship, where a single text becomes sacrosanct even if much of it is outdated, aspiritual, and unmoving' (Hoffman 2020).

Through Zoom and other platforms, new elements have been introduced: video clips, artwork, photography, active captions for Hebrew songs, interactive communal engagement through the 'chat' facility—radically new departures in Jewish worship. In addition there is the possibility of worldwide participation in any prayer service: when geographical location is no longer relevant, suddenly the tradition-based 'we' formulation of liturgical prayers has taken on a new immediacy. And for specific liturgical occasions, such as funerals and the memorial *shiva* prayers that follow a death, the comfort of connecting with distant family or friends who might otherwise not be able to participate in such events has been experienced as a particular blessing that has, quite unexpectedly, arisen out of the new global realities.

What further technologically enhanced elements of creativity in Jewish worship will be developed—or will remain—after the worldwide pandemic subsides remains to be seen. Yet for the first time in Jewish history forms of hybrid services—i.e., in-person and online—look set to become an established part of many Jews' experience of worship as the twenty-first century unfolds.

As we journey on, new questions arise: can the experience of the divine be conveyed, mediated, instilled, elicited, through a glass screen? Can *kavanah* be maintained in a virtual community? Is the lived presence—the kinesthetic experience—of other bodies in space around one an essential medium for the soul at prayer in community?

The 'truly immense journey' of inhabiting the living dialectic between tradition and innovation in Jewish worship—with no provisions available other than what we receive on the way—is, 'fortunately,' set fair to continue.

BIBLIOGRAPHY

Assembly of Rabbis ed. 1985. *Forms of Prayer for Jewish Worship, volume 3: Prayers for the High Holy Days*. London.

Buber, M. 1958. *Hasidism and Modern Man*, trans. M. Friedman. New York.

Buber, M. 1987. *I and Thou*, trans. R. G. Smith. New York.

Friedland, E. L. 2013. 'From Marks to Magonet: The Prayerbook Creator at Work,' in *Welcome to The Cavalcade: A Festschrift in Honour of Rabbi Professor Jonathan Magonet*, ed. H. Cooper, C. Eimer & E. T. Sarah, 127–134 London.

Glatzer, N. ed. 1953. *Franz Rosenzweig: His Life and Thought*. New York.

Green, A. 2010. *Radical Judaism: Rethinking God and Tradition*. New Haven, CT.

Hoffman, L. 2020. *Open Letter To My Students 9: Seriously Speaking* https://blog.lawrenceahoffman.com/page/2/ October 7, 2020

Kafka, F. 1973. *Parables and Paradoxes*, New York.

Kimelman, R. 2020. 'The Theology of the Daily Liturgy,' in *The Cambridge Companion to Jewish Theology*, ed. S. Kepnes, 77–101, Cambridge.

Lerner, M. 1995. *Jewish Renewal: A Path to Healing and Transformation*. New York.

Magonet, J. 1988. 'The Question of Identity,' in *Soul Searching: Essays in Judaism and Psychotherapy*, ed. H. Cooper, 187–192, London.

Millgram, A. 1971. *Jewish Worship*. Philadelphia.

Chapter 12

The Jewish Year

Metaphor and Meaning

Jeremy Schonfield

The events of the Jewish calendar, whether biblical or post-biblical, are usually seen as individual occasions scattered around the year. This chapter draws
on traditional sources and psychological theory to suggest how the familiar
agricultural and ritual cycles can be viewed as symbolically re-enacting the
developmental structure of a traditional family, and how emotional problems
raised by the passage from birth to new parenting may be faced and in some
cases overcome. Beyond the dynamic within families, the narrative refers to
power relations in general, irrespective of gender and age. It is hoped that
this study will serve as a model for exploring parallel narratives in other
faith traditions.

The philosopher Franz Rosenzweig (1886–1929) argued that the feasts
and fasts of the traditional Jewish calendar encompass a core sacred narrative
spanning creation, revelation and redemption (Rosenzweig 1971: 112, 156,
205). But while the first two elements appear explicitly and the third implicitly in the Pentateuch (Lev 26, Deut 28–9), and all three feature in the liturgy
(the Shema blessings), the calendar seems more complex than Rosenzweig
suggests. From the springtime start of the harvest to its autumn climax, most
ritual events are based on the seasonal agricultural cycle of the now-lost Holy
Land, but these are interwoven with multiple historical narratives apparently
unrelated to nature, extending from creation and the Exodus to the fall of
the Temple, and only rarely arranged in chronological or thematic order.
Theological ideas such as repentance are also enmeshed with the natural
and narrative elements. Strikingly, several major biblical events are absent,
including some for which dates might be identified. There is no reference

to the entry into the Promised Land, and the only scenes included from the Patriarchal period are the Banishment of Ishmael and the Binding of Isaac.

I wish to argue that the rabbinic authorities who oversaw the evolution of the calendar included a variety of narrative elements that, while not explicitly reconciled, harmonize symbolically with the human life cycle from youth to parenting and then to old age. Rabbinic writers explicitly linked feasts and fasts during the six months from Passover to the autumn feasts to human life-events. Noting biblical references to children in the context of Passover in spring, they elaborated a drama based on the lifecycle from youth in the spring to parenting around the start of the new cycle in the autumn. The other half of the year, from autumn until spring, can be integrated to this scheme by noting how biblical readings selected by rabbinic authorities for recital on *Rosh Hashanah* in the autumn suggest links to birth, infancy and weaning, while rabbinic themes of Passover in the early spring allude to adolescence. The two halves of the year complete an annual narrative of human birth, maturity and eventual decline that runs parallel to the agricultural cycle. A similar pattern is reflected in the annual Torah-reading cycle that begins with creation and ends in the autumn, prior to entering the Promised Land.

In order to understand the impact of this observation better we can point to Bruno Bettelheim's psychoanalytically based argument (Bettelheim 1979) that European traditional stories throw symbolic light on different moments in the lifecycle, to help those who tell and listen to them to survive the painful and problematical experiences of life transitions. I wish to suggest that the agricultural and lifecycle elements of the Jewish ritual calendar similarly address problems faced while moving between stages in life, and that they tell a universal story in a Jewish accent (see table 12.1). When these cycles are read as a layered whole, a new narrative can be seen to emerge. The lifecycle scheme outlined here seems not to have been proposed before, but might appear familiar to rabbinic thinkers precisely because the parts newly proposed echo the approach that rabbis took to the period from spring to autumn.

In the following discussion I will briefly describe the biblical and rabbinic sources of each event, and then suggest their symbolic implications for the human lifecycle.

The ritual year begins with the anniversary of creation at the autumn new moon of *Tishri*, described biblically as the 'day of trumpeting' (Num 29:1) and 'day of remembering the trumpeting' (Lev 23:24), which inspired the rabbinic ritual of sounding a *shofar*, a ram's horn. In rabbinic thought this is *Rosh Hashanah*, 'New Year,' that lasts like other festivals for two days to reflect ancient uncertainty about its precise date. This festival's themes include judgement for deeds of the previous year and their reward or punishment over the coming year, perhaps recalling Adam and Eve's first sin. The liturgy includes prayers asking for God's attribute of paternal mercy to dominate

Table 12.1. The Jewish Calendar, Agricultural Year and Lifecycle

Jewish months	Feasts & fasts	Festival narrative	Agricultural cycle	Life-cycle narrative
Autumn				
Tishri	Rosh Hashanah	Creation, judgement		Infant vulnerability
	Tsom Gedaliah	Exile		Trust abused
	Yom Kipur	Atonement		Survival anxiety
	Sukot	Desert survival	Harvest ends	Playing at exile & return
	Hoshanah Rabah			Circular patterns
	Shemini 'Atseret		Need for rain	
	Simḥat Torah	Renewing Torah cycle		Recurring cycles
Ḥeshvan				
Winter				
Kislev	Ḥanukah	Temple saved	Coldest season	Victory idealized
Ṭevet	10 Ṭevet	Jerusalem siege		Separation & exile anticipated
Shevaṭ	Tu Bi-Shevaṭ	Trees New Year	New blossom	Promise of growth
	Shabat Sheḳalim	Counting soldiers		Value of life
Spring				
'Adar	Shabat Zakhor	Remembering Amalek		Owning agression
	Ta'anit Ester	Esther's fast		
	Purim	Book of Esther		Adolescent violence
	Shabat Parah	Purification		Reflecting on violence
	Shabat Haḥodesh	Nisan New Moon		Safety of home
	Shabat Hagadol	Future rescue		Hope of perfection
	Pesaḥ	Exodus	Grain harvest	Home symbolizing safety, education, passion
	'Omer			Separation anxiety
'Iyar	33 day of 'Omer	Plague ends		
Sivan	Shavu'ot	Revelation	Fruit harvest	Marriage achieved
Summer				
Tamuz	17 Tamuz	Golden calf, Jerusalem breached	Hottest season	Conflict
'Av	9 'Av	Spies, Jerusalem falls		Mourning loss & death
	15 'Av	Love, landlessness	Grape harvest	Mature love experienced
'Elul	Seliḥot	Preparing for Judgement		Forebodings for the next year

that of kingly severity, attributes illustrated in the scenes of childhood and parenting in the Torah readings. The following interpretation of these readings, while not traditional, attempts to explain why these particular passages were selected. In the reading for the first day (Gen 21) Abraham banished his concubine Hagar and Ishmael her son, his firstborn, believing the boy had abused Abraham's hospitality by mistreating Isaac, his second and preferred son. Their exile was proposed by Isaac's mother Sarah, Abraham's wife and half-sister (in rabbinic writings their father Terah had a record of filicide). The text implies that Abraham was unaware that both survived their exile. In the reading for the second day (Gen 22) Abraham was told by God to sacrifice his preferred son, Isaac, thereby re-enacting the ordeal of Hagar and Ishmael. Abraham was narrowly prevented from killing Isaac, and, when he saw a ram caught in a bush, sacrificed it instead without being told to do so. If sounding a ram's horn recalls its death-cry, the ritual would symbolically recall all these scenes of parental aggression and childhood vulnerability, alluding also to the disparity between divine and human power.

The next day, 3 *Tishri*, is the fast of Gedaliah, commemorating the assassination of a Babylonian-appointed Judean governor, over a thousand years after Abraham, which hastened the Judean exile to Babylon, and echoes the Temple's destruction that dominates the end of the Jewish year. The name of the killer, Ishmael, the only biblical figure of that name besides Abraham's son, links it to New Year. He had just eaten with Gedaliah, suggesting that both Ishmaels abused hospitality (2 Kgs 25:22–6).

Yom Kipur, 'Day of Atonement,' falls on 10 *Tishri*, eight days after the first day of the New Year, the same time interval as between birth and circumcision. Rabbinic thinkers interpret the biblical instruction to 'afflict your souls' (Num 29:7) as a direction to fast, while rabbinic texts report that this was when Abraham circumcised himself, suggesting that aggression is now redirected towards the self. The liturgy opens by cancelling verbal statements, as though to silence scenes like those seen previously. Its morning Torah reading (Lev 16) describes how forgiveness is secured on this day by sending one goat into the desert bearing sins, and sacrificing another in the Tabernacle, later replaced by the Temple on Mount Moriah, the site of the binding of Isaac. The goats therefore symbolically echo the trajectories of Abraham's sons, although the sons, unlike the goats, survived. The afternoon Torah reading (Lev 18) lists forbidden degrees of marriage, again alluding to the abuse of power, while the prophetic reading, the book of Jonah, describes how that prophet pitied his protective leafy *sukah*, 'shelter,' more than the repentant city of Nineveh whose destruction he seemed to welcome. Symbolism of the period from New Year to the Day of Atonement, known as 'the Ten Days of Penitence,' implies that mercy does not inevitably defuse severity. Although judgement for the year is passed on this day, anxiety persists until the sentence is sealed on the seventh day of the next feast.

Five days later, on the biblical fruit-harvest festival of *Sukot*, 'Tabernacles,' Jews leave home to live for seven days in a *sukah*, a leafy hut (Lev 23:42), like those used by the Israelites in the wilderness (and also like Jonah's shelter). The first and last days (or two of each in the diaspora) are fully festive, and the others informally so. Here parents and children jointly experiment with homelessness, and also bring it to an end. The symbolic exile of leaving home is tolerable because one knows that order will soon be restored, much as in children's games thinking takes the form of play (Winnicott 1971). Annual rituals in this way can exemplify developmental patterns on the level of the individual, family, and community. The feast as a whole is described liturgically as 'the time of our rejoicing,' as though to conclude the challenges of New Year and Atonement.

Its other biblical symbol is a bouquet of willow, palm, myrtle and citron ('the four kinds'; Lev 23:40) which in rabbinic ritual is shaken to the four compass points and then up and down while reading verses of Psalm 118, perhaps symbolizing the sphere of moral responsibility around each individual (Babylonian Talmud, *Berakhot* 8a, *Eruvin* 48a). It is also processed round the synagogue once daily, but seven times on the concluding seventh day, *Hosha'anah Rabah*, 'the Great Hosannah,' when willows are also beaten to strip off the leaves, before Jews leave their leafy huts for home. In rabbinic thought these completed circles mark the sealing of the sentence passed on the Day of Atonement.

The pattern of circuits that underlies the minor biblical reading for the feast, Ecclesiastes, symbolically recalls the sacred narrative's pattern of exile and homecoming, anticipated in the departures of Ishmael and Isaac at New Year. This is here echoed by leaving the safety of home for a *sukah*. The prophetic reading for the second day implicitly aligns the huts with home and with Solomon's Temple, suggesting multiple cycles of departure and return (1 Kgs 8:2–21) throughout history, human life and the year.

The day after *Sukot* is the biblical feast of *Shemini 'Atseret*, 'the Eighth Day of Solemn Assembly,' which lacks ritual symbols, but features the annual prayer for rain. Its Torah reading details the annual festival cycle (Deut 14:22–16:17), and the prophetic reading the building of Solomon's Temple (I Kgs 8:54–66), implying the importance of cycles of building and of completion both within the year and the sacred narrative. On its second day, *Simḥat Torah*, 'Rejoicing of the Torah,' the annual cycle of reading the Pentateuch is completed, symbolized by seven ritual circuits of the synagogue with Torah scrolls. This, the last of the seven events in *Tishri*, the seventh month of the biblical year, marks the end of the harvest that determines survival over the coming year. Much as infants hope to survive adult power, so Israel emerges intact from potential divine severity.

The next month, *Marheshvan*, the only one with no event, looks forward to the eight-day minor midwinter feast of *Hanukah*, 'Dedication,' on 25 *Kislev*, when the sun is lowest and the moon smallest. This post-biblical celebration of the Hasmoneans' rededication of the Temple falls on the same date as its desecration three years earlier, but focuses on the rededication rather than the desecration. Lighting one flame on the first evening, and an additional one on each of the others, pierces the midwinter darkness, augments the warmth and security of the home, and heralds the return of sun- and moonlight. As with loss of home at *Sukot*, the desecration of the sanctuary seems survivable.

Eight days later—echoing the interval between New Year and Atonement—the fast of 10 *Tevet* recalls biblical reports of the start of the Babylonian siege of Jerusalem, aggravating the dangers highlighted by the previous event and anticipating the final fall of the Temple in midsummer (2 Kgs 25:1).

The full moon on 15 *Shevat* marks the minor rabbinic feast of 'new year for trees' when new blossom appears. This was first introduced for taxation purposes, and concludes the anxious cluster of winter events that opened with *Hanukah*. In botanic terms it suggests the confidence inspired by the prospect of the fruit harvest, and is paralleled by the joy of young childhood, a rebirth of hope that culminates in *Purim* one month and *Pesah* two months later.

Five rabbinically established special Sabbaths around *Purim* and before *Pesah* may survive from the ancient triennial cycle of synagogue reading, which began and ended at *Pesah*. Annual reading was adopted in the Middle Ages. As will be seen, each such Sabbath received texts reflecting seasonal themes.

The first of two before the minor feast of *Purim* is *Shabat Shekalim*, 'the Sabbath of Shekels,' prior to the new moon of *'Adar*. Its minor Torah reading (Ex 30:11–16) commemorates the building of the Tabernacle sanctuary in the wilderness, when half-shekel contributions were collected from men of military age, described as 'ransom' for their souls, implying the value of the life even of an enemy.

Shabat Zakhor, 'the Sabbath of Remembrance,' immediately before *Purim*, features the biblical command to wipe out the memory of Amalek for attacking the Israelites in the wilderness (Deut 25:17–19), a reading that paradoxically ensures their remembrance. The prophetic reading (1 Sam 15:1–34) evokes the killing of Agag, an Amalekite king, one of whose descendants is central to the next event.

The fast of Esther, commemorating dangers faced by Esther in protecting her people, falls the day before the minor feast of *Purim*, 'Lots,' on 14 *'Adar*. This feast's reading, the book of Esther, describes an attempt to destroy the

Jews, and presents the paradoxes involved in vengeance. It is celebrated both by hearing the story and by making gifts of food, primary gestures of fellowship. The name of the enemy in this book, Haman, a descendent of Agag the Amalekite, is 'wiped out' during the public reading by booing and whistling. But equally forgotten are the vengeful massacres at the end of the book. Once it was known that the king had changed his mind about ordering his subjects to kill the Jews and told them to defend themselves, Jews would have been in little danger, especially as royal officers assisted them and some Persians posed as Jews to escape hostility (Esther 8:17, 9:3). Yet 75,811 Persians were massacred in pre-emptive revenge that is challenged neither by the book nor by rabbinic commentators. This contrasts with the hesitation to kill implied on *Shabat Shekalim*. Moral confusion is supported by the rabbinic instruction to drink "until you cannot distinguish 'blessed-be-Mordecai' from 'cursed-be-Haman'" (Babylonian Talmud, *Megillah* 7b; Hebrew sentences with the same numerical value), and there is an atmosphere of excess as people drink and wear fancy dress. *Purim* symbolically echoes characteristics of adolescence, high in energy and low in reflection, unlike the maturity of young adulthood featured in the next major feast, *Pesah*.

Three more rabbinically ordained special Sabbaths precede that festival. On *Shabat Parah*, 'the Sabbath of the [Red] Heifer,' immediately after *Purim*, the minor Torah reading (Num 19:1–22) describes ritual purification after coming into contact with death. The prophetic reading (Ezekiel 36:16–38) concerns national ingathering from the impurity of exile. Both texts may respond to the killings on *Purim*.

The second is *Shabat Hahodesh*, 'the Sabbath of the [New] Month,' immediately before the new moon of *Nisan*, two weeks before *Pesah*. Its minor Torah reading (Ex 12:1–20) describes the first Passover in Egypt, and the prophetic reading (Ezek 45:16–46:18) the future rituals of the rebuilt Temple. Both allude to the symbolic merging of home and sanctuary over *Pesah*.

On the third, *Shabat Hagadol*, 'the Great Sabbath,' immediately before *Pesah*, the special prophetic reading (Mal 3:4–24) views the messianic rescue as a sequel to the Exodus, encompassing past and future redemptions.

Pesah, 'Passover,' a seven-day biblical commemoration of the Exodus that begins on the full moon of *Nisan*, recalls the Israelites' lamb sacrifice on the eve of their departure, during the lambing season. Leaven is prohibited throughout the week, pointing to the start of the grain harvest. On the first day the prayer for dew is recited. Like *Sukot*, six months earlier, only the first and last days of *Pesah* (or two days in the diaspora) are fully festive. After the fall of the Temple the rituals were transferred to the home, and are still performed at a family gathering known as a *seder*, 'order,' on the eve of the first day, or two days in the diaspora. A home liturgy including symbolic foods, called the *Hagadah*, 'Recounting,' is recited in response to the biblical instruction to 'tell your child on that day' about the Exodus (Ex 13:8), linking the event symbolically to educating the young. This is the seed from which the rabbinic spring-to-autumn drama grew. But rather than recounting the Exodus story in full, the *Hagadah* encourages mature discussion by offering alternative approaches to the Exodus designed for different kinds of hearer. A midrash embedded in it describes the types of child needing to be addressed as wise, wicked, simple, and incurious (Schonfield 2005). There follows a meal followed by a grace which renews an awareness of exile, as though merging the Exodus with present homelessness. Concluding songs look forward to messianic times, so that the narrative spans the remote past, present, and ultimate future.

The Torah reading for the opening day relates to the Exodus (Ex 12:21–51), and the prophetic readings for both days to later celebrations of *Pesaḥ* (Josh 5:2–6:1; 2 Kgs 23:1–9, 21:5). That for the intermediate Sabbath describes the reviving of the Valley of Dried Bones (Ezek 37:1–14), while on the last day the text is a messianic vision of perfection (Isa 10:32–12:6). The minor reading for *Pesaḥ* is the Song of Songs, implying the passionate love of Israel and God (Jer 2:2), which reflects the rabbinic seasonal narrative of maturation.

Unlike the mood of guiltless war-gaming at *Purim*, texts for *Pesaḥ* avoid vengeance, summarized in the biblical instruction: 'do not hate the Egyptian, since you were strangers in his land' (Deut 23:7–8). Drops of wine are removed from cups during the *Seder* in memory of the plagues and of the drownings in the Red Sea, signs of emotional maturity that recall Melanie Klein's psychoanalytic view of emotional development from the 'paranoid-schizoid' to the 'depressive' positions. While *Purim* features infantile rage that leaves no room for understanding the other, *Pesaḥ* invites patience in achieving gratification and developing reflective relationships (Schonfield 1999).

The second evening of *Pesaḥ* sees the start of the biblically commanded ritual of counting seven weeks of the '*Omer*, 'Sheaf [counting]' (Lev 23:15–16), a time of semimourning that coincides with the grain harvest. Daily offerings were brought to the sanctuary reflecting anxiety about completing the harvest. Rabbinic texts associate this with the developing relationship between God and Israel, particularly the period between falling in love and the commitment of marriage. Rabbinic legend relates a pause in mourning on the thirty-third day to mark the end of a plague among students of the second-century Rabbi Akiba, caused by enmity between study-partners (Babylonian Talmud, *Yevamot* 62b). The prophetic reading for the Sabbath before its end (Hos 2:1–22, for the first pericope of Numbers) compares the return of an adulterous wife to the end of Israel's idolatry, symbolizing the way a relationship based on mutual idealization and passion, in this case between God and Israel, cannot be sustained.

The counting ends on the eve of the next biblical festival, *Shavu'ot*, 'Weeks' or 'Pentecost,' on 6 *Sivan*, the only annual event to begin on the sixth of a month. This ends the grain harvest and starts the fruit harvest which will last until *Sukot* (Exod 34:22, Lev 23:16–21). Since the Middle Ages it has been associated with the revelation at Sinai, described in the Torah reading for the first day (Exod 19:1–20:26). The prophetic texts for both days are heavenly visions (Ezek 1 and 3:12, Hab 2:20–3:19). Rabbinic thinkers, who view the Torah as Israel's marriage contract with God, may have chosen the book of Ruth as the minor reading to suggest how loyalty and marriage now replace the passion of the Song of Songs seen at *Pesah*.

The next period, spanning the summer, contains no festivals, but fast days and a time of mourning and reflection that commemorates events in both the Exodus and the Temple narratives. Rabbinic thinking about this period suggests the growing strains and conflict between God and Israel, and describes how they may be survived. Three periods of forty days span the summer from *Shavu'ot* to the Day of Atonement. The first of these ends on 17 *Tamuz*, now a fast day, when Moses brought the Ten Commandments from Sinai, found the people worshipping the Golden Calf and broke the tablets. Midrashic writers suggest that he did so to annul Israel's marriage with God and spare her the death penalty for adultery (Rashi on Exod 34:1). Idolatry can be conceptualized as concretizing a relationship with God that should be dynamic and fully expressible only inwardly, like human love. In rabbinic thought the Tabernacle alone appropriately represented the divine presence without depicting it, with an ark at its centre containing the broken and whole tablets that recall both failure and success in relating to God (Schonfield 2006: 95).

Moses restored order in the camp for the next period of forty days until 1 *'Elul*, a month before New Year, and then mounted Sinai for a last period of forty days, after which he brought the second set of tablets on 10 *Tishri*, the Day of Atonement. God's 'thirteen attributes of mercy' (Exod 34:6–7), revealed at that concluding moment, were truncated by liturgical editors to disguise the severity implied at the end. The statement 'I will be gracious to whom I will be gracious, and merciful to whom I will be merciful' (Exod 33:19) implies the random nature of providence.

In rabbinic thought a parallel time-scheme is in operation, as the calf episode is worked through during the seven 'Sabbaths of Consolation' between 9 *'Av* and *Rosh Hashanah*. Sephardim recite *selihot* (pentitential prayers) on weekdays from the start of *'Elul*, and Ashkenazim from the Sunday before *Rosh Hashanah* itself. The *shofar* is sounded each morning, anticipating the theme of divine and human severity that dominates the ten Days of Penitence and is resolved only when the second set of tablets was received on the Day of Atonement, the time of judgement ten days into the next year.

The fast in memory of the calf episode on 17 *Tamuz* is followed by the 'Three Weeks' of semimourning that is intensified during the concluding 'Nine Days' between the New Moon of *'Av* and the rabbinic fast of 9 *'Av*. These feature the 'Sabbaths of Misfortune,' with prophetic readings on exilic themes. On 9 *'Av*, at the end of the Three Weeks, Israel's 'marriage' with God was undermined once more by the return of the spies with negative reports of the Holy Land (Num 13–14). Moses saved the people from destruction by reciting the 'thirteen attributes,' aligning this episode with that of the calf (Num 14:18), but the generation of former slaves was condemned to wander for forty years until they died, only their children entering the Land. The episode of the calf could therefore be resolved while that of the spies could not. Love between God and Israel takes priority over entering the land, since territory is divine property and is held by humans only conditionally (Deut 11:17).

These two summer fasts are associated also with the fall of the Temple, centuries later, anticipated by the fasts of Gedaliah and 10 *Tevet*. Rabbinic readings of biblical texts date the breaching of the walls of Jerusalem by Babylonians and Romans to 17 *Tamuz*, and the destruction of both Temples to 9 *'Av*. The Torah reading for the first of these recounts Moses' descent with the second tablets (Exod 32:11–14, 34:1–10) and that for the second a statement of inevitable landlessness (Deut 4:25–31). Dirges are recited on both days, and on 9 *'Av* the book of Lamentations, describing the fall of the first Temple in 586 BCE. Its first verse compares Jerusalem to a mourning widow, reapplying the seasonal marriage theme. Exile symbolizes both the temporary failure of God's relationship with Israel and the idea of permanent universal landlessness. Rabbinic writers link other later disasters to these dates, presumably because of the destructive heat and waterlessness of Near Eastern summers (Mishnah, *Ta'anit* 4:6).

The Temple-period minor feast of 15 *'Av*, recently revived in Israel, which falls exactly six months after celebrating the innocence of new life at 15 *Shevat*, follows a five-day interval, like that between Atonement and Tabernacles. It does not form part of the traditional calendar, but illuminates themes that have developed around the year. On this day young men and women courted in vineyards (Babylonian Talmud, *Ta'anit* 30b–31a; *Baba Batra* 121a), emphasizing the shift from suffering to joy, and symbolically restoring God and Israel's interrupted love. It is rabbinically associated also with the story of the daughters of Zelophehad (Numbers 27, 36), after which Israelites could marry partners from different tribes, privileging love over maintaining traditional land boundaries. The generation of slaves then also stopped dying out in the wilderness. Its celebration may have lapsed due to the narrative mismatch between midsummer and the theme of love, a theme which returns after the second tablets are brought on the Day of Atonement.

The failure to mark the entry into the Promised Land by the end of the year suggests an ongoing state of loss described by Freud as 'melancholy' (Freud 1917). Eight days after the end of New Year, on the Day of Atonement, tensions over the calf are relieved, but land remains unattainable. The lifecycle implicit in the calendar seems here to acknowledge the renewal of love with God, but not territorial homecoming. As the summer events show, Joshua's invasion of the land is replaced in the Jewish year by midsummer fasts for exile. Perhaps the entry into the land involved massacres of the inhabitants that were too painful for Jews—who themselves had suffered exile—to contemplate.

No calendrical moments seem clearly identified with old age and death, although these are implied on the Day of Atonement. By the end of the year, loving relations between couples, and symbolically between God and Israel, are underpinned by the birth of children, although God's patience was challenged by the newly created world just as young children tested that of parents in the Torah readings for the New Year. Behind the potential dangers of infancy and young parenthood alluded to in the Torah readings for *Rosh Hashanah* lies the theme of exile implied by Abraham's departure from his own land (Genesis 12:1), an image that dominates the annual cycle.

This developmental narrative of the individual within the family and society may be summarized as follows. From birth around *Rosh Hashanah* the vulnerable child is at risk from the abuse of power. Conflict over power is resolved by recognizing the vulnerability of the home, and by symbolically enacting cyclic patterns of exile and return at *Sukot*.

Individual and communal identity is established through conflict with external powers, and victory is idealized at *Ḥanukah*. But identity is soon endangered on 10 *Ṭevet*. Growth, physical maturity and fertility are celebrated around 15 *Shevaṭ*, after which Purim shows the aggressively destructive side of adolescence. Sabbaths between *'Adar* and *Nisan* highlight further developments that culminate in the sense of security gained through education and passionate relationships formed at *Pesaḥ*.

Anxiety about love is reflected in the *'Omer*, but resolved at a symbolic wedding on *Shavu'ot*. Conflict and fears about betrayal and survival strain the relationship to breaking point in midsummer with the destruction of home and departure into exile. After happiness is briefly glimpsed on 15 *'Av*, the couple seek rapprochement in *Elul* by taking joint responsibility for the relationship. Failed relationships and the death of individuals introduce the theme of judgement at *Rosh Hashanah*, which also sees birth, as was recognized at the start of the previous cycle.

It cannot be proven that those who arranged the Jewish year intended to comment on the lifecycle in this way, but the similarities between the agricultural and the human cycles suggest fine discernment of human developmental stages. This topic deserves book-length treatment, but even this summary illustrates how the combined agricultural, theological and historical narratives delineate a nonlinear process of growth taking place against a backdrop of conflict and ambivalence.

The present model for thinking in psychological terms about a religious calendar is offered in the hope that others will find analogous lifecycle structures in their own calendars, sacred narratives and theological structures.

Acknowledgments: I am grateful to Lawrence Kilshaw, Tony Kitzinger, Yoav Landau-Pope, Andrew Levy, Tamar Schonfield and Rabbi Deborah Silver for their help.

BIBLIOGRAPHY

Bettelheim B. 1979. *The Uses of Enchantment*. London.
Freud S. 1917. 'Mourning and Melancholy,' in *The Standard Edition . . . Works of Sigmund Freud* xiv: 243–58. London.
Rosenzweig F. 1971. *The Star of Redemption*, tr. W. W. Hallo. New York.
Schonfield J. 1999. 'Esther: Beyond Murder,' *European Judaism* 32/1.
Schonfield J. 2005. 'One Haggadah, or Four?,' in *Studies in Jewish Prayer*, eds R. Hayward & B. Embry. Oxford.
Schonfield J. 2006. *Undercurrents of Jewish Prayer*. Oxford.
Winnicott D. 1971. *Playing and Reality*. Harmondsworth.

Chapter 13

The Psalms in Orthodox Christian Worship

Yves Dubois

One of the strange characteristics of the Bible is that, frequently, the middle point of one of its books gives the sense of it all. In the Psalter, that midpoint is verse 11 of Psalm 77, 'It is my failing that the High One's right hand has changed' (Robert Alter's translation). In other words, things are not what they used to be! Not so long ago, in the twentieth century, during the years of the Nazi and the Soviet regimes, that wistfulness of the Psalms was particularly appropriate. It united Jews, Orthodox Christians, and many others who were victims of oppression.

Traditionally, the Psalter is closely associated with David for spiritual rather than historical or authorship reasons. When Saul was king of Israel, he was often overcome by a spirit of gloom and deep anxiety, which would eventually drive him to suicide. The only way Saul could be freed from the clutches of that spirit was by asking David to play the harp and sing for him. The Psalms are therefore a powerful spiritual tool to vanquish the forces of death *by praising God*. From the outset, the Psalms are a door to the Resurrection because the joy of praise holds in germ, spiritual renewal. An early image of that victory is David dancing ecstatically before the Ark of the Covenant (2 Sam 6:14).

The text of the Psalter makes it obvious that it is the song book of the people of Israel. This is unquestionable, like the fact that what Christians call the Old Testament is the Jewish Scriptures. Christians share their Scriptures with the Jews. In spite of centuries of anti-Jewish attitudes among many Christians, this common element has never been denied. The Psalms repeat God's commandment in Deuteronomy 30:19, 'life and death I place before you, blessing and curse; now choose life!' (Everett Fox translation), since from Psalm 1, we are made aware of the two opposed ways, the way of light, of God's Law, and the way of iniquity, darkness, and death which rejects God's eternal life. In the Psalms, through the voice of the people of Israel, we find a voice to express every aspect of our relationship to God: joy, pain, anger.

The four Gospels borrow much of their vocabulary from the Jewish Scriptures even when they do not quote their sources. The Psalms are omnipresent, central to the spiritual life of Jews and Christians not only because of their role in the liturgical life of both faiths. Their message—God's ultimate victory over the powers of darkness—unites the two communities.

Christians read the whole Bible through their relationship with Christ. Jesus applied to himself the beginning of Psalm 22 as he was dying on the Cross, 'My God, my God, why have you forsaken me?' Christians go farther and apply to Christ all Psalms of struggle and victory. Since Christ is the supreme embodiment of God's redemptive work within his creation, there is no mutual exclusion between what Christ achieves and suffers, and what the Church and the Jewish community achieve and suffer. Just as the Suffering Servant in Isaiah is both one specific individual and the whole nation of Israel, so the main actor in the Psalms is both the unique person of Christ and all God's righteous servants.

In trying to explain the place of the Psalms in Orthodox Christian worship, I shall focus on those aspects of the Psalter experienced frequently by the average Orthodox Christian worshiper. The Psalms permeate all aspects of the liturgical life of the Orthodox Church, making it impossible to give an exhaustive account of their use in one short chapter.

There are two different uses of the Psalms in the Orthodox Church. On the one hand, the Psalter is appointed to be read each week in its entirety. To that effect, it is divided into twenty sections called *kathismata* (a plural Greek word meaning *sessions*, the singular being *kathisma*, because the people sit during the reading of the Psalms), of approximately seven psalms each. One *kathisma* is read at Vespers, and two at Matins. On the other hand, individual Psalms recur at each celebration of Vespers, Matins and the Eucharistic Liturgy. Because they are so frequently heard, those Psalms are spiritual landmarks in the life of practicing Orthodox Christians.

For the average faithful, the liturgical reading of *kathismata* is not part of the daily rule of prayer. It tends to be used privately at home outside of liturgical services, in two ways. On the one hand, in the morning prayers, the penitential Psalm 51 is read before the Creed, and in the prayers of preparation for communion, Psalms 23, 24 and the second half of Psalm 116 are read. On the other hand, as a form of intercession for specific people who are sick or in danger, one person or a group of friends may decide to read each day (perhaps at an agreed time) one or more *kathismata*, group of psalms in sequence, as intercession to God. Why use Psalms read in succession and without reference to any link between the situation prayed for and the actual contents of the Psalms? This is due to the origin and nature of the Psalms as songs of joy and praise which bring spiritual renewal. Praise is the human response to God's constant life-giving creative action.

As far as liturgical services are concerned, the day begins at sunset, because of the Church's symbolic understanding of the unfolding of each day as a statement about God's creative work. God initiates his creative activity in the late afternoon. Soon, the creation experiences the darkness of this world, where it struggles towards the light of dawn, then the glory of midday. The first chapter of Genesis should not be understood as a questionable scientific description of the beginnings of time, but rather as the deep discernment of the meaning of life. The Biblical approach to God's creative action is not the deists' view that by creating, God set the universe into motion, before wandering away, leaving his creation to its own devices. The biblical understanding of creation is that everything receives its existence from God at each moment. If God ceased creating, the universe would cease to exist. A day, any day, is the reflection of the drama of God's creation, journeying into darkness and struggling towards the light.

For that reason, we begin Vespers with the reading or singing of Psalm 104, which blesses God for looking after all aspects of the natural world. That Psalm, like Genesis 1, looks at all aspects of creation. Light is the first aspect of creation. Then come the heavens, the oceans, vegetation, birds, fish, land animals and finally people. The difference between the two texts is that Genesis 1 presents creation as a succession of divine activities, and the Psalm describes what goes on night and day throughout creation.

In parish life, Vespers is celebrated on Saturday evening, the beginning of Sunday, the first day of the week and the commemoration of Christ's resurrection. Therefore, after Psalm 104 we read Psalm 1, 'Blessed is the Man.' Verse 1 of Psalm 1, 'the Man who has not walked in the counsel of the wicked,' brings to mind the person of Christ, the New Adam. This does not set him in opposition to everyone else, but on the contrary, he is the example for every man or woman, the entire human race without exception. Christ is Emmanuel, God *with* us, and cannot be a screen between God and any human being. It would be self-contradictory to use our allegiance to Christ as justification for hostility towards anyone.

The people of Israel remain beloved of God because 'the gifts and the calling of God are irrevocable' (Rom 11:29). From a Christian point of view, this is the essential aspect of Jewish–Christian relations. And we can extend the same ethical attitude to all human beings, because every person is made in the image of God (Gen 1:26–28, 5:1–3, 9:6) and the entire human race is included in God's Covenant with Noah (Gen 9:9). God does not call on anyone to condemn or judge those of other nations or other faiths, as we learn from the last verses of Romans 11 (verses 33–35): 'O the depth of the riches and wisdom and knowledge of God! How unsearchable are his judgements and how inscrutable his ways! For who has known the mind of the Lord? Or who has been his counselor? Or who has given a gift to him, to receive a gift in return? For from him and through him and to him are all things. To him be glory for ever. Amen.'

The message of Psalm 1 is that the righteous meditate day and night on the Torah of the Lord (verse 2). That precludes side-lining Judaism. It also points to the heart of spiritual ethics: the righteous 'do not sit in the assembly of the scornful' (Ps 1:1). Being dismissive about others, labelling people, so one can despise them, opens the door to injustice and oppression. The first and most important step in the spiritual life is to train the heart and the tongue to refrain from such attitudes.

The next Psalms at Vespers, Psalms 141 and 130, are meant to coincide with dusk (for practical reasons, the Saturday evening service takes place at the same time throughout the year). They talk of our prayer ascending to God as incense and they are accompanied by the censing of the whole church building. The singing of these Psalms is a cry of anxiety at the onset of darkness. We see the logic of the Psalms in this: worship and praise are the way through and out of times of trial.

Our parish follows the Russian liturgical tradition. Others follow the Greek tradition, which celebrated Matins on Sunday morning before the Eucharistic Liturgy. In our parish, Matins follows Vespers without interruption on Saturday evening. The two make one service called the *Vigil*. From October to March, by the end of Vespers it is actually night. It is the perfect time to begin Orthodox Matins which is not a morning prayer but a night prayer, meant to begin in deepest night. On Mount Athos, all the monasteries start Matins around midnight and conclude it with the Great Doxology when the sun shines through the East window in the altar space. In that way, the monks uphold the world throughout the hours of darkness. This is their primary task.

Immediately after the end of Vespers, the Six Psalms (3, 38, 63, 88, 103, 143) are read aloud by the reader who stands in the middle of the church. At that time the lights have been turned off, the candles have been blown out and only the voice of the reader is heard. It is a time of deep concentration and complete immobility, a communion with the tragedy of much of the world, with those who are alone, slandered, hungry, at death's door or in a hostile environment.

The Six Psalms are accompanied by twelve *Prayers in Deepest Night*. Traditionally, these are read silently by the priests during the Six Psalms, but some parishes encourage the members of their communities to use them when they pray late at night. This is one of the prayers: 'Master, holy God beyond our understanding, at your word light shone out of darkness. Your loving kindness intercedes better than our prayers. We prostrate in worship before you. We give you thanks according to our strength. Grant us all our petitions which are unto salvation. Show us to be children of the light and of the day, heirs of your eternal good things. Protect those who are in danger, keep us all safe in soul and body, that with boldness we may glorify your wonderful Name.'

From the lowest point of darkness, at Matins we toil in prayer towards the light. At the Saturday evening Vigil we make our pilgrimage towards the proclamation of the Resurrection Gospel. Immediately after the Six Psalms, we proclaim verses from Psalm 118, showing our trust in God's victory when there is no other source of liberation.

Before the Resurrection Gospel, we sing verses of praise from Psalms 135 and 136. After the Resurrection Gospel, we read a long poetic text praising Christ's and our resurrection. We see the purpose of our life accomplished and show our joy by the singing of Lauds, a shortened form of the last three Psalms, 148 to 150. This immediately precedes the Great Doxology, the greatest liturgical praise used throughout Christendom, and which concludes our Matins.

There is a contrast between the Vigil service, which dramatizes the ups and downs of our earthly life, and the Eucharistic Liturgy, which is pure Thanksgiving (the meaning of *Eucharist*) and Communion with God and one another. However, before the beginning of the Eucharistic Liturgy, while the congregation trickles into the church building, the reader (in Russian he or she is called a *psalomshchik*, as psalm reader) reads the third and sixth liturgical Hours, made up mainly of Psalms. The role of the Psalter is modest in the Liturgy, where the emphasis is less on the struggle between light and darkness, and far more on the enjoyment of God's salvation.

At the beginning of the Eucharistic Liturgy we sing the blessings found in Psalms 103 and 146, except at festivals which have their own Antiphons not taken from the Psalms. In the Liturgy we are rejoicing in the fact that 'we have found the true Light, we have received the heavenly Spirit, we have found the true faith.' The emphasis is not on tension, but on the Gift of eternal life. The Bread and Wine of the Liturgy are called the Holy Gifts: we give our humble bread and wine, our world, and God transfigures us and our tragic world into victorious life. Jewish theologians like Richard Rubenstein rightly remind us of the grave danger of imagining *facile* victory over unmentionable tragedy. Yet it is essential to assert that the powers of death have not succeeded, and will never succeed in destroying meaning, goodness, life. Otherwise our minds would fail to rise above chaos. Our human nature by itself shows that ultimate reality is anything but meaninglessness. The human heart has instinctive hope, because God is present in its deepest recess. That is what we mean by the image of God in all people.

The entire Psalter is a call for the transformation of society through goodness and justice. As songs of the heart, the Psalms purify us from spiritual
darkness, asserting the ultimate victory of God's light and love. Our Orthodox
Church and all faith communities can rejoice in God, since praise is the spiritual calling of all humanity, the foundation of our relationship to God and all
his creation: 'How precious is your steadfast love, in your light we see light'
(Ps 36:7, 9).

BIBLIOGRAPHY

Alter R. 2009. *The Book of Psalms, A Translation with Commentary*. New York.
Fox E. 1995. *The Five Books of Moses, a New Translation with Introductions,
Commentary and Notes by Everett Fox*. London.

Chapter 14

Are there Christian Cultural Elements in Jewish Practice?

Michael Hilton

Out of the ashes of the ancient Israelite way of life, after their cultic cen-ter was twice destroyed—first by the Babylonians and later, finally, by the Romans—arose two new faiths, which we now call Judaism and Christianity. Though differing sharply in their thinking about how God's revelation had come to the world, both offered answers to the difficult questions of how human salvation, both personal and communal, was to be achieved (Segal 1986, Hilton and Marshall 1988: 114–18). Jews and Christians both believed themselves to be the 'true Israel,' inheritors of the biblical tradition. Both devoted themselves to a life of prayer, of communal organization and welfare, of self-searching and repentance. For Jews the central act of worship became the reading and translation of the Torah: for Christians, it was the sharing of 'the Lord's supper,' a special time of communion with God. At times, teach-ing either of these twin new faiths was prohibited by the Romans, and many Jews and Christians suffered horrible deaths as martyrs. The names of many who died in the early centuries of our era are remembered by the faithful to this day.

Once the Roman Empire became officially Christian in the fourth century, life for Jews living under Christian rule became much more difficult. From then on the history of Jewish–Christian relations became largely a story of misunderstandings, polemic, persecutions, and pogroms. Across Europe from the Inquisition in the West to the Bohdan Khmelnytsky massacres in the East, across time from the Rhineland massacres on the way to the first crusade to the Holocaust of the twentieth century, Jews were slaughtered. The gradual recognition by many Christian groups, particularly the Roman Catholic

Church, of this hateful past, has paved the way for the positive dialogue of our own time (Bowden 2005: 683–7).

But it is not possible that every Christian hated every Jew; for how could Jews have survived? There is also a more benign narrative, of dialogue and disputation, of cultural exchange and borrowing, and ways to find means to live together. For Jews living in Christian lands, their customs, practices, and even interpretations of the Bible have been shaped by the surrounding culture. Indeed, the relationship goes further than that, as each of the two faiths has measured, weighted, and proclaimed doctrine and customs which are taken from or respond to the other faith. Christianity and Judaism pursue parallel paths through history, never completely merging or diverging. This chapter gives a few examples, mainly in areas where Christianity has influenced Judaism, since that is far less well known than the influence of Judaism on Christianity.

At the heart of the theological differences between the two faiths is the nature and role of Jesus Christ. At worst, Christian teachings have seen Jews as living examples of a rejection of God, and even violence against God, as proclaimed in the notorious words 'His blood be on us, and on our children' (Matt 27:25 KJV). The best of today's Jewish scholars lecture on the contemporary Jewish context of the parables, sayings, and miracles of Jesus, explaining carefully how they can be fitted into what we know of late Second Temple Judaism, even before the major reshaping of the faiths mentioned at the start of this paper. Much of the dialogue and dispute between the two faiths over two thousand years has centered on whether or not Jesus was the future king foretold by the Hebrew prophets, who would one day arrive to lead his people, bring peace on earth, and initiate a golden age. This figure has become known in Hebrew as *mashiach*, or by the equivalent Greek *christos*, in English Messiah, words which mean 'anointed,' a reference to the ancient practice of a new king, priest or prophet being anointed with oil. In my book *The Christian Effect on Jewish Life* I argued that the figure and doctrine of the Messiah is not really central either to Judaism or Christianity, but has been kept alive by centuries of debate between us (Hilton 1994: 63–84). We Jews are still waiting for an era of peace and reconciliation—the 'days of the Messiah' have not yet arrived; and Christians have had many other ways of designating Christ, most importantly as Son of God and part of the Trinity (Bowden 2005: 661). It seems likely that, following the failure of the Bar Kokhba revolt against the Romans in the year 135 CE, at the time of the persecutions by the emperor Hadrian, messianism fell out of favor. Bar Kokhba, it was said, had been hailed as the Messiah by none other than Rabbi Akiva (Jerusalem Talmud, *Ta'anit* 4:8/27). His martyrdom and the failure of the rebellion put an end to the belief that the promised redemption would come soon. And so we find that in the foundation text of rabbinic Judaism, the Mishnah, there is almost no reference to messianism, and when it is mentioned, it is now placed in the distant future (Mishnah, *Berakhot* 1:5; Jerusalem Talmud, *Sotah* 9:15). But in the two Talmuds, the Babylonian and Jerusalem, which have plenty to say about the Messiah, there is a new idea: the Messiah has already been born, perhaps even on the day the Temple was destroyed, but is hiding somewhere until the right time comes. This more elaborate doctrine can be seen as a rabbinic response to a dominant Christianity (Kessler & Wenborn 2005: 291–2). And yet, in the Barcelona disputation of 1263, where the Messiah was the main topic, Rabbi Moses ben Nahman (Nahmanides) puzzled his audience by suggesting that the Messiah was not really so important to Jews: 'My Lord King, hear me. The Messiah is not fundamental to our religion . . . You are a king, and he is a king.' Nahmanides objected to Moses Maimonides making the messiah one of the thirteen principles of the faith, but Maimonides' formulation has been popular, and a version of it has become associated with Jewish martyrdom: 'I believe with perfect faith in the coming of the Messiah, and though he tarry, I wait daily for his coming.' We may well conclude that 'had it not been for Jewish–Christian debate *neither* faith would have since been so preoccupied with messianism. Official religious leaders would not otherwise have accepted a doctrine so threatening, so potentially subversive and so revolutionary, and so rooted in popular culture' (Kessler and Wenborn 2005: 292).

Jews and Christians share a common scripture, but with the definitive texts in different languages. Although the first translation from the Hebrew, the Greek Septuagint, was made by Jews in Egypt, it was abandoned by the rabbinic tradition because it came to be the definitive text for the Christian Old Testament, at first in the Greek, and then in the Latin translation known as the Vulgate. Jewish exegetes thus restricted their own range of possible interpretations by steering well clear of both the texts and the themes adopted by the Church.

In his book *A History of the Bible: The Book and Its Faiths* (2019) John Barton has a wonderfully clear chapter, 'The Theme of the Bible,' explaining in simple terms the two quite different readings of our common scripture which have emerged in Christianity and in Judaism. For Christians, he suggests, the Old Testament 'begins in history but ends in prophecy' (Barton 2019: 312). The most important prophecies are about the coming of Christ, and the books are arranged with the prophetic books at the end, so the reader can turn the page and read on to their fulfillment as described in the Gospels. For Jewish readers, he suggests, the Bible is much more about providential guidance and how to live a faithful life. It is the Torah which is the interpretative key to the whole Bible, not the Prophets.

What Barton misses is how much both these interpretations have been shaped over the centuries by Jewish–Christian dialogue and disputation. Take for example the 'Suffering Servant' poems in Isaiah 53: 'he was wounded for our transgressions, he was bruised for our iniquities: the chastisement of our peace was upon him; and with his stripes we are healed. All we like sheep have gone astray . . . and the LORD hath laid on him the iniquity of us all' (Isa 53:5–6 KJV). Acts 8:32 identified the 'Suffering Servant' with Jesus; in contrast, some rabbinic texts identified the servant with the future Messiah, as did Targum Jonathan in the third or fourth century CE. 'While in the Christian sources such texts are referred to the lifetime of a Messiah who had already lived and died, in the homilies of the Sages the allusions are to the Messiah who has still to come' (Urbach 1987: 686). But medieval rabbinic commentary repeatedly denied that Isaiah 53 had anything to do with messianic hopes. God's innocent servant was thought of as one of the people of Israel. 'He was wounded for our transgressions' came to mean that the innocent among Israel suffer along with the guilty. Christopher North explained it like this: 'Jews abandoned the Messianic in favor of the collective interpretation as a means of defense against the Christians' (North 1948: 18).

This summary is but one example of how the need to argue against Christian claims led Jews to rethink the way we read our own Bible. Meanwhile, many Christians continue to place great emphasis on Isaiah's prophecies, and they are frequently used by Christian missionaries to Jews.

A second example of centuries of dialogue and disputation can be seen in the parallel Jewish and Christian interpretations of the Song of Songs. Teachers of both faiths viewed this series of erotic love poems as a series of spiritual marriage hymns. For rabbis they showed the love of God for the people of Israel, and for Church Fathers the love of Christ for the Church. The third-century Rabbi Yohanan has been shown to have answered many of the comments made by Origen in his commentary point by point (Kimelman 1980). St Bernard of Clairvaux (1090–1153) used the Song as the basis for sermons proclaiming the path of love as central to Christian spirituality. Imagery from the Song can be seen in the mystical commentary, the Zohar's, portrayal of Torah as a beautiful maiden whose love must be sought (Zohar 2:99a). The Virgin Mary often appears in Christian iconography with roses or lilies in her hands, based on Song 2:1–2. Christian influence can be seen in the use of the rose in the Zohar as one of the symbols of the *Shekhinah*. The very opening sentence of the Zohar quotes Song 2:2 (Pardes 2019). European exegetes from both faiths were quite unafraid to portray their love of God using the imagery of these ancient love poems. They did not openly reference one another, but they drew from the same well of ideas.

The first Christians were Jews who observed Jewish festivals. Later these were abandoned by the Church, and the liturgical year came to revolve around Christmas and Easter, celebrating the birth and the resurrection of Christ. But rabbinic Judaism also remodeled the biblical festivals and some of this was in response to Christian claims or, later, to adapt to Jewish life in Christian lands. Such adaptations are the most obvious evidence for Christian influence on Jewish practice, much of which is rooted in popular culture rather than rabbinic legislation.

Rosh Hashanah, the Jewish New Year on the first days of the autumn month of *Tishri*, attracts the largest crowds of the year in our time. But in the biblical festival calendars the description of the day is brief, and the sounding of the *shofar* is the only distinctive feature. As Judaism was reborn as a synagogue-based religion, Rosh Hashanah and Yom Kippur (the Day of Atonement on the tenth day of *Tishri)* found a new role. The rabbis developed and popularized these festivals as a corrective to Jewish bickering and hatred of each other *(sin'at hinam)*, which they blamed for the destruction by the Romans. They took up the words of the prophets, asking for prayer, the offerings of the lips, to be accepted in place of the sacrifices of old. Gradually, these two days became the most important days of all, days of self-reflection, days of self-examination, days of soul-searching, days of solemnity, days of denial, days of public and repeated confession so that the people should have respect for themselves and for each other and should never again descend to the depths of madness and hatred. At the heart of this new approach is the principle of *teshuvah* (repentance). The two festival days were linked up by making them the start and end of ten days of repentance, and later the whole of the preceding month of Elul became a time of preparation (Pirkei de Rabbi Eliezer 46), making a total of forty days in the penitential season, mirroring the forty days of Lent.

At the same time early Christians were teaching a similar message: repent and be saved. Something was in the air, a new way of looking at spiritual experience, a path of personal searching, a route to personal salvation. But for Christians, the connection with the time of year was lost. Although some have seen scapegoat imagery in Matthew, neither Rosh Hashanah nor Yom Kippur are mentioned in the Gospels, suggesting perhaps that they were not particularly important at that time. Origen *(ca* 184–253 CE) urged contemporary Christians not to participate in Yom Kippur, and the Church took the festivals out of the calendar, arguing that it was wrong to have a special day for repentance and atonement, because forgiveness through Christ can be sought at any time. Many of the motifs of the season, particularly those of the sacrifices and the imagery of the scapegoat, were transferred to Lent and to Easter (Ben Ezra 2003).

A legend was told about the tenth-century Rabbi Amnon of Mainz. Martyred by the Church, as he was dying he composed a special prayer which has come to be used at the heart of the High Holyday liturgy. On this day God decides who will live and who will die, but repentance, prayer and charity can avert the evil decree. From this prayer comes the designation of the two days of Rosh Hashanah and Yom Kippur as the *yamim nora'im*—the Days of Awe or the High Holy Days. This profound prayer reminds us of how small we are in God's sight, and that our lives are in God's hands. At a time when martyrdom was an important inspiration to Christians to repent and believe, so it was to Jews. The arrival of this prayer into the Ashkenazi liturgy marked a profound change in how the High Holy Days were viewed, a shift to something darker, a time when hope was tinged with a fear that reflected the troubles of Jews. Both faiths shared the emphasis on sin and atonement, 'and both formulated the ritual and theological answer to this need in terms of Yom Kippur' (Ben Ezra 2003:333).

Although Chanukah and Christmas have such very different themes, they were probably connected in antiquity by the ways in which they came to be dated (Hilton 1994: 18–20; Roll 1995; Hilton & Schick 1997). The origin of the festival of Chanukah is found in 1 and 2 Maccabees, books preserved by the Church in Greek. It is the only ancient Jewish festival which is non-Biblical in origin. It is celebrated by the lighting of candles, and has never been part of Christian observance, though it is mentioned briefly in John 10:22. Although a minor festival, it has taken on increasing significance in modern times as a Jewish alternative to Christmas. Chanukah decorations, presents, feasts, bazaars, pageants, plays, balls, and parties began in the USA in the 1860s and continue to this day. In 1859, Rabbi Isaac Mayer Wise ran a serialized account of the Chanukah story in the *American Israelite* which ran to thirty-nine episodes. During the late 1880s and early 1890s, the Young Men's Hebrew Association sponsored a 'Grand Revival of the Jewish National Holiday of Chanuka' which was held in New York at the Jewish Academy of Music (Plaut 2012: 41–64). Today, the Prime Minister of Great Britain and the President of the United States take part in public Chanukah candle lightings every year. Some have argued that all this is a mockery of a festival designed to celebrate Jewish distinctiveness, while others have suggested that such public acknowledgment is a fitting demonstration of the survival of the Jewish spirit.

The central feature of the festival of Purim is the reading of the Book of Esther from the Hebrew Bible. The story tells of Haman, an antisemitic government official who pursued vengeance against the whole Jewish people because of his dislike of a single Jew. The tables were turned, and the Jews took vengeance on their enemies. Over the centuries, the celebration of the festival has had a difficult history in the story of Jewish–Christian relations. At various times and in various places effigies of Haman were burned at the celebration. From time to time, Christians complained that it was an effigy of Christ which was being burned. Perhaps they were misled by the Septuagint translation of Esther, in which the King orders Haman to be killed, using the word *staurotheito* (Esther 7:9), the same Greek word later used by the Gospel writers for 'crucified.'

In 1543 Martin Luther described in *On the Jews and their Lies* how much the Jews love the book of Esther 'which so well fits their bloodthirsty, vengeful, murderous greed and hope' (Horowitz 2008). The perception of ongoing Jewish violence had marred the festival. No wonder that the Liberal Judaism of my own childhood refused to have anything to do with Purim.

Today, Purim is normally celebrated in fancy dress. The costumes, plays and parodies and general atmosphere of fun is reminiscent of Carnival. Lenten carnivals take place to this day across Europe a couple of weeks before Purim. In many places Jews were not allowed to take part: in Rome Jews were forced to, and were humiliated. It is therefore not surprising that Jews decided to use the opportunity of Purim to hold their own carnivals. The earliest pictures we have of Purim entertainers are from the fifteenth century, and the first published Purim play is from Frankfurt in 1708. Since the eighteenth century, Jews have popularized Purim by making fun of themselves, and plays were and still are written which satirize communal life (Hilton 1994: 24–9).

The story of Passover is central to the Christian narrative. In Matthew, Mark and Luke, the last supper Jesus shared with his disciples is a Passover meal, but in John the supper takes place on the night before Passover, and Jesus is crucified at the very hour of the Passover sacrifice. By a play on words in Greek, the Paschal Lamb became the suffering lamb, as shown in the title of Melito's *Peri Pascha* (Bokser 1984: 27). In Second Temple Judaism, the center of the celebration was the eating of the roast lamb or goat in Jerusalem, accompanied by singing. After the destruction, the Passover meal was celebrated at home, and a new ritual arose, based around the asking of questions, the telling of the story, and the sharing of symbolic foods which reminded those present of aspects of the story. Christians today who attend a Jewish Passover meal seeking to understand the Passion narrative are often disappointed to hear that, apart from the Psalms, the entire text we use was written later than the time of Jesus, and apart from Hillel, the rabbis mentioned were all from the second century of the Christian era.

The ascendancy of Christianity and Jewish life in Christian lands has influenced the celebration in several important ways, most obviously by the abandonment of the eating of roast lamb, although that tradition is still maintained by Jews living in non-Christian countries. Many avoided the eating of lamb in ancient times, because there was no official Passover lamb without the Temple where it was slaughtered, but it was no doubt the link with Jesus which finally took it off the menu. But it was not until the thirteenth century that we find a reference to the placing of a lamb bone on the seder plate in place of the Paschal lamb of old (Hilton 1994: 36). By that time Easter had become another difficult time between Jews and Christians. From 1144 up to the time of the Reformation, Jews across Europe faced accusations of killing Christian adults or children and using their blood to bake matzah, the so called 'blood libel.'

The seder can only be properly understood once it is realized that many of its key statements reflect a desire for liberation by their authors or by their readers: 'Now we are slaves; next year may we be free.' 'In every generation they rise against us and seek our destruction.' 'In every generation one must look upon himself as if he personally had come out from Egypt' (Riskin 1983: 45, 70, 106). The celebration became a moment of light for an oppressed people, reiterating the message that freedom will come again, and hope must not be lost. In our time the message is extended to others, and there are many discussions of modern slavery around the seder table.

Viewing foods in symbolic terms is common to both the eucharist and the seder. Although the bread and wine used on an ordinary Sabbath are simply food and drink, the salt water, the *haroset*, the bitter herbs and the matzah at the seder are linked to the story. For early Christians, the symbols of the eucharist helped them cope with the loss of Jesus, and for Jews, the symbols of the seder helped them cope with the loss of the powerful temple ritual (Hilton 1994: 35).

Shavuot, or *Yom habikkurim* ('the feast of weeks' or 'the festival of the first fruits') was purely a harvest festival in biblical times and in Second Temple Judaism. But as farming gradually declined among Jews, a new role needed to be found for the festival. Building on the narrative in Exodus 19 which states that in the third month, around six weeks after leaving Egypt, the Israelites arrived at Mount Sinai, Rabbi Elazar ben Pedat (third century) declared: 'It is the day on which the Torah was given' (Babylonian Talmud, *Pesahim* 68b). This chronology meant that the time of the *Omer*, the counting of seven weeks from the Exodus, became a reminder of the journey through the desert from Egypt to Sinai. It came to be observed as a time of moderate mourning, during which no weddings took place. It is noteworthy that the Church came to observe the forty days leading up to Easter as a time of abstinence and repentance, known as Lent. What had been a happy time of year for Israel became a sad time for the Church, and vice versa.

The reworking of Shavuot as the anniversary of the giving of the Torah gave it a new designation in the prayer book as *zeman mattan toratenu* ('the season of the giving of our Torah'). By making Shavuot a celebration of God's revelation it came to parallel the Christian reworking of the festival as a commemoration of the narrative in Acts 2, where the disciples who were gathered in an upper room started speaking in languages they did not know. This is the foundation story of Christian mission, a hugely important event.

The new Jewish festival of the giving of Torah was a clear response to the Christian claim. Central to the Jewish–Christian debate was the question of whether the Torah should continue to be observed, and the related question of which of the two faiths represented the true heritage of the ancient people of Israel. Although the rabbinic texts do not refer directly to Christian claims, this heritage dispute can be discerned as an underlying theme, particularly in the fourth century *Bereshit Rabbah* (Neusner 1987: 29–58).

Many life cycle customs in Judaism have Christian origins or were developed in contradistinction to Christianity. Notable examples are the replacement of the Sabbath oil lamp by two white candles, and the lighting of *yahrzeit* candles on the anniversary of the death of a close relative. It was not just the candles but even the term *yahrzeit* which was borrowed from Rhineland Christians. Several wedding customs appear to be adapted from Christian practice, most notably the shattering of a glass, and the sixteenth century introduction of wedding canopies. These were modelled on those used for Church processions (Gutmann 1989).

The celebration of bar mitzvah began in Christian Normandy around the twelfth or thirteenth centuries. At first it consisted simply of the boy's father saying a one-line blessing, and there is no evidence that it was a common practice. When researching my book *Bar Mitzvah: A History* I looked at many different possible cultural influences in an attempt to explain the new ceremony. It may perhaps have begun as a special blessing for thirteen-year-old boys leaving home to study in a *yeshiva*, the Jewish boys' boarding school of the day: a *yeshiva* of the time has been excavated at Rouen in Normandy. But by the time bar mitzvah became popular, and was no longer the preserve of studious families, it is possible that it was viewed as a parallel to Christian confirmation. The Council of Trent of 1545 suggested ten to twelve as a suitable age for confirmation, whereas earlier it had been done at a younger age. In Germany the new Lutheran Church proposed a period of instruction, followed by an exam, for boys seeking confirmation, representing a remarkable parallel to bar mitzvah as it developed. Two important new elements were added to the *bar mitzvah* ceremony: in addition to the call-up to the Torah and the father saying a blessing, there was to be a family or community celebration meal; and at the meal the boy would give a *drosha*—a speech explaining an aspect of Torah to show off his learning (Hilton 2014: 35–53).

In Germany, at the start of the nineteenth century, a remarkable new ceremony was introduced to Jewish communities, known in German as *Einsegnung* and in English as confirmation. This Jewish confirmation began as a class graduation ceremony for thirteen-year-olds in the new modern Jewish schools of their day. With few exceptions it has remained a group ceremony. In the nineteenth century it consisted of both boys and girls giving well-rehearsed answers to questions about the Jewish faith, many of which were published in books called *catechisms*—a term clearly borrowed from Christianity. From the start many of the Jewish confirmation ceremonies took place at the festival of Shavuot, just as the Christian ones often did at Pentecost (Hilton 2014: 74–105). Another imitation of Christian practice was wearing white for the ceremony; this has survived, especially for girls in smaller Jewish communities around the world, as published photos indicate (Vinick & Reinharz 2012).

Although Jewish confirmation was originally intended to replace *bar mitzvah* completely, the old ceremony was revived in Reform and Liberal synagogues in the twentieth century, and a parallel ceremony for girls was introduced (*bat mitzvah*), following the same traditional pattern of Torah reading, speech and party as the boys' ceremony. By this time, confirmation ceremonies were held at the age of fifteen or sixteen instead of thirteen, because young people were staying in school for longer. This change made it possible to celebrate twice—first *bar* or *bat mitzvah*, and then confirmation (Hilton 2014: 106–34)

My conclusion is that Judaism and Christianity are faiths which depend on each other, pursuing parallel but distinct paths through history, never completely diverging or joining, and each being enriched by the relationship. To the question posed in the title of this chapter, the answer is a firm 'yes.'

BIBLIOGRAPHY

Barton J. 2019. *A History of the Bible: The Book and Its Faiths*. London.

Bokser B. M. 1984. *The Origins of the Seder*. Berkeley.

Bowden J. ed. 2005. *Christianity: The Complete Guide*. London.

Gutmann J. 1989. 'Jewish Medieval Marriage Customs in Art: Creativity and Adaptation,' in *The Jewish Family: Metaphor and Memory*, ed. D. C. Kraemer, 47–59. New York.

Hilton M. & G. Marshall. 1988. *The Gospels and Rabbinic Judaism: A Study Guide*. London.

Hilton M. 1994. *The Christian Effect on Jewish Life*. London.

Hilton M. & Schick P. 1997. 'Signs from Heaven and the Date of Chanukkah,' *The Journal of Progressive Judaism* 9, 39–57.

Hilton M. 2014. *Bar Mitzvah: A History*. Philadelphia.

Horowitz E. S. 2008. *Reckless Rites: Purim and the Legacy of Jewish Violence*. Princeton.

Kessler E. & N. Wenborn, eds. 2005. *A Dictionary of Jewish–Christian Relations*. Cambridge.

Kimelman R. 1980. 'Rabbi Yoḥanan and Origen on the Song of Songs: A Third-Century Jewish–Christian Disputation,' *Harvard Theological Review* 73:2, 567–95.

Neusner J. 1987. *Judaism and Christianity in the Age of Constantine*. Chicago.

North C. R. 1948. *The Suffering Servant in Deutero-Isaiah: An Historical and Critical Study*. London.

Pardes I. 2019. *The Song of Songs: A Biography*. Princeton.

Plaut J. E. 2012. *A Kosher Christmas: 'Tis the Season to be Jewish*. New Brunswick.

Riskin S. ed. 1983. *The Passover Haggadah*. New York.

Roll S. K. 1995. *Toward the Origins of Christmas*. The Hague.

Segal A. F. 1986. *Rebecca's Children: Judaism and Christianity in the Roman World*. Cambridge, MA.

Stökl Ben Ezra D. 2003. *The Impact of Yom Kippur on Early Christianity: The Day of Atonement from Second Temple Judaism to the Fifth Century*. Tübingen.

Urbach E. E. 1987. *The Sages: Their Concepts and Beliefs*. Cambridge, MA.

Vinick B. & Reinharz S. 2012. *Today I am a Woman: Stories of Bat Mitzvah from Around the World*. Bloomington.

FURTHER READING

Doniach N. S. 1933. *Purim or The Feast of Esther: An Historical Study*. Philadelphia.

Levine A.-J. & M. Z. Brettler, eds. 2011. *The Jewish Annotated New Testament*. New York.

Chapter 15

Anti-Judaism and Orthodox Liturgy

Michael G. Azar

Throughout the year, the Orthodox liturgy unveils a natural and unquestioned continuity between the *ecclesia* of Israel before Christ and the *ecclesia* of Israel now. Hebrew patriarchs and prophets are commemorated on the church calendar (a practice not reflected in the West) in the same breath as martyrs and spiritual elders of recent years. The God who blessed 'Abraham and Sarah,' 'Isaac and Rebecca,' 'Jacob and all the prophets' (and a host of others) is petitioned to bless new couples in marriage; the God of 'our forefathers' Abraham, Isaac, and Jacob is asked to bless those who have fallen asleep. The springtime commemoration of God's saving act of deliverance is, for Orthodox, still 'Passover'—*Pascha*—rather than 'Easter.' In church architecture, one commonly finds Christ at the center of the dome surrounded most immediately not by his apostles, but by his prophets. It is undoubtedly this continuity—the frequent invoking of the God of Abraham, Isaac, and Jacob in distinctly Eastern Mediterranean tones—that constitutes one of the many reasons Jews can easily find in Orthodox liturgy something strikingly familiar, despite the many differences.

Yet there is much in Orthodox liturgy that brazenly continues a 'negative' counterpart to this continuity: the sense that God has chosen 'us' but not 'them.' 'We' are Israel, his royal priesthood, his royal nation; 'they' are the Greeks (*ellenes*), the 'Gentiles/nations' (*ethne*). Toward the end of Holy Week, this 'us versus them' dynamic takes on an infamously distinct dimension, as the liturgical hymns come to present 'Jews' regularly, but not consistently, as the notable other, alongside the 'Gentiles,' as those who had resisted and rejected the God of Israel. These texts, though rare in Orthodox liturgy, provide easy fodder for antisemitic pockets within the Orthodox world and offer the most significant problems for contemporary Jewish–Christian relations.

Though the Eastern Christian commemoration of the Lord's Pascha (Exod 12:11) stretches back to well before the fourth century, it was not until then that the feast began to be partitioned into a week-long sequence of commemorations leading up to his resurrection (probably first in Jerusalem in connection with the holy sites). Most of the week's unique hymns developed in the centuries thereafter and now constitute the final third of the *Triodion*, a liturgical collection, primarily of Palestinian and Constantinopolitan origin from roughly the sixth to the fifteenth centuries, though the basic structure was in place by the ninth (Mother Mary and Ware 2002: 42). While the historical origins of these hymns are of tremendous significance—especially in light of their vastly different chronological and geographic contexts—the focus here is on the *Triodion*'s current shape, which comprises three parts: the pre-Lenten hymnography (beginning over three weeks before Lent with the Sunday of the Publican and the Pharisee), the Lenten hymnography (which concludes on the Friday prior to Holy Week), and Holy Week itself.

An underlying motif throughout the *Triodion* is the inward person, whose failure to keep God's commandments perpetuates an ongoing state of exile, as Israel in the wilderness, but who nonetheless hopes to (re)enter God's promised kingdom. Thus, in words quite reminiscent of parallel Jewish traditions, the first Sunday of the *Triodion* asks God to 'open unto me' the 'gates of repentance: for early in the morning my spirit seeks your holy temple, bearing a temple of the body all defiled.' On this Sunday, the pride of the Pharisee is condemned while the humility of the Publican is extolled as a model of repentance (see Luke 18:10–14). However, one does not here find the image of the Pharisee common in some Christian traditions: that of the paradigmatic legalist bound by a dead 'law.' Instead, the *Triodion* on this Sunday recognizes the Pharisee repeatedly as one who was 'exalted by the works of justification,' who had 'spent his life in virtue' and attained the 'riches of righteousness,' but who fell through vainglory and pride. The people are thus exhorted to 'follow the Pharisee in his virtues and to emulate the Publican in his humility' and to 'hate what is wrong in each of them: foolish pride and the defilement of transgressions.' The people are not exhorted to condemn the Pharisee's way of life or whitewash the Publican's; they are pushed, rather, at the onset of a season replete with increased asceticism and righteous works, to learn from both a fundamental point: 'Every good deed is made of no effect through foolish pride, while every evil is cleansed by humility.' The hymns offer the Publican and Pharisee to the people as a means to awaken their own meekness and humility: 'Weighed down by a great multitude of sins, I have surpassed the Publican in an excess of evil, and I have also made mine own the boastful delusion of the Pharisee. I am utterly devoid of all good things: Lord, spare me' (Matins, Sunday of the Publican and the Pharisee).

When the church enters the second part of the *Triodion* and Lent begins, the biblical theme of exile and return directs the general flow and feel of the forty days. The people are cast out of paradise at the beginning, spending the season striving to be let back in. The weekdays focus, unlike the rest of the year, on Old Testament readings, with no weekday reading prescribed from the New Testament (except to commemorate the Annunciation on March 25/ April 7). Once, however, the third part of the *Triodion* begins and the church enters Holy Monday, the weekday New Testament readings reappear (namely, in the Bridegroom Matins services), as the liturgical themes flow from and toward the final days, hours, and minutes of Christ's life.

By Holy Friday in particular, the hymnography begins to present Jews more jarringly and negatively than in the days preceding and, indeed, any other time of the year: It is 'Jews' who nail Christ to the cross; it is 'Jews' who have become a 'lawless nation'; it is 'the nation of the Jews' who become 'murderers of God' (Matins, Holy Friday 'Service of the Twelve Gospels'). Even without the poignancy of these particular hymns, the image of Jews and Jewish practice that appears in Orthodox Holy Week is overwhelmingly negative. Nevertheless, for the majority of their indictments against Jews, the hymns, like the Synoptic Gospels (and even John in key moments), foreground not Jews *in toto*, but the leaders specifically: 'lawgivers of Israel, scribes and Pharisees' seek Christ's demise (or earlier in the week, the 'priests and scribes'). But on Holy Friday, the hymnography, as aggadic midrash in general (there is hardly a better way to describe the exegesis), hardly sticks to the actual, surface parameters of the biblical text. Instead, the hymns pull out of the basic narrative a multiplicity of features not directly evident, in this case typically exacerbating both the underlying intentions and motives of Jews who oppose Christ and the significance of their actions. Three primary elements shape this presentation: Byzantine rhetorical culture, biblical precedent, and, especially, a theological emphasis on the juxtaposition of the divine and human in the economy and person of Christ (much of the following is adapted from Azar 2015).

Primarily of Byzantine composition (whether Palestinian or Constantinopolitan), the hymns regularly employ *psogos* (invective), a rhetorical mode long established in Greek culture for speaking of one's opponents, particularly to expound their 'evil attributes' (Aphthonius, *Progymnasmata* 10.27). Such a rhetorical form, perhaps most well-known from John Chrysostom's *Against the Jews*, was well established in Byzantine textbooks as a way of *speaking*, but not *acting*. It was not to be confused with *koinos topos*, which proposed punishment; rather, *psogos* contained 'mere slander alone' (Aphthonius, *Progymnasmata* 10.27). Thus, in Holy

Week, Jewish leaders do not merely hand over Christ to be crucified; Jews, rather, become a 'lawless nation'; they become 'murderers of God,' even while God is petitioned to forgive them. This rhetorical motif—which is employed, it should be noted, against Gentiles as well—is consistent with late antique Greek standards of speaking of one's opponents, but hardly with more recent standards of public discourse, especially in those countries where Jewish–Christian relations have taken shape. One simply does not speak of one's opponents as a 'pack of dogs' or a 'swarm of God-Slayers' anymore (Matins, Holy Friday).

The hymns are also deeply biblical and so find their way of speaking of Christ's opposers not only in the Byzantine textbooks, but also in the laments of destruction and rejection and hopes for redemption found in the Psalms and Prophets. They intentionally and directly draw upon the Prophets in particular, including the sometimes hyperbolic accusation that *all* of God's people had rejected him and his prophet. As the prophets had provided images by which Christ was to be later understood (most famously, the suffering servant of Isaiah), so also they provided images by which the reaction to Christ is to be comprehended.

Nonetheless, a far more important factor in Holy Week's presentation of Jews is the *theological emphasis*, of which the rhetoric, however biblical or Byzantine, is merely a vehicle. Overall, Orthodox theology, which is most fully expressed in the liturgy, typically marvels in paradoxical statements about the juxtaposition of the human and divine: the Virgin who gives birth, the God who suffers, the incorruptible assuming the corruptible, the Author of Life becoming subject to death. On Holy Friday, as throughout Orthodox liturgy and art, the compositions go to great, often unnatural, lengths to communicate a theological message about the nature of Christ: it is not merely a man who is crucified and buried, but God himself, the one who freed Israel from Egypt and led Israel through the wilderness (Bucur 2017).

One finds this love of dissonant juxtaposition forcefully expressed in the Holy Week and Pascha texts, as the hymns often and unabashedly mold the biblical passages in order to highlight the divine–human paradox. One does not hear merely the mundane details of Jesus's judgment before Caiaphas and Pilate, but that *God* specifically stood before a *priest*; that *the Judge of All* stood before *a temporal judge* (Vespers, Holy Friday), that the 'Lawgiver' was crucified 'as lawless' (Matins, Holy Friday). The hymns do not tell the congregants simply that the man who suffered was innocent, but that the man who suffered was God. As the well-known hymn sung during the dramatic procession of the cross on Holy Thursday night proclaims,

Today is suspended upon the tree,
      he who suspended the earth amid the waters;
A crown of thorns crowns him,
      who is the King of the angels;
He is wrapped in the purple of mockery,
      who wraps the heavens in clouds;
He receives buffetings,
      who freed Adam in the Jordan;
He is transfixed with nails,
      who is the Son of the Virgin.
We worship your passion,
      O Christ.
Show us also your glorious resurrection. (Matins, Holy Friday,
served Thursday night)

Or again, from Vespers on Holy Friday afternoon,
  A fearsome and marvelous mystery is today coming to pass:

    The incorporeal one
      is being held;
    The one freeing Adam from the curse
      is bound;
    He who tries the inner hearts and thoughts of man
      is unjustly tried;
    He who sealed the abyss
      is shut up in prison.
    He before whom the powers of heaven stand with trembling
      stands before Pilate;
    The Fashioner
      is struck by the hand of the fashioned;
    The Judge of the living and the dead
      is condemned to the cross;
    The Despoiler of Hades
      is closed up within a tomb:
    O forbearing Lord,
      compassionately enduring all things
      and saving all from the curse,
      glory to you.

Such is typical of the way Orthodox theology regularly employs stark juxtaposition in order to communicate Christ's great *sunkatabasis*. Often translated as 'condescension' or 'considerateness,' this word is central to patristic thought and exegesis as a literary means through which to express God's singular work of salvation from creation onward. God led his people to salvation by 'condescending' to a cloud, fire, or to their state itself. One finds the refrain, 'Glory to your *sunkatabasis*,' sung repeatedly on Holy Friday as a summarizing praise of Christ's passion. When the hymns of Holy Week relate the gospel accounts and marvel at what is done to Christ, they do so in a manner that explicitly highlights the absurdity of his *sunkatabasis*, well beyond what the Gospels themselves do. The point is not merely to retell the gospel narrative, but to marvel theologically and intellectually at God's mercy.

Thus, the hymns accentuate the paradox and *sunkatabasis* of the eternal Judge tried before a temporal judge, of the God who was crucified on the tree that he created. And it is chiefly this accentuating that produces the overwhelmingly, but not entirely, negative picture of Jews. In the same way that he who fashioned the heavens is struck by the hand that he fashioned, and he who is suspended on a tree is he who suspended the land upon the waters, so also he who gave the law is condemned as lawless by those to whom he gave the law and turned over to those who have no law. This motif is a chief reason why Pilate's culpability is notoriously diminished and that of the Jews increased: God's rejection by a pagan is nothing remarkable; God's rejection by *his own people* is; this is the paradox of the God-Man's *sunkatabasis*. While Pilate is by no means exonerated, his treachery is not the focus because a Gentile breaking the law is not as significant to the hymnographers as the law-bearers themselves becoming 'lawless' (*anomos* or *paranomos*—vocabulary that again reveals the liturgy's inspiration in the Psalms and Prophets).

But Holy Friday's indictment against Jews does not happen all at once, and it is not monolithic or simple. At first, the hymns of Holy Friday Matins continue a juxtaposition that had been building since Palm Sunday between the unnamed sinful woman who anoints Jesus and the disciple who betrays him, leaving before one's soul one of two routes to seek. When the hymns begin to speak more historically of the actual events of the crucifixion, they do so at first by blaming the religious leaders. Their inspiration is an adapted form of Psalm 2:2, a verse that occurs repeatedly in the course of the service: 'The rulers of the people took council together against the Lord and against his anointed.' However, the sharp turn of events comes with the Sixth Antiphon (after the second gospel reading):

> Today, the Jews nailed to the cross
> > the Lord who divided the sea with a rod and led them through
> > the wilderness.
> Today they pierced with a spear
> > the side of him who for their sake smote Egypt
> > with plagues;

> They gave him gall to drink,
>> who rained down manna on them for good.

The hymn, as several others throughout Holy Week, commemorates the Lord's Pascha as one (whether in Exodus or the Gospels) and, in so doing, marvels at the *sunkatabasis* of the God-Man. 'The Jews' are presented as the *very same* people whom *Christ* freed in the Red Sea and fed with manna, as the hymn is replete with imagery that highlights the paradox: the tangible tools used (nails and a rod), the act of violence (piercing and smiting), and the offering of food (gall and manna). The same people whom Christ (according to Orthodox art and liturgy) led through the Red Sea at the Pascha of exodus now turn away at the Pascha of crucifixion.

In the Eleventh Antiphon (after the fourth gospel reading), the indictment strengthens, and the guilt of those who condemned Christ is underscored:

> In return for the good things that you granted, Christ,
>> to the offspring of the Hebrews,
> they condemned you to be crucified,
>> giving you vinegar and gall to drink.
> But render unto them, Lord, according to their works,
>> for they have not understood your *sunkatabasis*.

The 'offspring of the Hebrews' are thus indicted because they have not understood Christ's *sunkatabasis* specifically, and the precedent provided by Lamentations provides the means to express this. The author of Lamentations laments the destruction of Jerusalem and its temple by enumerating the sins of his own people, but, despite his recognition of the failings of his own people, the author wishes the Lord to 'pay [the destroyers] back for their works' (Lam 3:64). The hymns of Holy Week bear a similarly dissonant tension between the recognizably sinful souls of *the* congregants (perhaps *the* central theme of the entire *Triodion*) and the sins of those who actually helped to spur the destruction of this temple, Jesus.

Of all the Holy Friday texts in which the Jews appear negatively, the most striking are the *improperia* or 'reproaches' (as they are commonly known in Western liturgy): the hymns within the Antiphons that comprise first-person addresses on behalf of Christ toward the people, especially those who crucify him. Once again, the hymns are molded by biblical precedents: First, there are the words of Christ himself in John 10:32, where he says to 'the Jews' who are about to stone him, 'I have shown you many good works from the Father. For which of these are you going to stone me'? (NRSV). Second, and perhaps more important, there are the numerous first-person addresses of the Lord (that is, in Orthodox theology, *Christ*) toward his people who have wronged him found in the Psalms and, especially, Prophets. Jeremiah's fifth lament serves as one example, in which Jeremiah asks, *not* coincidently as far as the Holy Friday hymns are concerned, why the people who are 'plotting' and taking 'counsel' against him are repaying him 'evil' for 'good' (18:20).

The first of these first–person addresses arises in the Twelfth Antiphon of Friday Matins:

> Thus says the Lord to the Jews:
> 'My people, what have I done to you,
>   or how have I wearied you?
> To your blind, I gave light;
>   Your lepers, I cleansed
>   Your paralytics, I raised up.
> My people, what have I done to you,
>   and how have you recompensed me?
> Instead of manna, gall;
>   instead of water, vinegar;
> Instead of loving me,
>   you nailed me to the cross.
> No longer do I endure;
>   I will call the nations [*ethne*] to me,
> And they will glorify me with the Father and the Spirit;
>   and I will grant them eternal life.'

Within this litany of prophet-like reminders of all the good 'the Lord' has given 'the Jews' is an allusion to Psalm 69:21, which one finds in the Gospels as well: 'They gave me gall for food, and for my thirst they gave me vinegar' (NRSV). But here the Twelfth Antiphon makes an important change by explicitly recalling the exodus, in which the Lord had provided manna and water. Thus, rather than repeating this verse more accurately, the hymn proclaims, '*Instead of manna*, gall; *instead of water*, vinegar.' The change serves to accentuate the paradox and juxtaposition between the Pascha of the exodus and the Pascha of Christ's passion—or, more to the point, the juxtaposition between two incarnations of one event: *the Lord's* Pascha.

The first sticheron of The Praises after the ninth gospel reading from the same night similarly employs the Prophets:

> Israel, my first-born son,
>   committed [*epoiēsen*] two evils:
> He forsook me,
>   the source of living water,
>   and hewed out for himself a broken well;
> He crucified me on the tree
>   and asked for the release of Barabbas;

> The heavens were aghast at this
>> and the sun hid its rays;
> Yet, you, Israel, were not ashamed,
>> but delivered me to death.
> Forgive them, Holy Father,
>> for they do not know what they have done [*epoiēsan*].

Spoken by the very same Lord who both freed Israel from Egypt and was crucified, the first line is a direct quotation of Jeremiah 2:13. With these words, the Lord calls for Israel to repent by providing a stark juxtaposition between the God who freed from Egypt and the Israelites who repay with rebellion. Similarly to Jeremiah and others (Ezek 43:10), these words from Holy Week call for Israel to be ashamed. But even with such a call, the last line encapsulates a notion as prominent in these services as that of the individual's sinful soul: repentance and forgiveness (Luke 23:34). Similarly, at the sixth of the Royal Hours of Holy Friday morning, the congregants are exhorted to behold what the 'lawless priests' have plotted with Judas, in order to—note the juxtaposition and *sunkatabasis*—'judge the immortal Word guilty of death' and deliver him to Pilate. Yet, the hymn again ends with a surprising request on Christ's behalf:

> Suffering these things,
>> our Savior cried out saying,
> 'Father, forgive them this sin,
>> that the nations [*ethne*] may know my resurrection from
>> the dead.'

Soon after in the same service of the Royal Hours on Holy Friday morning, the people recite the following words, demonstrating once again the continuity of Orthodox worship that susurrates throughout the year: 'Do not forsake us utterly, for your holy name's sake, and do not annul your covenant. Take not away your mercies from us, for the sake of Abraham your beloved, and Isaac your servant, and Israel your holy one' (Ninth Hour, Holy Friday, Prayer of Azariah 11–12). To follow the harsh presentation of Jews and Jewish practice above with words such as these may seem ironic or dissonant, but in the context of Orthodox worship that assumes a natural continuity throughout Israel's ongoing history, it is almost entirely unremarkable.

None of the hymns addressed above occur alone or in the abstract; they are, rather, 'movable' portions interspersed throughout various scripture readings and the abundant 'immovable' portions of Orthodox liturgy (i.e., the designated litanies, prayers, psalms, and hymns that appear in every type of Orthodox service). Moreover, in those churches where these Holy Friday hymns occur (which is *not* all of them), many are read or sung by the people while they stand or kneel before Christ crucified—in the case of many churches *literally*, as a life-sized icon of Christ is actually mounted on a wooden cross at the front of the church, venerated by the people, and later physically taken down, wrapped in a white cloth, and 'entombed.' This setting undoubtedly affects the impact of the hymns, as it is physical liturgical actions such as these, combined with the instructive sounds, abundant smells, and stirring sights of Orthodox worship, that define the worshiper's actual *experience*. While it is the worshiper's experience of the hymns that is of central concern to Jewish–Christian relations, it is not an experience that can be fully communicated merely through a literary analysis of the hymns' imagery in regard to Jews. And the latter, it must be said, is all I have provided here.

Nonetheless, whatever the experience, liturgical texts are always a principal source for Orthodox theology, and thus the Holy Week hymns, as they currently appear in most Orthodox churches, present a major problem for Orthodox Christian–Jewish relations. Already at the first bilateral dialogue meeting between Orthodox Christians and Jews in 1972, the participants recommended the formation of a joint study, 'with a view toward reviewing or revising negative or hostile references to the Jewish people and Judaism in certain readings in the liturgy' ('Recommendations' 1977). And at subsequent meetings, Jews turned toward Orthodox participants more than once with similar requests. At the fourth international meeting in 1998, the Orthodox participants were careful to admit a possibly 'anti-Jewish' impression in the hymns but did little toward calling for any sort of revision. On the whole, while many of the authors cited below, and even Ecumenical Patriarch Bartholomew himself, have admitted some sort of need for revision, the Orthodox world generally resists significant liturgical changes.

In light of this resistance, any calls for revision—particularly from outside of the Orthodox fold—must bear in mind a few points if they are to be careful and effective. First, liturgical revision in the Orthodox Church cannot be viewed through the prism of liturgical revision in other Christian traditions. As a series of entirely autocephalous churches with no universal, centralized administrative structure and, perhaps more important, no universal official catechism, the Orthodox Church's common liturgy (despite variations) has for centuries provided Orthodox Christians the chief mode of instruction and unity. For centuries under Communists, Ottomans, Crusaders, and Caliphates, Orthodox communities have survived in part by holding tenaciously to their liturgy. That liturgy thus justifiably holds a special place in the hearts of many Orthodox Christians that goes well beyond 'traditionalism' or 'legalism.' As such, hesitancy to remove those elements problematic to Jewish–Christian relations (especially according to Western standards) is easily and often rooted in something having little to do with anti-Judaism or antisemitism. The presence of the latter in the Orthodox world assuredly does not help the possibility of liturgical reform, but neither can be said to be the cause. The situation for the Orthodox has been considerably different than that of those churches who have enjoyed centuries of relative freedom and power in Europe and elsewhere. And the situation is complicated further still should one call to mind the Orthodox Churches in the Arab world, where encounters with Jews in recent decades have come chiefly through Israel's military superiority.

Second, despite claims otherwise, the Orthodox Church has in fact often revised its liturgical texts and observances for a variety of reasons. In Holy Week alone, one could mention the procession of the cross during Holy Friday Matins (Holy Thursday night)—one of the most distinct and memorable moments of Orthodox Holy Week, but one that was not added until the nineteenth century (and not in all practices). With regard to the negative presentation of entire groups, one could mention the contemporary practice in many places of no longer proclaiming the 'Synodikon of Orthodoxy'—a text that originates in the triumph against iconoclasm and is now proclaimed on the First Sunday of Lent (the 'Sunday of Orthodoxy')—with the more original censures against 'the Greeks.' To choose to remove negative references against Jews is not far from this, and to choose to amend liturgical texts is not, historically speaking, unorthodox (Azar 2015). There is therefore much precedent in Orthodox history for removing or amending those passages in Holy Week that are also the most problematic vis-a-vis Jews—that is, those that employ *psogos*, but otherwise contribute very little to the hymns' main theological focus: the mystery of Christ's *sunkatabasis*.

Third, Orthodox bishops have a considerable amount of freedom in what they wish churches under their purview to do, and in many places, steps have already been taken to 'adjust' the Holy Week hymns—whether generalizing references to Jews (e.g., 'lawless Jews' has become 'lawless people') or 'Jews' has changed to 'Judeans' to reflect better the sociopolitical, and not just religious, meaning of *Ioudaioi* in Greek. To change these translations is, nevertheless, a question different and less challenging from that of changing the original Greek or Slavonic.

Orthodox practice reveals a salient and distinct continuity with the Israelite past and preserves a variety of Second Temple elements otherwise unknown in contemporary Christian, or even Jewish, traditions. Yet, much of its Holy Week hymnography employs *psogos* against Jews, which one can easily and especially do without, while nonetheless preserving the central theological points of Holy Week. In seeking liturgical revision, one must not wrongly understand or portray the Holy Week hymns as mere products of 'Gentile,' anti-Jewish fervor, rather than products of theological encounters with the God-Man, the Author of Life who became subject to death and so redeemed all of humankind, Jews and Greeks. The victory is over not any particular people, but over death and darkness, as proclaimed on the day of the Lord's Pascha:

> It is the day of resurrection;
> Let us be made bright in the festival,
>   and let us embrace one another;
> Let us say, 'brothers,'
>   even to those who hate us;
> Let us forgive all things in the resurrection,
>   and thus let us exclaim,
> 'Christ is risen from the dead,
>   trampling death by death,
>   and to those in the tombs, bestowing life.' (Matins,
>   Holy Pascha)

BIBLIOGRAPHY

Primary Sources

Mother Mary and K. Ware, trans. 2002 (orig. 1977). *The Lenten Triodion*. South Canaan, PA.

Papadeas G. L., comp. 2007 (orig. 1963). *Hai Hierai Akolouthiai tēs Megalēs Hebdomasos kai tou Pascha/Greek Orthodox Holy Week and Easter Services*. New English trans. South Daytona, FL.

Secondary Literature

Azar M. G. 2015. 'Prophetic Matrix and Theological Paradox: Jews and Judaism in the Holy Week and Pascha Observances of the Greek Orthodox Church.' *Studies in Christian–Jewish Relations* 10: 1–27.

Bucur B. G. 2017. 'Anti–Jewish Rhetoric in Byzantine Hymnography: Exegetical and Theological Contextualization.' *St. Vladimir's Theological Quarterly* 61: 39–60.

'Recommendations Adopted by the Greek Orthodox–Jewish Scholars Colloquium, January 25–26, 1972.' 1977. *Greek Orthodox Theological Review* 22: 155–56.

SUGGESTIONED FURTHER READING

Azar M. G. Forthcoming. 'Israel: The People of God on Palm Sunday in the Orthodox Church,' in *The Byzantine Liturgy and the Jews*, ed. Alexandru Ionita.

Caneri S. 2006. 'Les sources juives de la liturgie byzantine.' *Contacts* 216: 399–422.

Groen B. 2008. 'Anti–Judaism in the Present–Day Byzantine Liturgy.' *Journal of Eastern Christian Studies* 60: 369–87.

Ionita A. 2014. 'Byzantine Liturgical Texts and Modern Israelogy: Opportunities for Liturgical Renewal in the Orthodox Church.' *Studia Liturgica* 44: 151–62.

Ionita A. 2019. 'Byzantine Liturgical Hymnography: A Stumbling Stone for the Jewish–Orthodox Christian Dialogue?' *Review of Ecumenical Studies Sibiu* 11: 253–67.

Moga I. 2019. 'Jüdische Elemente in der Tradition der orthodoxen Kirche: Ein Beitrag im Zeichen des Dialogs.' *Review of Ecumenical Studies Sibiu* 11: 167–79.

Pentiuc E. 2014. *The Old Testament in the Eastern Orthodox Tradition*. Oxford.

Theokritoff E. 2003. 'The Orthodox Services of Holy Week: The Jews and the New Sion.' *Sobornost (Incorporating Eastern Churches Review)* 25: 25–50.

Tonias D. E. 2019. 'Fulfillment in Continuity: The Orthodox Christian Theology of Biblical Israel.' *Review of Ecumenical Studies Sibiu* 11: 209–36.

Chapter 16

The Blood Libel in the
Russian Orthodox Tradition

John D. Klier

In December 1994 I received a most unusual commission. I was conducting research for a popular book on the fate of the Russian imperial family, executed by the Bolsheviks in Ekaterinburg in 1918. I interviewed the Deputy Prosecutor of the Russian Federation, Vladimir Solov'ev, who had been assigned to investigate the remains, allegedly those of Tsar Nicholas II and his family, which had been found in a mass grave in a wood on the outskirts of Ekaterinburg. Newspaper stories reported that the Patriarch of the Russian Orthodox Church, Aleksei, had asked the Prosecutor to investigate the possibility of a ritual element underlying the murder of the royal family. It was apparent to all what was meant: the Russian political Right had long embraced the claim that 'The Jews killed the Tsar,' and that he and his family were martyrs for the Orthodox faith. This assumption was reinforced by the belief that evidence found at the scene indicated that a ritual element was involved. Moreover, at the time of Solov'ev's investigation, there were claims circulating in Right-wing circles within the Church that Orthodox clergy had recently been murdered by fanatical Jews, apparently with a religious objective, and in ritual ways. When I expressed concern that the Patriarch might actually suspect that a ritual element was involved in the Tsar's murder, Soloviev invited me to provide him with a report on the subject, which I did.

I tell this story to illustrate the resilience of this cultural motif even in the modern history of the Russian Orthodox Church. For many observers, there would seem to be nothing remarkable in continued Church sponsorship, however indirectly, of the Blood Libel. Late imperial Russia, in which Orthodoxy was the state religion, was the site of a number of celebrated ritual murder accusations. It is widely assumed that the Orthodox clergy played a role in these affairs, and that the Blood Libel was an established motif of Orthodox belief.

In fact, I shall argue, the Blood Libel was slow to infiltrate Orthodox belief, remaining essentially a 'western' cultural motif. When it was finally adopted by Orthodox clergymen, its sources were not theological, but political. For most of the period of imperial Russian rule over a Jewish population (1772–1918), the Orthodox Church viewed the Jews in abstract theological terms, as 'Christ-killers,' Deicides, or part of a divine plan for apocalyptic redemption. In practical terms, the Orthodox Church was most concerned at the alleged threat posed by proselytizing Jews to the integrity of belief of the peasant masses. The more sophisticated themes of western anti-Judaism, such as the Blood Libel, the Host Desecration charge, and a theological obsession with the Talmud, were absent from Russia. Moreover, in the absence of significant numbers of Jews living in the Russian land for much of Russian history, Orthodox views of the Jews remained theological, directed at biblical Jews, and abstract and vague when dealing with actual Jewish communities.

This situation changed when the partitions of Poland began to bring Jews under Russian rule. Along with Jews and Poles came prejudices and beliefs about the Jews that had long existed among Catholic Poles and, to a certain extent, among Eastern Rite Catholics, the so-called Uniates. These included the theme of Blood Libel, which was well-established in Poland–Lithuania. This was the source from which this belief entered the Russian Empire. Even then, it was usually viewed with suspicion by most Russian officials (with a few singular exceptions) and was slow to spread. Only as the belief in the Blood Libel became well-established in Russian society, as part of the development of Russian Judeophobia throughout the nineteenth century, did it spread to the Church, an organization that was of course embedded in society itself, and a servitor of the Russian state. By the end of the century, belief in the Blood Libel was common in Orthodox circles, although in an unsystematic way. Largely through the medium of the modern, empire-wide press, belief in the Blood Libel also became established in popular belief, even in areas where there were few, if any, Jews.

Despite the popular perception of the Russian Empire as a hotbed of the Blood Libel, cases which had a national resonance or serious consequences were rare. A brief examination of the most important ones will allow us to make some general observations about the charge in 'Orthodox Russia.' Virtually all the incidents conformed to a general model: accusations would appear at the local level, usually among a Catholic or Uniate congregation; the local police authorities approached such cases with the a priori assumption that Jews were capable of carrying out ritual murder; a role was usually played by Jewish apostates, of the most dubious moral character (and quite without pretensions of scholarship). Only at this point did the Russian authorities at the center become involved. They usually regarded the charge with skepticism, but at the same time considered it a possible criminal matter, and demanded a thorough criminal investigation, which constituted the foundation of the case. The authorities in the capital also found it necessary to commission a report on the veracity of the concept itself.

The Orthodox church was seldom consulted: criminal investigations were outside its responsibility, the population was not Orthodox, and the church had no ritual murder expertise. There is not a single case where the Orthodox church was the moving force behind the charge.

The major Blood Libels in Russia were:

The Grodno Affair (1816–17), in which Jews near the town of Grodno, Grodno province in Belorussia, were accused of murdering a four-year-old girl, Maria Adamovicha, for ritual purposes. The authorities were aided in compiling their charge by a Jewish convert to Christianity, one Savitskii, who presented elaborate claims regarding the use to which Jews put Christian blood. The ritual element of the Grodno investigation (and a number of other accusations which were apparently prompted by it) was ended by order of Emperor Alexander I, who commanded that 'the real culprits be found.' He was responding to the interventions of the so-called 'Deputies of the Jewish People.' Alexander later confirmed an order of his Minister for Religious Affairs, Golitsyn, that the authorities were not to launch criminal investigations on the basis of ritual murder claims.

The Velizh Affair (1823–35) arose from the presumed murder of a three-year-old boy, Feodor Emelianov, near Velizh, Vitebsk province. A renegade Jew, Grudinskii, produced 'evidence' from Jewish religious books in the later stages of the affair. The governor played a major role in pushing the affair forward. The accused Jews were finally released in 1835, although Tsar Nicholas expressed his concern that the practice really did exist among the Jews.

The Saratov Affair (1852–6) was the first Blood Libel to appear outside the Pale of Settlement. Two young boys were found murdered, with signs of an apparent circumcision. The moving force in keeping the affair going was a bureaucrat of the MVD, Durnovo. The accused were soldiers in the local garrison who had converted from Judaism to Christianity. The investigation implicated all Jews in the region, and over forty were ultimately arrested. The authorities began an investigation of all the Jewish manuscripts and books that they could find, which were examined by a special commission. The accused were found guilty. The affair prompted a member of the commission, Professor Daniel Khvol'son, to publish his book *Concerning Several Medieval Accusations against the Jews* in 1861. On the whole, however, the Saratov Affair was not widely publicized.

The Shavel Affair (1861), in Shavel district of Kovno province, was distinctive for a number of reasons. It was the first Blood Libel where the Jewish press played a role in attacking the veracity of the charge. The young *maskil* (partisan of the Jewish enlightenment movement, the Haskalah) and future Hebrew poet, Lev Gordon, played a major role in defending the Jews. This affair introduced the motif into Russian journalism.

The Kutais Affair (1879) was the first Blood Libel to be heard by the new court system in Russia, set up in 1865. A young girl, Sarra Modebadze, disappeared from her home in rural Georgia the day before Passover, and was later found dead. The accused were nine Hasidic Jews. The only basis for suspicion was their passage along a road near where the girl disappeared. The ritual element, implicit in the original indictment, was downplayed when the case came to trial, and the accused were all acquitted. The case was heavily reported in the Russian press, and helped to spread the idea of the Blood Libel throughout Russia. The Kutais Affair prompted an outpouring of literature on ritual murder, including a reissue of Khvol'son's book in 1880.

The Nizhnyi Novgorod Pogrom (1884) was one of the most violent pogroms of the period 1881–4. A number of Jews were hacked to death with axes. The *pogromshchiki* were stirred up by the claim that Jews had kidnapped a Christian child. The Jewish community in Nizhnyi Novgorod was very small, and far from the Pale of Settlement. The event reflected the power of the press to spread the accusation.

The Blondes Affair (1900–1902) saw an assault charge enlarged into a Blood Libel against a Jewish barber, David Abramovich Blondes, by a servant woman, Grudzinskaia, who had heard that the Jews 'obtain blood for their *matzo*.' Blondes was convicted, but an appeal to the Senate resulted in an eventual acquittal. The legal process took place against the background of worsening relations between Poles and Jews in the Kingdom of Poland and in the Pale.

The Kishinev Pogrom (1903) occurred during Orthodox Easter Week in Kishinev, the capital of the province of Bessarabia. One of the factors was said to be a ritual murder accusation made in the town of Dubossary, Kherson province, about twenty-five miles from Kishinev. The atmosphere was inflamed by the reporting of the case by the local newspaper, *Bessarabets*. 14-year-old Mikhail Rybachenko was the presumed victim.

The Beilis Affair (1911–13), which took place in Kiev, was the most notorious Blood Libel in Russian history. This was because agents of the central government, and especially the Ministry of Justice, were deeply involved in seeking to ensure the conviction of Mendel Beilis for the ritual murder of a local boy, Andrei Iushchinskii. Defenders of the Jews hailed Beilis's acquittal, ignoring the fact that the jury, while acquitting him, allowed for the possibility of a ritual murder having taken place.

Two other Blood Libels were also known about in Russia. The first was the notorious Damascus Affair (1840) which was discussed by Khvol'son; the second was the Tisza-Eszlar Affair, in Hungary in 1883, which attracted massive attention in the Russian press.

On the basis of the above cases, it is possible to make a number of generalizations about the history of the Blood Libel in Russia.

Firstly, the Russian state was the prime mover in the investigation of Blood Libels, and rarely called on the Church for expertise in this regard. The Russian elites, including the Tsar, tended to be skeptical about the Blood Libel in general, but willing to investigate specific accusations. For example, on 6 March 1817, at the behest of Jewish communal representatives, the Deputies of the Jewish People, and in response to the Grodno Affair, Alexander I confirmed an instruction which had been sent to all the governors by Prince A. N. Golitsyn, the Minister for Education and Spiritual Affairs, which decreed that Jews were not to be accused of ritual murder, 'without any evidence, but only on the basis of the prejudice that they have a need for Christian blood, but if there should be an incidence of child-murder, and suspicion should fall upon the Jews, without the prejudice that it was carried out in order to secure Christian blood, then an investigation should be carried out following the legal procedures that are followed when investigating people of any other religion, when they are accused of murder' (Gessen 1923: I, 183–4).

Yet Alexander failed to follow his own guidelines. In 1825, when passing through Velizh, at the time when the Blood Libel there was just taking shape, he accepted a petition from one of the accusers of the Jews, and ordered the matter to be investigated in depth. The provincial authorities used the Tsar's command to instigate an investigation which dragged on for years, and led to the arrest and detention of much of the local communal leadership and the closing, by imperial order, of the Velizh synagogue. The more the authorities looked for Blood Libel cases, the more they found. The problem was that these became ever more elaborate and exotic, and thus liable to refutation. Upon reading a report on the investigation, Tsar Nicholas I queried in 1827: 'It is absolutely necessary to find out who these unfortunate children were; this ought to be easy if the whole thing is not a miserable lie.'

On this occasion good sense prevailed, and in 1835 Nicholas signed the protocol of the Council of State which finally ended the affair by ordering the release of the accused Jews and the punishment of their accusers. However, at the same time Nicholas rejected the recommendation of the Council of State that Golitsyn's 1817 instruction to the governors should be reissued. The Tsar noted ominously:

> ... sharing the opinion of the Council of State that in this case, due to the vagueness of the legal arguments, no other conclusion was possible than the one found

in the verdict I have confirmed, I nonetheless consider it necessary to add that I have, and cannot but have, an internal conviction that the murder was carried out by Jews. The numerous examples of such murders with those characteristics, but always unresolved because of the impossibility of meeting the legal criteria for proof, and even the present very strange case in Zhitomir demonstrate, in my opinion, that there truly exist among the Jews fanatic or sectarians, who consider Christian blood necessary for their rites; and this can be considered all the more possible because, unfortunately, such sects exist among us, Christians, which are no less horrible and incomprehensible; for example, self-immolators and suicides, such as the case I encountered in Saratov province. In a word, not thinking for a moment that this custom is common among the Jews, I cannot deny that there must exist such horrible fanatics as exist among us, Christians (Gessen, 1923: II, 27).

(This note of the Tsar perhaps lay behind the investigation launched by the Ministry of Internal Affairs which produced the survey of ritual murder cases later published as *Zapiska o ritual'nih ubiistvah* ('A note on ritual murders') in St Petersburg in 1914, which was commonly attributed to the lexicographer V. I. Dal.')

This link to Russian Orthodox sectarianism goes far to explain the ease with which Russian rulers, and the general public, accepted the possibility of the Blood Libel. An entire literature in Russia provided hysterical descriptions of the horrendous practices of sectarian groups such as the Skoptsy (Self-castrators), Khriltsy (Self-flagellators) and Molokane (Milk-drinkers). Common sense and balance suggested that the Jews—widely viewed as fanatics—must be capable of the same. As the leading liberal newspaper *Golos* explained in 1863:

All religions not yet cleansed from superstition show examples of [human sacrifice], and since all religions have their fanatics, it is in no way unbelievable that among the followers of the teachings of Moses are to be found their own brand of fanatics. It is likely that these people do not know the Talmud very well, but having heard of the superstition about Christian blood, resolved upon cruelty and murder (188:23NII/1863).

I. G. Shcheglovitov, the Minister of Justice responsible for engineering the Beilis Affair, is reported to have justified his efforts by declaring that 'do we not know that even among Christians there are sects of this kind; why should it be impossible among the people of Israel?' (Rogger 1992: 51).

The search for Jewish fanatics who might be capable of ritual murder had a sinister undertone, because of a parallel investigation within the Ministry of Interior of just such putative fanatics. The existence of the Hasidim had over the years come to the attention of the authorities. They were briefly discussed in Derzhavin's 'Opinion.' The recognition of the sectarian in-fighting between Hasidim and Mitnagdim had resulted in a special clause in the Statute for the Jews of 1804 permitting the existence of two synagogues in every Jewish community. In the 1840s, the movement again came to the attention of the authorities in the provinces of the Northeast (where Hasidim was less common that in the Southwest, and thus perhaps more noticeable). The provincial government asked the local police to investigate the activities of the Hasidim, with a view to establishing if they were a 'harmful sect.' This was the legal term used for the extreme Orthodox sectarians that were so feared by the central government. The consensus of the local police on this occasion was that the Hasidim could not be considered a 'harmful sect,' but the link had been established (National Archive of the Republic of Belarus, coll. 295, manuscript 1, act 1151 (185153), ll. 113). Moreover, to anyone acquainted with the rhetoric of the Russian Haskalah, denunciations of the 'fanaticism' and 'obscurantism' of the Hasidim would have been very familiar. It was widely noted in the press, in the course of the Kutais Affair, that the accused were Hasidim. Nor has this concept disappeared from history: an article in *Pravda* in 1993 accused Hasidim of the ritual murder of Orthodox clergymen in Russia.

As indicated by the above survey, members of the Russian Orthodox Church played very little role in these investigations, either as instigators or specialists. The communities that produced the accusations were usually Catholic or Uniate. When confronted with general claims about the Blood Libel, the clerical elite was cautious. Thus, in 1854, a conference of staff of the St Petersburg Ecclesiastical Academy was asked to evaluate a pamphlet written by a military chaplain, Father Eoll Remizov, and designed to expedite missionary work among Jewish cantonists. Perhaps in response to the Saratov Affair, which involved converted Jewish soldiers, Remizov appended a chapter in which he claimed that the Jews murdered a Gentile on the eve of Passover and drank his blood. The committee's uncertainty about the ritual murder claim was one of the reasons for rejecting the manuscript. It is worth noting that Fr Remizov was a priest at the Church of St Theodosius at the Kiev Monastery of the Caves, where Catholic influence was not unknown. Four faculty members of the St Petersburg Ecclesiastical Academy were called upon to help assess the Jewish books and manuscripts seized in the course of the Saratov Affair. Their judgement was that they 'did not find anything that would indicate that Jews, or any individuals among them, made use of Christian blood in the pursuit of any religious or superstitious goals' (*Evreiskaia entsiklopediia*: 14,7–8).

The various investigations of the Saratov Affair produced contradictory outcomes. The civil investigation led indirectly to a literary fantasy, disguised as an historical event, that assumed the existence of ritual murder in the seventeenth century (Kostomarov 1883). The clerical investigation inspired the most influential debunking of the charge in nineteenth-century Russia (Khvol'son,1861). It is useful to remember that in the case that appeared to be most closely linked to the Orthodox Church, the Beilis Affair, the Church itself was unwilling or unable to provide an expert witness for the trial in Kiev. The 'expert' brought in to testify was Father I. E., Praniatis, a Catholic priest living in Turkestan. Three professors at Orthodox seminaries, A.A. Glagolev, I. G. Troitskii and P. K. Kokovtsev, spoke out against the accusation (*Delo Mendela Beilisa* 1999: 18).

Secondly, Russian Orthodox churchmen did not play a prominent role in the elaboration or spread of the Blood Libel motif. Orthodox theologians and official Church publications played very little part in the creation or spread of this literature—indeed, Orthodox presses produced some works of literature against the libel.

The relaxation of Russian press censorship in the early years of the Reform Era permitted the widespread journalistic discussion of the Jewish Question. At the same time, the Saratov Affair was drawing to its unsatisfactory conclusion (the convictions of the 'murderers' were upheld, and confirmed by the new Tsar, Alexander II).

Thereafter the theme of ritual murder reappeared periodically in the press. The individual who more than any other popularized the idea of the Blood Libel among the Russian reading public was a Pole, Ippolit Liutostanskii, a classic example of the type of charlatan so often connected with the accusation in the modern period. As far as his notoriously unreliable biography can be reconstructed, Liutostanskii (born 1835) was baptized a Roman Catholic, ordained a Catholic priest in 1864, and defrocked in 1867 for sexual misconduct. He converted to Russian Orthodoxy, and was briefly in an Orthodox monastic order. In the early 1870s, he appeared in Moscow and began to produce a series of theological works designed for the general public. In 1876 Liutostanskii published his first *succès de scandale, The Question of the Use by Jewish-Sectarians of Christian Blood for Religious Purposes, in Connection with Questions of the General Attitudes of Jewry to Christianity*. It is important to note that all of Liutostanskii's works were published by private presses; none of them had any Orthodox Church connections. This work, like his later *The Talmud and the Jews*, was largely a rehash of little-known earlier publications. It offers the usual pretence of erudition by offering lengthy citations from Jewish texts, invariably mistranslated and incorrectly cited.

Whereas semiliterate renegade Jews often played a pivotal role in Blood Libel affairs, by providing expertise and validation of the charge, a cadre of converted Jews in late-imperial Russia proved to be its most articulate opponents. We have already encountered Daniel Khvol'son, a Professor at the St

Petersburg Ecclesiastical Seminary, who was relentless in his attacks on the Blood Libel.

Another example is provided by the career of A. A. Alekseev. Alekseev was born Vul'f Nakhlas into a Hasidic family. He was given as a recruit into the notorious cantonist battalions of the Russian army, where he converted to Russian Orthodoxy. He became an ardent Christian missionary among the Jews, both in the army and after he was invalided out of the service. Learning about the Saratov Affair from one of his former officers (the accused were converted Jews in the army, stationed in Saratov), Alekseev devoted much time and energy trying to convince the authorities of the falseness of the charge. In 1886 he published a book entitled *Do the Jews Use Christian Blood for Ritual Purposes?* The historian Iulii Gessen contends that the simplicity of the language and the lack of sophistication of the argument (for Alekseev was a complete autodidact) made it a very effective refutation of the charge for a general audience. Alekseev's book on ritual murder, along with his other books designed to convince Jews that Jesus Christ was the Jewish Messiah, were published by a church press in Novgorod. He also published periodically in an intellectual Orthodox magazine, *Strannik*.

Another Jewish convert to Orthodoxy, and would-be missionary, Iakov Brafman, has a far more sinister reputation in Russian Jewish history. Brafman was the author of *Kniga Kagala (Book of the Kahal),* a tendentious translation and interpretation of the record book of the Jewish community (*kahal*) of Minsk in the first years of Russian rule. Brafman's claims of the existence of a 'secret talmudic municipal republic' which controlled all Jews and sought to undermine the Christian world, is one of the classics of nineteenth-century European antisemitism, and a direct predecessor of (and influence on) the *Protocols of the Elders of Zion*. Brafman's missionary activities were sponsored by the Orthodox Church, and he briefly taught Hebrew in an Orthodox seminary. He was thus well placed to play a malevolent role in the spread of the Blood Libel. Despite all his attacks and denunciations of the Jews, however, Brafman never gave the slightest credence to the Blood Libel. Nor were official church publications propagators of the Blood Libel. In 1877 *Strannik* published a review of Liutostanskii's Blood Libel book, written by the publication's editor, Father S. V. Protopopov. The priest criticized the one-sidedness of Liutstanskii's sources, offered a negative but balanced view of the Talmud, and urged Christians to be charitable in the rejection of false accusations.

It cannot be claimed that the Blood Libel had no resonance within the Church, but the charge was made by Orthodox laymen rather than the clergy. N. P. Giliarov-Platonov, the editor of the conservative newspaper *Sovremennye Izvestiia*, had been educated at the Moscow Theological

Seminary, where he later held a chair. The ritual murder charge was a mild obsession of his, and featured frequently in his paper.

Perhaps the most notorious use of the motif was in the work of V. V. Rozanov which owed much to *fin de siècle* Decadent movement and was far too eccentric to enter the intellectual mainstream. K. P. Pobedonostsev, the notorious reactionary and bureaucratic head of the Russian Orthodox Church in his guise as Ober-Procurator of the Holy Synod, apparently gave credence to the Blood Libel. He attempted to introduce the cult of Gavriil Zabludovskii, a ritual murder victim, into the Orthodox Church calendar. Pobedonotsev met resistance from the bishops on this score, apparently because St Gavriil was a 'Uniate' saint (Dubnov 1916a).

This may provide one clue as to the discomfort of the Orthodox Church with the Blood Libel: the motif was quite obviously 'western' and 'Catholic' in its main features, with little resonance for the Orthodox, for whom the motif of 'deicidal Jews' offered a solid basis of prejudice.

The third point is that the Blood Libel was not as strongly associated with the outbreak of pogroms as is commonly assumed.

Contemporaries and later historians have noted the proximity of anti-Jewish pogroms, which became a familiar phenomenon in Russia in the reigns of the last two Tsars, to the celebration of Russian Orthodox Easter, or Paskha. The situation was made worse, it is assumed, when the Jewish Passover fell within the Pascal calendar. There have been claims that the Orthodox Easter service, which recalls the passion and death of Christ, stirred up religious hatred that erupted into pogroms.

There is no question that the Pascal season was a time of tension between the Empire's diverse religious communities. The Jewish secular leadership were very sensitive to references to the Blood Libel in proximity to Easter and protested indignantly when Russian newspapers carried incorrect reports of the kidnap of Christian children in 1881. Once the pogroms broke out, however, no Jewish publicist attributed them to Blood Libel agitation. There is an obvious contrast here with events in Kishinev in 1903, when publicists emphasized this charge as part of a wider antisemitic campaign (For 1881, see Klier 2005: 433; for Kishinev, see Judge 1992: 44–8 and Dubnov 1916b, 3:70–1). The city of Odessa, where Orthodox Greeks and Jews lived in the same vicinity, was notorious for Easter-time brawls and street scuffles in the best of years, and pogroms in the worst (1859, 1871). On the same day of the Easter season that witnessed the outbreak of the first anti-Jewish pogrom, in Elisavetgrad, there was pogrom-like violence between Muslims and Christians in Baku. As I have argued elsewhere, however, the proclivity for mass violence was not so much a product of articulated antireligious prejudice as an outgrowth of the raucous overindulgence, especially in alcohol, of so-called 'Bright Week' (Klier 2002:157–70).

Far from encouraging violence, the Orthodox clergy were one of the principal vehicles employed by the regime to quiet minds (Aronson 1990:140). No less an antisemite than Pobedonontsev ordered the clergy to preach against pogroms and himself drafted an antipogrom sermon to be read in all Orthodox churches in 1881. A total of thirty-two Orthodox clergymen were given state decorations because of their initiative in opposing pogroms in 1881–2. Even when the hierarchy stood accused of passivity, as was the case of Iakov, the Metropolitan of Kishinev, in 1903, there was no real evidence of clerical agitation or instigation. To imagine otherwise is to misunderstand the function and status of the state church in the Russian Empire.

BIBLIOGRAPHY

Aronson I. M. 1990. *Troubled Waters: The Origins of the 1881 Anti-Jewish Pogroms in Russia*. Pittsburgh.

Delo Mendela Beilisa 1999. St Petersburg.

Dubnov S. M. 1916a. 'Tserkovnye legendy ob otroke Gavriile Zabludovskom.' *Evreiskaia starina*, VIII 4–8, 309–16.

Dubnov S. M. 1916b. *The History of the Jews in Russia and Poland*. Philadelphia.

Gessen I. V. 1923. 'Na arene krovavogo naveta v Rossii,' *Evreiskaia letopis'* I, 8–10.

Judge E. H. 1992. *Easter in Kishinev: Anatomy of a Pogrom*. New York & London.

Khvol'son D. A. 1861. *O nekotorykh srednevekoyykh obvineniiakh protiv evreev*. St Petersburg.

Klier J. D. 2002. "Christians and Jews and the 'Dialogue of Violence' in Late Imperial Russia," in *Religious Violence between Christians and Jews: Medieval Roots, Modern Perspectives*, ed. A. S. Abulafia, 157–70. Houndmills.

Klier J. D. 2005. *Imperial Russia's Jewish Question, 1855–1881*. London.

Kostomarov N. I. 1883. 'Zhidotrepanie v nachale XVIII v.' *Kievskaia starina*, I,3. Natsional'nyi Arkhiv Respubliki Belarus,' fond 295, opis' 1, delo 1151 (185153).

Rogger, H. 1992. 'Conclusion' and 'Overview,' in Klier, J. & S. Lambroza, eds, 'Pogroms: anti-Jewish violence in modern Russian history.' Cambridge.

Chapter 17

Jewish Responses to the Blood Libel in Countries with Historic Orthodox Christian Traditions

Considerations for Dialogue

George R. Wilkes

In 1840, the Chief Rabbi of Rhodes, Michael Jacob Israel, was released from prison after weeks of interrogation on charges of having conspired to kill a Christian child for ritual purposes. In his next public sermon, Rabbi Israel called his congregants to repentance—the blood libel, he said, was punishment for the sins of the community, and chiefly for the sins of dissension and division (Angel 1978: 39; Angel 1991: 146). A first goal of this chapter is to explore the widespread traditional teaching according to which causeless hatred amongst Jews prompts divine punishment in the form of hatred from the enemies of the Jews.

To 'explore,' because there are numerous, diverse lines of reflection on the link between blood libels and division amongst Jews. At the time of the Beilis case (1911–13), for instance, a leading Polish traditionalist, Elchonan Wasserman, wrote that the recurrence of the blood libel through the ages could not have occurred without some kind of truth behind the charge. This truth was evident from the biblical passage describing the denouement of the first ever 'blood libel,' after Joseph's brothers smeared goat's blood across his coat to persuade their father Jacob that he had been killed. Confronted in Egypt with a still-living Joseph, now in control of their destiny, the first words of the brothers were not a confession of their guilt, but 'What is this that G-d has done to us?' (Gen 42:28). Far better, argued Wasserman, that we acknowledge our guilt when confronted with even these more recent fabricated accusations, for the blood libels are our punishment for the sin of the brothers (Wasserman 1982: 284, 318).

When in the nineteenth century the blood libel became increasingly widespread in communities traditionally associated with Orthodox Christianity, from Russia to the Balkans and the Middle East, centuries of blood libels had exerted a deep impact on the self-understanding and organization of Jewish communities in Europe. Long afterwards, Jewish scholars recalled how the expulsion of Jews from West Europe between the twelfth and fifteenth centuries was promoted by the spread of the blood libel, notably in England and in Spain, and at this early stage often not in connection with Passover (Po-Chia Hsia 1988; Dundes 1991). In 1580, the revival of the blood libel in Poland prompted the creation of one of the most influential early modern Jewish communal organizations, the Council of the Four Lands (Fram 1997). In the eighteenth century, the Hasidic movement was born in Poland amid a renewed spate of libels (Hundert 1991). Libels brought retribution against whole Jewish communities, and the resultant martyrdoms marked the Jewish liturgical calendar, particularly during the period from Purim to Passover. It is sometimes maintained that the blood libel prompted the reordering of the Passover meal in the twelfth century, shifting the ceremonial opening of the door from the beginning of the service (a gesture of welcome) to the middle (commonly claimed to be an attempt to show that no ritual slaughter or consumption of blood was taking place). Many communities, notably in Poland, substituted white for red wine at the Passover table to underline that there was no ritual need for Christian blood at Passover (Domnitch 1997:40). The ceremony is nevertheless accompanied in many Jewish households with a prayer from Jeremiah, 'Pour down Thy Wrath upon the nations that know thee not,' hardly an invitation to greater understanding.

The resurgence of the blood libel in the nineteenth and early twentieth centuries returned Jewish thinkers and communal leaders to this recurrent dimension of Jewish history. Many of the defensive organizations established then were created after blood libels: B'nai B'rith and later the Alliance Israélite Universelle, after the Damascus and Rhodes libels in 1840 and the Saratov trial of 1859; the Centralverein deutscher Staatsbürger jüdischen Glaubens, in 1893, after the ritual murder trial in Xanten; the American Jewish Committee and the East European traditionalist party Agudath Israel in 1912, at the time of the Beilis trial in Kiev. Across the Jewish world, writers penned tracts against the blood libel, analyzing its origins and causes while at the same time drawing out the lessons and meaning of the blood libel for Jews of their generation. A broad cross-section of thinkers judged the revival of the blood libel in the modern world to be the harbinger of a renewed 'medievalism,' of ancient ignorance and hatred, against which Jews could no longer be silent: 'Cease to be martyrs,' the Russian Hebrew poet Zalman Schneour wrote after the Beilis trial, 'learn to be heroes! The Middle Ages draw near' (Spiegel 1963: 293f.).

In what follows, we will see how this long history shaped Jewish religious responses during the resurgence of the blood libel in countries with historic Orthodox traditions. Jewish commentators reviewed the causes of the entire history of the blood libel, casting the relationship between blood libels and Christianity in strikingly different ways. While some Jewish writers have had a sense of the historic differences in attitude of Orthodox and other Christian churches, in many respects the distinctive relationship between Orthodox Christianity and Judaism was peripheral to the majority of writers whose response to the blood libel was shaped instead by other challenges. We will conclude with a reflection on what this history may offer for the promotion of greater understanding of the relationship between Jewish and Orthodox Christian dialogue partners.

Throughout its history, the blood libel has been treated by religious Jews as a deliberate attack on Jews as a collectivity, as an attack on rabbinic textual tradition, and thus on Judaism itself. In the wake of the first nineteenth-century libels, treatises which countered the insinuation that Judaism permits the consumption of blood multiplied. Some, such as *Efes Dammim* by the Russian Jewish writer Isaac Baer Levinsohn, were presented as dialogues with Christians, though they were primarily aimed at a Jewish audience. Others, such as *Rekach Yayin* by the last Chief Rabbi of Crete, Avraham Evlagon, were cast as guides for Jewish readers while concentrating on material designed to persuade Christians of the untruth of the charge (Stavroulakis 2003). Little attention was paid to the distinctions between accusations of ritual murder and the legend that Jews consumed Christian blood on Passover, though these sets of accusations had developed separately. Evlagon and Levinsohn both link these two facets of the 'blood libel' to other blood-related charges made against the Jews as well.

One of the striking features of this literature is the resort to the Bible as a basis for dialogue with Christians on the subject—a source of authority which political and religious leaders were assumed to respect, and which Christians, it was assumed, would view as definitive for Jews as well. The Bible was a natural resource for the celebrated and successful attempt of Manasseh ben Israel to persuade Cromwell, faced with the reassertion of anti-Jewish polemics in public, including assertions of the veracity of the blood libel, to readmit Jews to England (Davis Perry 2019: 123). The persistence of resort to the Bible is more remarkable in later times, when blood libels were commonly accompanied by the assertion that ritual murder was only practiced by extremists following the Talmud or Hasidic teaching 'literally.' In order to combat the allegations of the renegade Catholic priest who was star witness for the prosecution at the Beilis trial, leading figures associated with the nascent Agudath Israel sent interpretations of difficult post-Biblical Jewish texts often used in attacks on 'Talmudic' literature, and these were presented as testimony at the trial by the Chief Rabbi of Moscow, Jacob Mazeh (Schwartz & Bulka 1992: appendix). One claim made was that Jews believed that Gentiles were not truly human, not true descendants of Adam (though the Mishnah affirms the contrary). In a particularly celebrated communication, Rabbi Meir Shapiro of Galina argued that Jews might be referred to in a unique sense as *adam* (man), as they were in the Talmud, because they responded to such blood libels as one person, a single *adam*, as if a charge against one was a charge against all (Schwartz & Bulka 1992: appendix). Rabbinical responses to the blood libel commonly dared to highlight interpretations which underpinned the continuing unique relationship between the Jewish people and the Biblical text. Thus Manasseh ben Israel related to Cromwell that the recurrence of false charges of ritual murder was foretold in the statement of Moses (Deuteronomy 28:61) that Jews would be punished for not listening to God with plagues 'not written down in the book of this teaching' (Davis Perry 2019: 123). In traditionalist tracts, such as Chief Rabbi Evlagon's *Rekach Yayin*, the blood libel was commonly attributed to Satan or to the progenitors of the Jews' enemies, Amalek and Esau, motivated by hatred or by jealousy of Israel's divine mission.

The sin of Joseph's brothers is the source to which some of the most developed religious responses to the blood libel hark back. Indeed, the Hebrew and Yiddish phrase for the blood libel, *alilat dam* (literally: 'blood plot'), stems from the recurrent reference to plotting in the Biblical text of the Joseph story (Zornberg 1995: 263ff). There has been a rich disagreement among Jewish commentators as to what aspect of the sin of the brothers constituted the first 'blood plot,' a 'plot' often construed as implicating both Joseph and God as well. In Talmudic literature, the sin of the brothers was held to be responsible for the torture and killing of ten leading sages at the hands of the Romans, Rabbi Akiva among them, an event marked on the Day of Atonement and the Ninth of Av, as well as during the days between Passover and Shavuot (Pentecost), along with the deaths of Akiva's students, a divine judgement prompted by their 'causeless hatred' and 'dissension.' The link between the Joseph story, the ten martyrs and communal unity is a persistent one in post-Biblical Judaism. The ten were a frequent point of reference for the writers lamenting the martyrdoms during and after the First Crusade. In his *Guide of the Perplexed* (3: 46), Maimonides noted that in the Temple a goat was sacrificed as a communal sin offering because the goat, which was substituted for Joseph, remains a symbol of the hatred and violence that existed in the consciousness of the whole people. According to the nineteenth-century Baghdad rabbi Yosef Hayyim, the two times at the Passover Seder at which 'dipping' occurs represent first the dipping of Joseph's coat in blood after the archetypal sin of brotherly hatred and, secondly, the passage of the Angel of Death over those houses in Egypt marked with sheep's blood. According to his commentary *Ben Ish Hai*, the Haggadah refers to with the word *agudah* (association, union) because this latter dipping of blood was a remedy for the sins of disunity and gratuitous hatred which had plagued the Children of Israel in Egypt since Joseph's day (Hayyim 1898 Vayeshev).

Kabbalistic interpretations of the precise sins of the brothers and the punishments meted out against subsequent generations are explained, karmic style, by reference to the belief that Jews suffer in order to purge the sins of the biblical brothers whose souls have been reincarnated in them. The sixteenth-century kabbalist Isaac Luria and his disciple Hayyim Vital give two accounts of the legacy of this first 'blood libel.' In the first, they argue that the death of the ten rabbinic martyrs, reincarnations of the ten biblical brothers, was atonement for the sale of Joseph into slavery, but that we are still paying for the anguish they caused their father Jacob by showing him Joseph's bloodied coat (Luria & Vital Chapter 1, 31). In the second (Luria & Vital Chapter 1, 34), Luria noted that Joseph himself caused the brothers to sell him, and thus caused all that happened to him as a result, through his own tale bearing about his brothers. The resurgence of torture and massacre associated with ritual murder trials in mid-eighteenth-century Poland was interpreted by the nascent Hasidic movement in the light of this tradition. In 1753, a key founder of the movement, Israel Baal Shem Tov, responded to news that a group of prisoners accused of ritual murder were beginning to be killed with such agonized prayer to God that the spirits of the ten martyrs came to tell him of the commotion he had caused in heaven (Hundert 1991: 40). On this occasion, it was not enough: the prisoners were all killed.

A long-established feature of Jewish responses to the blood libel was the trust placed in the effect of an active response on the part of Jewish religious leaders, aimed at Christian leaders, in spite of the objections that a response could dignify the accusation and that the accusers would not listen and often did not themselves believe their charges (Golinkin 1996: 232). One of the means by which rabbis attempted to impress their views on a Christian audience through the centuries was through the vow commended by Manasseh ben Israel, swearing 'I have not seen it and it is not so.' Since the ritual murder charge was so purely negative, he noted, no evidence from witnesses could clear the Jews of the charge and all that was left in their defense was such an oath. When the heads of the Jewish community in Damascus faced an impending trial for ritual murder in 1840, the Chief Rabbi of Britain, Solomon Hirschell, repeated the oath (*The Times*, 6 July 1840). In 1903, the Cairene Rabbi Elijah Hazzan spearheaded an international rabbinical conference in Cracow which opened with a solemn ceremony before the open ark of the synagogue at which Sephardi and Ashkenazi rabbis from Europe and the Middle East swore that no Jew anywhere had ever committed such an act (Stillman 1995: 44; Angel 1991: 198–200).

In 1840, Yehuda Alkalai, a Sephardi rabbi from Sarajevo, published a tract (*Minhat Yehuda*) which cast the Jewish response to the 1840 Damascus blood libel as a portent of the imminent redemption. The injustice of the charge and the maltreatment of the prisoners in Damascus convinced Alkalai of the need for Jews to be able to live in safety in their own land, and the success with which Moses Montefiore and Adolphe Crémieux were able to negotiate the release of the Damascus prisoners convinced him that leaders of the Jewish community might persuade the great powers to support the return of the Jewish people to the land of the Bible. *Minhat Yehuda* came to be seen as a classic text in the Zionist movement some five decades and more later.

Alkalai's eulogy for the activity of the British and French Jewish community leaders was echoed by rabbis from across the Ottoman Empire (Palaggi 1845). They were joined by Jewish writers across Europe, echoing a familiar theme of the antitraditionalist Maskilim: that the plight of the Jewish people was gravely exacerbated by a leadership unwilling or too timid to stand up for the rights of Jews (Lederhendler 1989: 102–3, 107; Frankel 1997).

In part, this newfound confidence rested on a historic shift in the nature of trials of Jews accused of ritual murder: in the nineteenth century, states were no longer open to the extraction of confessions by torture and the martyrdoms which commonly ensued. Perhaps as significantly, the spirit motivating these appeals demonstrated a belief that the provision of favorable information could make a decisive impact on the political and religious leaders who held sway in the lands where the blood libel was resurfacing. *Efes Dammim*, one of the most influential of these tracts and widely praised among traditionalists and Maskilim in Eastern Europe and the Ottoman world, was written in 1833 as a response to a Polish blood libel. The Christian protagonist of *Efes Dammim*—Simmias, the Greek patriarch in Jerusalem—is constructed to show exactly how important rational dialogue amongst Jews and Christians can be. Though Simmias is sympathetic to Jews, intelligent, extremely well-read, and willing to be proven wrong, he has received information from a co-religionist in Poland which makes him believe that there may be extremists who do practice ritual murder. It takes a discussion of all related aspects of the history of the blood libel before Simmias can be persuaded that there is no truth in the claim. After the Damascus libel, the book was translated by the secretary who accompanied Moses Montefiore to the Middle East, Louis Loewe. Loewe's preface reiterates Levinsohn's insistent theme that 'ignorance'—the bugbear of the Maskilim—undergirded the modern resurgence of the blood libel.

Such was the optimistic view which accompanied the creation of the main mid-nineteenth century humanistic defense organizations, B'nai B'rith and the Alliance Israélite Universelle. The latter became the main body identifying and responding to blood libels in the Balkans and the Middle East. Not for these Western, modern campaigners the prism of biblical enemies and hatreds: instead of Amalek, injustice and the human rights abuse; instead of Joseph's brothers, the pettiness of club and nation, obstructing the achievement of peace and harmony between peoples of all religions.

By the turn of the century, however, Jewish thinkers were often less sanguine about the prospects of eradicating the blood libel and other prejudices through education. The blood libel appeared to suit the agendas of antisemitic political extremists, bolstered by the economic greed of embattled business rivals, as in the Rhodes and Corfu blood libels (Angel 1978: 37–9; Stavroulakis 2003: 65), or indebted former gentry, as in Poland (Levine 1991:137–9, 159, 185f.). The leading cultural Zionist Ahad Ha-Am, writing in Odessa at the time of the Beilis trial, penned a celebrated essay finding 'consolation' in the revival of the blood libel. Of all antisemitic accusations, this one was so widespread and yet so ridiculous that Jews could not feel bound to respond to it with a sense of moral inferiority and thus with further assimilation. The blood libel was a reminder that even when all the world seemed to say that Jews were guilty, the Jews could nevertheless be in the right (Simon ed. 1912/1962: 195–204).

Knowing something of the religious and political agendas that have colored different Jewish responses, the complexities of Jewish attitudes to the relationship between Christianity, Christians and the blood libel now present themselves in greater relief.

Two examples will suffice to indicate how these factors affect Jewish perceptions of the late resurgence of the blood libel in areas where Orthodox Christianity has traditionally been strong. The details of the Beilis trial were first known among many English readers through Bernard Malamud's novel *The Fixer*, published in 1966 in the wake of renewed Western interest in the situation of Soviet Jews. While Malamud partly based his work on a Yiddish novel by Sholom Aleichem, *Bloody Hoax*, written in installments during the Beilis trial, he added passages which suggested an Orthodox Christian inspiration behind the accusations; whereas Sholom Aleichem went to some lengths to underline the distance between the instigators of the libel and the bulk of Orthodox Russian society. Malamud's novel is written with evident distance from all religious traditionalisms. Sholom Aleichem, by contrast, provides a sympathetic insight into both Jewish and Orthodox Christian religious identification (Sholom Aleichem 1991; compare also essays penned by An-sky after attending the Beilis trial, Safran 2010: 206f.). However, Malamud's evocation of the plight of innocent Jewry at the hands of a callous and conspiratorial regime appeals to a theme that was expressed more and more strongly in nineteenth- and twentieth-century Jewish responses to the blood libel, the isolation of the Jew in the face of uncontrolled barbarism, and the consequent need for international pressure in defense of the weak. Any discrepancy between the diplomatic version written at the time and the later more critical account might easily be read as a reflection of the declining pressure for Jews to adapt to the dominant attitudes in their surroundings.

Some of the most accessible literature written about the propagation of the blood libel within Orthodox Christian communities in the Balkans and Middle East presents a comparably undifferentiated picture. The late Stanford Shaw presented a well-known extreme according to which the explosion of blood libels at the hands of Greek and Armenian 'communities' was fed both by a combination of antisemitic nationalism and by traditional Christian anti-Judaism—the very first blood libel made against Jews, he asserted, was by the ancestors of these Greeks (Shaw 1991: 3–4, 16, 84–6, 194f.). Similarly, in some recent accounts of the fate of Jewish communities in the Balkans and Middle East, the blood libel appears simply as an expression of Greek Christian prejudice (Gubbay 2000: 111, 118), easily dated back to the first charges of ritual murder and blood consumption from Greeks in the Ottoman Empire in the sixteenth century (Shaw 1991: 84–6, 127, 198). Thanks to the exercise of Ottoman power, blood libels were suppressed, and the renewal of the Ottoman *firman* condemning the blood libel in the nineteenth century also had to be read in churches in the empire. A good number of works written on the nineteenth- and twentieth-century blood libels in Balkan and Middle Eastern Greek communities are more deliberate in differentiating local interests and external causes, Catholic influence being one of the more commonly identified factors (Barnai 1988: 189–94). Nevertheless, in the absence of a great deal of scholarly material covering wider aspects of Jewish–Christian relations in these countries, the blood libel remains one of the most prominent prisms through which these relations are seen.

How different the picture we have from Avraham Evlagon, Chief Rabbi of Crete at the time of the greatest explosion of blood libels in Greek communities, at the turn of the twentieth century, both within and outside Greece. *Rekach Yayin* notes the condemnation of the blood libel by clerics of Eastern and Western churches, and emphatically denies that the perpetrators of these libels are Christian, Muslim, or of any religion. They are animals, idolaters who (like Amalek) are so reprehensible that they should not be named, pagans who seek to justify the sacrifice of their own sons in war through the allegation that it is the Jews who kill children.

Like many subsequent writers, Isaac Baer Levinsohn justified his appeal for Christian–Jewish solidarity against the 'blood plot' on the basis that the accusation was originally a pagan charge made against Christians. Levinsohn was also one of the first to argue that the charge was first directed against Jews in the Catholic West at the very time that Catholic doctrine affirmed that the Eucharistic wine and wafer really are the body and blood of Christ, consumed by his Church. The list of papal condemnations of the blood libel nevertheless testified to the authoritative Catholic position, a list which also appears in a majority of Jewish treatises on the blood libel, and which at various times inspired Jewish leaders from across Europe to request the Vatican's confirmation of the papal attitude (Levine 1991: 188; Frankel 1997: 379–81, 397; Kertzer 2001: 90, 105). The expectation that Orthodox clergy would also pronounce judgement on the blood libel led Jewish communal leaders to meet with leading figures in Orthodox churches virtually everywhere that the accusation led to trial or public violence. While few of these meetings have made their way into historical accounts, those Christians who weighed in against the blood libel were the object of widespread gratitude and affection within the Jewish communities of their countries.

In common with Levinsohn and Evlagon, many of the Jewish writers who called for Jewish–Christian solidarity in the face of the resurgence of blood libels presented the charge as not simply an outrage against civilization but also as an outrage against the Jew Jesus. Shortly before the start of the Beilis trial, the prominent Liberal rabbi Ignaz Ziegler of Carlsbad/Karlovy Vary (a cultural Zionist greatly influenced by Martin Buber) wrote to the *Allgemeine Zeitung des Judentums* calling for joint protests in cities across Europe: 'ask noble, truth-loving Christians, theologians as well as laity, to stand beside you; this concerns the honor of that religion which Jesus, too, loved with every fiber of his heart' (29 August 1913).

Until the nineteenth century, accusations of ritual murder and the consumption of blood were not common in the lands where Jews and Orthodox Christians lived alongside each other. At the turn of the twentieth century, blood libels swelled in number in Orthodox Christian communities from Russia to Greece and Egypt. From the collapse of Nazism, they almost disappeared from public view (though see, for instance Agursky 1988: 191–8). Jewish observers aware of these shifts have attempted to explain them with a number of (usually multicausal) explanations, which go to the heart of the difficulties of characterizing and in some respects defining the blood libel. Thus, in response to the trial of Beilis, a leading Conservative Jewish thinker, Louis Ginzberg, argued that it was wrong to assume that the reappearance of the blood libel signalled 'the return of medievalism,' since medieval Russia, to its credit, had been notably free of the accusation (Golinkin 1996: 232). With Ginzberg, many cast the revival of the blood libel in Russia as a creature of reactionary government politics—the same has been claimed of Bulgaria at the time (Tamir 1979: 113f.). By contrast, the upsurge of cases reported in Russia was viewed by other Jewish observers at the time—the correspondents of the *Jewish Chronicle* of London, for instance—as a by-product of the weakness and instability of Tsarist government. Jacob Barnai views the late nineteenth-century outbreak of libels in Greece and the Middle East in the same light, the consequence of political weakness and instability during the Greek–Turkish wars (Barnai 1988: 189–94). Were attention to shift from motivations for blood libels to the context in which they spread with ease, the divergence between the two perspectives would disappear. Moreover, either angle would make equal sense of the decline of the blood libel from the 1940s—a decline which may also reflect the decline in Jewish communities in these areas. The two contexts may imply different perspectives, however, on the challenge for increased understanding between Jewish communities and the churches. Bernard Malamud, convinced of the complicity of the Tsarist regime, deplored the weakness of Ukrainian church leaders in responding to the Kiev libel trial (Malamud 1966, compare Samuel 1967: 243–4). Barnai raises only the involvement of Greek priests in making the allegations. One framing of the need for dialogue might focus on the relationship between church leaders and the Jewish community while a very different discussion might turn on the varying local contexts where blood libels emerged.

If it has long been recognized that the blood libel was not native to the Orthodox Churches, that the leaders of the Orthodox Churches have not instigated blood libels nor given them active support, then one might legitimately wonder for what reason the blood libel would be a fitting focus for a Jewish–Orthodox Christian dialogue. Malamud's attitude suggests a somewhat different tack. Given that Orthodox leaders have not been doctrinally predisposed to accept the blood libel, why have instances of the blood libel in Orthodox communities not been dealt with more forcefully? Jews and Christians, with Malamud, may seek to understand how this recurrent attempt to mark the enmity of Jews for Christians and Christianity could have been dealt with more forcefully. It has been the objective of this essay to show, too, how wide the range of Jewish thinkers is who over the past five hundred years have responded to the blood libel made against Judaism and against religious Jews with attempts to bring the resources of Judaism and Christianity into contact, including in historically Orthodox Christian contexts, and these responses remain thought-provoking even when more recently expectations of Jewish–Christian dialogue have made greater room for secularism and modern ways of thought.

BIBLIOGRAPHY

Agursky M. 1988. 'The Beilis Case is not over yet,' *Ostkirchliche Studien* 37:2–3, 191–8.
Angel M. 1978. *The Jews of Rhodes: A History of a Sephardi Community*. New York.
Angel M. 1991. *Voices of Exile: A Study in Sephardi Intellectual History*. Hoboken, NJ.

Barnai J. 1988. "'Blood libels' in the Ottoman Empire from the Fifteenth to the Nineteenth Centuries," *Antisemitism Through the Ages*, ed. Shmuel Almog, 189–194. Oxford.

Davis Perry L.A. 2019. 'Satirizing the Blood Libel,' *Rocky Mountain Review*, 73/2 119–41.

Domnitch L. 1997. *Passover and the Colour of Wine*, 40. New York.

Dundes A. 1991. *The Blood Libel Legend*, Madison, WI.

Fram E. 1997. *Ideals face reality: Jewish law and life in Poland, 1550–1655*. Cincinnati.

Frankel J. 1997. *The Damascus Affair: "Ritual Murder," Politics, and the Jews in 1840*. Cambridge.

Golinkin D. 1996. *The Responsa of Professor Louis Ginzberg*, New York.

Gubbay L. 2000. *Sunlight and Shadow: The Jewish Experience of Islam*, London/ New York.

Hayyim Y. 1898. *Ben Ish Hai*. Jerusalem.

Hsia R. Po-Chia. 1988. *The Myth of Ritual Murder: Jews and Magic in Reformation Germany*, New Haven.

Hundert G. D. 1991. *Essential Papers on Hasidism: Origins to the Present*, New York.

Kertzer D. 2001. *The Popes against the Jews*, New York.

Lederhendler E. 1989. *The Road to Modern Jewish Politics: Political Tradition and Political Reconstruction in the Jewish Community of Tsarist Russia*, Oxford.

Levine H. 1991. *The Economic Origins of Antisemitism: Poland and its Jews in the Early Modern Period*. New Haven.

Levinsohn I. B. 1841. *Efes Dammim. A Series of Conversations at Jerusalem Between a Patriarch of the Greek Church and a Chief Rabbi of the Jews, Concerning the Malicious Charge Against the Jews of Using Christian Blood*. London.

Luria I. & H. Vital. 1573/1620. *Sha'ar HaGilgulim*.

Malamud B. 1966. *The Fixer*. London.

Palaggi H. 1845. *Derakav le-Moshe*. Salonika.

Safran G. 2010. *Wandering Soul: The Dybbuk's Creator, S. An-sky*. Cambridge MA/London.

Samuel M. 1966. *Blood Accusation: The Strange History of the Beiliss Case*. London.

Schwartz S. & S. F. Bulka. 1992. *Scapegoat on Trial: The story of Mendel Beilis*. New York.

Shaw S. 1991. *The Jews of the Ottoman Empire and the Turkish Republic*. London.

Sholom Aleichem. 1991. *The Bloody Hoax*, tr. A. Shevrin. Bloomington.

Simon L., ed. 1912/1962. *Selected Essays of Ahad Ha-'Am*. Philadelphia.

Spiegel M. 1963. *Restless Spirit: Selected writings of Zalman Shneour*. New York,/London.

Stavroulakis N. 2003. *The Jews of Crete III: Selected articles and essays: Rabbi Avraham Evlagon Constantinople 1846—Hania 1933*. Hania.

Stillman N. 1995. *Sephardi Religious Responses to Modernity*. Luxembourg.

Tamir V. 1979. *Bulgaria and Her Jews: The history of a dubious symbiosis*. New York.

Wasserman S. 1982. *Reb Elchonon: The Life and Ideals of Rabbi Elchonon Bunim Wasserman of Baranovich*. Rahway N.J.

Zornberg A. 1995. *Genesis: The Beginning of Desire*. Philadelphia.

Index

About the Editors and Contributors

Nicholas de Lange is Professor Emeritus of Hebrew and Jewish Studies in the University of Cambridge. A graduate of Leo Baeck College, he currently serves as Visiting Rabbi to Etz Hayyim Synagogue, Haniá, Crete.

Elena Narinskaya is an academic researcher in Abrahamic Religions and a founding director of Women's Ministries Initiative, an Orthodox Christian educational initiative open to everyone.

Sybil Sheridan is a freelance rabbi currently working with Newcastle Reform Synagogue. She has written and edited books and articles mostly in the area of women's studies and interfaith dialogue.

* * *

Michael G. Azar is Associate Professor of Theology/Religious Studies at the University of Scranton in Pennsylvania.

Howard Cooper is a graduate of Leo Baeck College, a psychoanalytic psychotherapist in private practice, the Director of Spiritual Development at Finchley Reform Synagogue, London, and a writer. He is the author of *The Alphabet of Paradise: An A–Z of Spirituality for Everyday Life* and blogs on psychological, spiritual, Jewish, and contemporary themes.

Daniel Davies is a Research Associate at Universität Hamburg. His publications include *Method and Metaphysics in Maimonides' Guide for the Perplexed*.

Yves Dubois was born in Brussels in 1938 and obtained a BD at King's College London in 1962. Ordained in the Orthodox Church (1966), he has worked in Orthodox parishes in England.

Michael Hilton is Rabbi Emeritus of Kol Chai Hatch End Reform Jewish Community, Senior Lecturer in Vocational Studies, Leo Baeck College, and Scholar in Residence at the Liberal Jewish Synagogue London. He has written on Jewish–Christian relations and the history of Jewish festive customs, and is currently researching the shared history of Judaism and Islam.

John D. Klier (1944–2007) was a historian of Russian Jewry. He was the Sidney and Elizabeth Corob Professor of Modern Jewish History at University College London.

Andrew Louth is Professor Emeritus of Patristic and Byzantine Studies at Durham University, and an archpriest of the Russian Orthodox Church.

Marcus Plested is Professor of Greek Patristic and Byzantine Theology and Henri de Lubac Chair in the Department of Theology of Marquette University.

Jeremy Schonfield is a Supernumerary Fellow at the Oxford Centre for Hebrew and Jewish Studies, and Professor of Liturgy at Leo Baeck College. His book *Undercurrents of Jewish Liturgy* was a finalist in the American National Jewish Book Awards in Modern Jewish Thought, 2006.

Norman Solomon was born in Cardiff and educated there and at St John's College Cambridge. He has served as rabbi to Orthodox congregations in the UK, founded and directed an institute for Christian–Jewish relations in Birmingham, taught at Oxford University and authored several books.

Kallistos (Timothy) Ware (Metropolitan Kallistos of Diokleia) was formerly Spalding Lecturer of Eastern Orthodox Studies in the University of Oxford and is a Fellow Emeritus of Pembroke College. His early book *The Orthodox Church* (1963) is still in print and widely read. He has translated many Orthodox texts, liturgical and spiritual, and is the author of many articles.

Daniel H. Weiss is Polonsky-Coexist Senior Lecturer in Jewish Studies in the Faculty of Divinity at the University of Cambridge.

George R. Wilkes has taught and written on interreligious dialogue, peace building, and ethics in conflict, and has a special interest in the development of Christian–Jewish dialogue in the modern period.

Lightning Source UK Ltd.
Milton Keynes UK
UKHW041537191022
410735UK00002B/110